INTERACTING WITH VIDEO

ADVANCES IN APPLIED DEVELOPMENTAL PSYCHOLOGY

IRVING E. SIGEL, SERIES EDITOR

INTERACTING WITH VIDEO

edited by

Patricia M. Greenfield

and

Rodney R. Cocking

ABLEX PUBLISHING CORPORATION
NORWOOD, NEW JERSEY

Printed in the United States of America.

ISBN: 1-56750-131-1 (cl) ISSN: 0748-8572
1-56750-152-4 (pp)

Ablex Publishing Corporation
355 Chestnut Street
Norwood, New Jersey 07648

Contents

Acknowledgments

This collection of articles would not have been possible without the support of a wide variety of organizations. These organizations understood that interactive video is contributing to the shape of human development and informal education at the end of the 20th century on a global level. Furthermore, they had the vision to support research to document the role of interactive video in the cognitive and emotional learning of children and youth. We would like to express our thanks and gratitude to the following organizations for translating this vision into financial support for the numerous studies that compose this book:

The Spencer Foundation, the Mary Ingraham Bunting Institute of Radcliffe College, the Office of Naval Research, UCLA Gold Shield, the University of Rome, North Atlantic Treaty Organization, UCLA College Institute, and the UCLA Academic Senate provided support to Patricia Greenfield.

The IBM Corporation, National Science Foundation, the McArthur Foundation, LEGO Company, Fukatake Company, and Apple Computer provided support to Yasmin Kafai.

The National Research Council and the U.S. Army Research Institute for the Behavioral and Social Sciences provided support to Sandra Calvert.

The University of Missouri provided financial support to Peter Frensch, while the Nintendo Corporation of America provided game equipment and software for the Okagaki and Frensch study.

The School of Cinema-Television and the Annenberg Center at the University of Southern California provided support to Marsha Kinder.

Chapter 2 is reprinted with permission from the *Journal of Popular Culture*, 1993, Volume 27.

Chapters 6–11 are reprinted with permission from the *Journal of Applied Developmental Psychology*, 1994, Volume 15.

Preface

IRVING E. SIGEL

This volume, edited by Patricia Greenfield and Rodney Cocking, is timely and fills a void in the policy-relevant research literature. The authors address a number of significant issues related to the role of interactive media in the emotional, social, and intellectual life of youths. The electronic media on which this volume focuses include video games and virtual reality games. During the past few decades, considerable research has been reported on the effects of television and film on children's behavior, most notably on their aggressive behavior, school achievement, empathic concern for others, and other social and antisocial characteristics. It is time to consider whether characteristics of film and television are impacting youth through interactive video media.

In this volume, the authors have directed concern to the media that are now consuming so much time and attention of the electronically "plugged-in" generation. Video games are attractive and engrossing. They capture the attention of children and youth who become immersed in the fantasy worlds of the games. What contributes to the staying power of these media, and what are the consequences of such total immersion for extended periods of time?

One of the main differences between video games and television or conventional movies is that video games are interactive—the player has some control over the action. Thus, rather than being a passive participant and letting the program provide the stimulation, the video game player has problems to solve and has to take action. Notable as this interaction may appear at first glance, the issue is the psychological relevance of such active engagement. It is this domain that Greenfield and Cocking address. To evaluate this aspect of the influence of video games, it is imperative that the content of the games be addressed. Some games have potential positive effects for learning decision-making rules and practicing problem-solving strategies, yet this learning often occurs in the context of hostile, aggressive, and violent content.

Greenfield and Cocking have collected a set of research studies that consider both cognitive and affective aspects of the topic. It is hoped that readers will be able to use these studies for a variety of purposes. Developmental sciences now encompass a broad set of disciplines, including clinical psychology, education, media development, and the like. In a future that is likely to be dominated by technology, studies such as those reported here are going to be increasingly important for guiding policy decisions. According to the editors, experiences with interactive media are likely to figure prominently in the cognitive socialization processes that prepare youngsters for their futures. How do we reconcile the learning potentials of these media with the harmful consequences reported so widely from other violent media sources, namely television and film? This is one of the important dilemmas facing parents and producers of the software products.

It is easy to get caught up in the rhetoric of the debates concerning the impact of media on the lives of citizens. The most prominent debates seem to be on the evils. But what of the learning opportunities of media that seem to be so engrossing for youth and seem to hold their attention occasion after occasion? It is time to address the positive learning effects in terms of impact on higher-order cognition, such as representation, problem-solving, computer literacy, and so forth. It is this perspective that I, as Editor of the Applied Developmental Psychology Series, aim to place before the research and policy readership. It is timely for behavioral sciences to discuss research contributions in a forum in order to acquaint practitioners and policymakers, as well as scientists, with relevant issues concerning both the benefits and dangers of interactive video.

It may be the case that video games can be accepted without equivocation when structured as educational or "just for fun" activities, because readers have an empirical basis from the literature for evaluating their conclusions. However, the evaluation of psychosocial consequences of video games needs to be viewed in broader sociocultural terms, such as effects on emotional and social development in the educational or workplace environments. A rational and reflective posture regarding these media is a responsibility of educators and parents if the new technologies are to be used effectively in educating children. In a world in which science and math developments are increasingly dependent on computer and technology literacies, this rational and reflective stance will be important.

In conclusion, let me say that I hope this volume will provide sources of material to stimulate new research on the various electronic media, setting new directions for creating new approaches, new contents, and new formats, all of which will point to constructive learning experiences. Already, Kafai's chapter strongly implicates the importance of integrating female programmers into the ranks of commercial game designers, if girls are not to be left out of the video revolution. It is probable that during the next decade there will be a need for greater collectivity among researchers, educators, and producers to provide the community with exciting new games.

Foreword

JOHN C. WRIGHT
Center for Research on the Influences of Television on Children
(CRITC)
The University of Kansas

It is a pleasure and a delight to contribute a foreword to this distinguished collection of research papers on the social and cognitive effects of video games and other interactive electronic media on their strongest devotees—children and young adults. One of the biggest questions addressed in this research, much of it conducted by Greenfield and her collaborators, is whether the playing of video games and involvement in other kinds of interactive media contribute to increased cognitive skills—especially spatial and iconic understandings and enactive precision and speed—or whether the resulting skills simply reflect greater capacity in those domains among those who are most drawn to interactive, electronic games. Clearly the answer is that both effects occur, heavily influenced by gender differences in initial skills and interest. It is significant that the positive effects of practice are as strong for girls as for boys.

Beyond noting the enormous majority by which male users of these interactive media exceed the skills of female participants, Patricia Greenfield does us a singular service by noting that such experience is a likely contributor to the development of both the requisite skills and the persistent fascination with interactive exploration that are likely to be needed for scientific and technical careers in our new century. Such experience and fascination may be the mechanism by which male dominance in these fields will be sustained. However, the data in this volume indicate that interest can be sustained for girls when they are provided with appropriate game content. Such game experiences may indicate both need and opportunity for working toward more game-androgynous qualities. Training in areas related to technical and scientific vocations through game design that is specifically targeted for young girls may provide the necessary early confidence that currently accounts for overwhelming male prowess in the game arena.

The seminal article by Yasmin Kafai should be singled out for special attention for its departure from the more typical research formats of the media effects literature. Instead of simply evaluating effects, she had boys and girls design and construct video games. While stereotypical gender differences were observed, the potential for getting all children into the logic of game design and construction was nicely demonstrated. There is hope out there when we let the kids do at least some of the creating.

One little jewel in this treasure chest is the article by Sandra Calvert and Siu-Lan Tan in which physiological and self-reported measures of arousal and hostility were used systematically to evaluate the one marker that popular wisdom says is critical about interactive technologies for play and learning: that they are interactive. Clearly, interactivity contributes in a major way to the power of these new technologies.

Also noteworthy in this volume is the valuable inclusion of articles from a special issue of the *Journal of Applied Developmental Psychology* whose editors, Rodney Cocking and Irving Sigel, have shepherded a number of these contributions into print. Thanks to these editors, these earlier scientific papers can now be brought to a larger audience.

Finally, there is one feature of this collection conspicuously lacking in previous integrated discussions of the field, one that may in the long run prove to be the most important of all: the social teaching accomplished by the interactive media, which have, by and large, failed to develop new content of a constructive and prosocial nature. The vast bulk of commercially available video games, as well as many computer programs for children's use, have followed the traditional themes of the entertainment media: power and domination, violence of both antisocial and allegedly prosocial origin, and overtones of sexism, racism, and interpersonal insensitivity.

Even if this timely volume does not alter some of the alarming trends in popular media culture, it may set the stage and define the issues for the next generation of research on children and media that might do so. Accordingly I wish to add my appreciation to the editors and authors whose work is so persuasively brought together in this provocative book.

Part I

Violence, Gender, and Video

Chapter 1

Effects of Interactive Entertainment Technologies on Children's Development

RODNEY R. COCKING
National Academy of Sciences

PATRICIA M. GREENFIELD
University of California, Los Angeles

Interactive entertainment technology, involving a variety of marriages between computer and television, is becoming an increasingly important part of play in our society, both for children and adults. What are the effects of these new and rapidly changing media on development? This question can be broken down into three conceptually distinct parts: What are the developmental effects of interactive media *content*? What are the developmental effects of *interactivity* itself? What are the developmental effects of interactive media *forms*?

Section I of the volume is subtitled *Violence, Gender, and Video*. The chapters in this section deal with the first two conceptual questions, the effects of media content and the effects of interactivity per se. This group of articles investigates the impact of violent game content on players' aggressive thoughts and feelings, and the role models that are portrayed in the games.

The first chapter explores the *culture* of video games and begins a theme that runs through most of the chapters of this section: Interpretations and assumptions that players bring to the game context. Gailey begins with a discussion of the role of games in society and how they reflect the values of a dominant culture, how these values are reinforced through play, and how games perpetuate socially approved models. The research question Gailey raises is whether or not the social values are *received* as *transmitted*. This discussion, of course, is at the heart of many video game debates currently waged: What values *are* conveyed in games; and how do children, as game players, interpret the play process and the game content? With reference to specific commercially available games, Gailey questions the messages received by children who play games that portray normal life as being replete with sexism, racism, class hierarchies, and a world that is a threatening place in which to live. What message is received from narratives that are based on the premise that one can't survive without killing? Gailey quotes a player who says that video game-playing is "good training for life."

The issue that interests most behavioral scientists in the area of media is the relationship between game playing and social behavior. Does such play promote aggressive behavior? Gailey's discussion puts this question into the context of the first two questions we raised regarding developmental effects of media content and interactivity. She reports that children who experience game control express less patience in real world situations that they don't control. But, she also asks: Do games reinforce individualism or do they encourage information sharing, excitement, and pleasure in others' successes and skill improvements? These are questions whose answers have to be evaluated against the backdrop of the cultural values that players bring to the game context (Greenfield, 1994). Thus, questions about the values that are conveyed by games cannot answer the question of how value-laden messages are *received*.

Violence in the media has taken on special significance in recent years for social scientists who are interested in prevention and intervention. Graphic violence in the media was initially a concern of television researchers who wanted to know more about the effects of watching the behaviors or others, but the issue of video violence has now become a broader concern of media researchers with the arrival of highly graphic video games, such as Mortal Kombat. The questions remain comparable to those asked about television violence, and the answers appear to be the same, too, according to latter-day philosophers, Calvin & Hobbes, by Bill Watterson. (See figure 1):

Does it glamorize violence? Sure.

Does it desensitize us to violence? Of course.

Does it help us tolerate more violence? You bet.

Does it stunt empathy toward others? Heck yes.

Does graphic violence in the media *cause* violence? Well, that's hard to prove.

The media industries, it would seem, have learned that the trick is to ask the right question.

Marcia Kinder writes about how violence in game media functions. She focuses on how humor mediates violent messages and through such portrayals

CALVIN AND HOBBES BILL WATTERSON

Figure 1 CALVIN AND HOBBES © 1995 Watterson. Reprinted with permission of UNIVERSAL PRESS SYNDICATE. All rights reserved.

makes the subtext of the game scenarios acceptable. She discusses how games empower players and how technical mastery of the skills is in itself empowering. Visual and sound effects that accompany surges of action have arousal qualities, and these sensory aspects of violent story narratives, in turn, become synonymous with story action. Each of these ancillary aspects of transforming story narratives into interactive video games lends an acceptability to violence. Kinder contrasts what players are *presumed* to like and what they are *expected* to do. She points out that these are two distinctly different sets of issues. The roles game players must assume, the actions they must engage in, and their position as game players must have important impact upon children's attitudes and beliefs.

Video games that are currently available are assumed to appeal to both girls and boys and the characters in the games are assumed to be appropriate models for both genders to emulate. The player's own position and place in the social context of the game narrative provides examples to draw from. These narratives, Kinder points out, often are formulated around a premise of conflict or evil to be avenged. The narratives also frequently portray the central character as a male hero whose purpose is to save someone (usually a female) or to obtain treasures. Clearly, these games are modeled on only half of the population, at most, and reflect the values and views of only one gender, according to the argument presented by Kinder.

In the chapter that follows, Kafai concludes that today's video games do not address girls' interests and concerns, a finding that echoes Kinder's claims. The chapter is based on a study with inner city fourth-graders, a large percentage of whom were Hispanic and African-American. Kafai found that girls are not attracted by the "kill" features that dominate most video game interactions. She found that the girls complained that females were rarely cast in the role of a main character. Further, the thematic embedding of hunts and adventures in the story narratives were not necessarily to girls' tastes. And, like Kinder, Kafai reports that games proceed at a rapid rate, embellished by sound and visual effects to accentuate the pace and to create arousal. For all their efforts at special effects, game designers, according to Kafai's findings, are not hitting the mark with girls, since females are reported not to prefer such quick-paced interactions.

Kafai's chapter provides an important new focus in behavioral research on *interaction* and *participation* as they relate to video games. The conclusions suggest alternatives to the games that are on the shelves at video stores. This study explored what players wanted in video games and then went the extra step to see what the players themselves produced when given the skills and opportunities to create their own games. Thus, *participation* means more than playing the video games and includes important insights into children's views of the game process, the relation between game-playing and the connective narrative, and reveals new ways to look at the creative processes behind game invention. The reader is in for some surprises as to how these young children invent and produce connective story narratives as they make the games more and more challenging for their peer players and for themselves. The gender differences that characterize game content and lack of such gender differences with respect to interest level and skills in game design should open industry eyes.

That video realism and production qualities are "hooks" to players there is no doubt. It is for exploring the importance of such realistic participation that the study of a virtual reality game, the next generation of interactive video technology according to some, is so important to this volume. The Calvert study asks whether the same video content has a different emotional impact, depending on whether the subject merely observes it, as in television viewing, or is part of it, as in a virtual reality game. As violence in "conventional" video games gets increasingly graphic (e.g., the recent game Mortal Kombat), developmental effects of "participating" in ever more realistic violent action through interactive media have become an issue of great social importance.

In television, the viewer *observes* the screen world; in video games, the player *interacts with* the screen world; in virtual reality, the player *becomes part of* the screen world (Calvert, 1994). It has been hypothesized (Sigel & Cocking, 1977) that as representational realism increases, the psychological distance between actor and medium decreases. In each of these three media, television, video games, and virtual reality, graphical quality is increasing to produce ever greater visual realism. CD-ROM, a medium not specifically included in this volume, is an important part of this trend, especially because it allows participants to interact with video footage photographed in the real world. As these real world images are incorporated into the play media of video games and virtual reality, research questions should focus on the developmental implications of ever decreasing psychological distance between person and medium.

Thus far, the scant empirical research on the subject contains an important paradox. Whereas Calvert reports that interactive involvement in a two-person, violent virtual-reality game augments aggressive thoughts in college students, others have found that a less realistic, two-person violent video game potentially reduces aggressive play in five-year-olds (Silvern, Williamson & Countermine, 1983). What is the source of this discrepancy? Is the crucial factor the augmentation of visual realism, the increased player involvement in the virtual reality medium, or the age of the subjects? Questions such as these imply that cognitive representation and symbolic processes of players need to be taken into account when discussing effects of media upon behavior.

The second section of this volume introduces some of these issues of cognition and representational thought. Section II of the book is subtitled *Cognitive Effects of Video Games* and deals with the remaining conceptual question with which we began this chapter, the developmental effects of interactive media forms. The five empirical articles in this section explore the cognitive and information processing effects of a variety of action video games, currently the mass medium of interactive technologies, especially during childhood. Some of the symbolic media forms that are explored in these studies are three-dimensional spatial representation on a two-dimensional screen, iconic imagery, and the simultaneous representation of events in more than one screen location. These symbolic forms found in video games are intrinsic to and all-pervasive in more "serious" computer applications. Consequently, practice in comprehending these distinctive symbolic forms through video game play provides a kind of cognitive socialization for using a crucial cultural tool, the computer.

Whereas the volume, in general, explores an interactive medium that has incredibly broad penetration in the United States and many other countries, we have included new interactive media, as well, such as virtual reality games, whose impact on childhood lies in the future. The pace of technological change is currently so rapid that this future will probably come about in the next few years. By including discussions of the developmental effects of the newer technologies, we can begin to explore this progression of interactive involvement and visual realism that reaches into the future. Social scientists' earlier interest in behavioral implications of watching violence portrayed on television may be replaced by concerns for the consequences of participating in vividly depicted acts of violence and aggression that are displayed in naturalistic or realistic contexts. At the same time, this more extensive exploration of the behavioral impact of video games provides an important portrait of interactive entertainment technologies as contributors to skill development, cognitive development, and elaborated thought processes that are based on the represented world through the use and creation of symbolic media. Studies in which children combined game invention with literacy skills of narrative development are important examples of the cognitive benefits derived from interactive media. All of these behavioral changes, both positive and negative, are currently most central in today's world of the developing child.

REFERENCES

Greenfield, P.M. (1994). Independence and interdependence as developmental scripts: Implications for theory, research, and practice. In P. M. Greenfield & R. R. Cocking, (Eds.), *Cross-cultural roots of minority child development*. Hillsdale, NJ: Lawrence Erlbaum Associates.

Sigel, I.E. & Cocking, R.R. (1977). *Cognitive development from childhood to adolescence: A Constructivist perspective*. New York: Holt, Rinehart & Winston.

Silvern, S.B., Williamson, P. A., & Countermine, T. A. (1983). *Video game play and social behavior. Some preliminary findings*. Paper presented at the International Conference on Play and Play Environments.

Chapter 2
Mediated Messages: Gender, Class, and Cosmos in Home Video Games

CHRISTINE WARD GAILEY
Northeastern University, Boston, Mass.

Video games, originally housed in arcades, have become commonplace in American homes.[1] Atari, which produced the first mass-marketed home video games,[2] has been eclipsed by Nintendo.[3] The basic package sells for around $100, which puts it as a luxury item within the reach of working and middle class parents. Nintendo comes with two games: "Duck Hunt," a skeet-type shooting game using a pistol attachment;[4] and "Super Mario Brothers," the company's original fantasy adventure game. Because the setup is fairly expensive for a toy, most sales are clustered in the months preceding the Christmas holidays, rather than the year-round sales we would expect if the games were primarily purchased as birthday presents.

The available games can be grouped into several distinctive genres, which for the most part echo television and film motifs: crime and violence, military or paramilitary adventures, sports, and cartoon/fantasy. In addition to the fantasy–odyssey adventure games, like Zelda, Link, and the Super Mario series, the several distinctive genres are urban jungle self-defense, gang warfare, law enforcement games, including Teenage Mutant Ninja Turtles; international paramilitary or military task force adventures; sports games; and gendered and gender-neutral spatial relations games, such as Paper Boy, Tetris (originally from the Soviet Union), and Marble Madness.

Games played in a society embody the values of the dominant culture; they are ways of reinforcing through play the behaviors and models of order rewarded or punished in the society. Debates in cultural studies center on the degree and kind of resistance that is possible when received messages are subverted at the point of consumption.[5] Like other messages from corporate culture, mass-marketed games, as opposed to customary or locally generated games, provide the participants with ways of playing at subversion. Play may invert the social order, or challenge the rules within a game format without fundamentally endangering the status quo.

In all stratified settings, dominant values are presented as common sense, derived from "human nature" rather than historical factors. A premise of cultural studies, however, is that culture cannot be shared uniformly when the society is composed of groups with decidedly different levels of control over their lives. The degree to which dominant values in any stratified society are shared,

---

This article is reprinted with permission. It originally appeared in *Journal of Popular Culture*, Volume 27, number 1, Summer, 1993, pages 81-97.

then, varies with the degree and kind of hierarchies present (e.g., class, racial, gender, ethnic, religious).

Games, then, particularly commercially successful ones, are apt to replicate in their structure the values and activities associated with the dominant ideology, with sufficient slippage to make playing them exciting. For this reason, studying commercial games at different time periods can give an indication of how corporate structures promote mass culture. Marketing strategies pinpoint market sectors by class, gender, age ethnicity, and lifestyle. The goal for corporations, of course, is expanded sales—customers eager for the next series of games. The effect of cultural domination—restricted control over the creation and deployment of cultural messages—can readily be seen.

But are the values received as transmitted? What role do audiences play in shaping messages to address their particular experiences? Because video games have widespread appeal to children and adults, I was led to ask, on the one hand, what values were conveyed in the games and, on the other hand, how children as players interpreted the play process and content of the games.

THE PROJECT

I came to this study as an aficionado of the games, part of the adult market Nintendo has sought to expand.[6] I became intrigued with home video games through courses I teach on aggression and on popular culture. As an anthropologist and a feminist, the intertwined representations of gender, class, ethnicity, and world view concerned me foremost. The aim of the project was to understand how the structure of the games represent ideas about human nature, gender, class, technology, and the general world view presented by a sector of the corporate structure. But because other studies I had done on the impact of cultural differences on the interpretation of home video films,[7] I supposed that none of the players would be passive recipients of messages coded in the games. As a rule, adults are accorded an intervening consciousness in cultural studies, but rarely have children been viewed as active subjects in interpretation. Whether game-playing is considered as having positive or problematic effects, almost all studies of children playing video games have presented these players as absorbing or rejecting—but not interpreting and thereby altering—values embedded in the games and play process.[8]

I therefore analyzed the content of a range of Nintendo and related home video games, trying to figure out what patterns existed in how the games depicted order and chaos, gender relations, social class, ethnicity, and technology. In doing so, the view of human nature underlying the range of games could be discerned. I also noted my own reactions to playing a range of games as my eye–hand coordination, problem solving, and reaction time improved.[9] These skills are acknowledged in both civilian and military circles as improving with regular video game playing.[10]

This aspect of the research was combined with a pilot project involving interviews with a small (N=21) snowball sample of urban parents and children in New York City and Boston. The nine adults included three single, working parents, one father and two mothers; the other six were married couples with dual incomes. All of the parents interviewed held professional positions. The children in the sample included the eight children of these adults and four friends of these children; five girls and seven boys, ranging in age from six to twelve. Three of the friends (two boys and one girl) had fathers and mothers who were skilled tradespeople or clerical workers. The other boy was the son of a single mother who is a doctor.

In addition to interviewing and observing the parents and children at play in their homes, separately and together, in some cases I played the games with children. Finally, I surveyed two stores renting and selling home video games in two ethnically heterogeneous and mixed-class urban neighborhoods, to see which ones were most popular. I asked clerks what kinds of customers rented or purchased which games, and I observed the traffic in the games over several evenings.

THE SPACE FOR INTERPRETATION:
WHAT GAMES OFFER PLAYERS

The new video games offer a way of closing out the real world, on one level, and controlling conditions not ordinarily in one's control, on another. They offer non-threatening competition with constant feedback. The player can repeat the game until a skill breakthrough occurs.[11] This sense of being in control in a society where such feelings are rare in everyday life, was a theme expressed by most of the adult players. All the children expressed pleasure at improving their skills through time, and several said they played the games when they were angry, to "let off steam." This contrasts interestingly with the findings of one study, which found that players of high-aggression video games showed heightened anxiety after play, compared with players of less aggressive games.[12] Most said they played the game instead of watching television, or when they wanted to avoid doing homework, or when they were happy and felt confident. After an initial period of intensive interest—ranging from three weeks to six months—most children did not seem to play the games to the exclusion of their other activities.[13] Most said they liked to play with friends, a parent, or alone, depending on their mood. A few said they liked to play alone when they were sad; as one boy explained, "I feel better when I win.[14]

The interactive quality of video games gives the player a sense of limitless choice. What the player does affects the outcome. But the perception of choice is largely illusory, since the framework—the range of possible moves and the outcome of each—is predetermined. In most cases, the player cannot reprogram the game. The princess is there to be saved; she cannot become a player.

ORDER AND CHAOS

On the surface, all of the games are morality plays, contests of good and evil, where the player is on the side of good. But the content of good and evil varies with the depiction of characters by class, gender, and race.

Some urban jungle games depict a complicated view of the relationship between chaos and social order. In those based on the film *Robocop*, for instance, the hero—seen as a kind of cosmic policeman—represents the bringer of order out of urban chaos and a defeater of evil.

One disturbing aspect of the class difference in the game genres is precisely the kind of winning involved in most of the urban jungle games; with the exception of the Ninja Turtle game, they seem to mimic the image we have of the reality of street gangs. Rival gang members seem to have no basic differences; they are enemies because they are enemies. If you win, you dominate the street, but the opponents are merely categorically bad—they don't represent any social vice or injustice. The urban world is chaotic, with few differences in power among enemies; the turf battle is among peers and is not about conditions of life.

What is missing from all the games is a sense of dramatic transformation: the task is to remove disruptive or corrupting influences, not invent a new universe or radically transform the previous order. The fantasy–odyssey games have clear goals with definitive rewards that are tied to the expulsion of the evil ones who have dominated the society and the restoration of a beneficent social order. The player can continue beyond the end in some cases, but the "new" game is merely a variant of the older one.

TECHNOLOGY

Technology in these games takes the form of superior weaponry, armor, or life-restoring medicine. It is clear in all of the adventure series that you cannot win unless you improve your technology. How you do this varies, but in general, urban-jungle, paramilitary, or fantasy–odyssey, the player is given superior weaponry upon achievement of ranked skill levels. In most games, a better weapon or greater strength comes your way when you kill a difficult enemy; in others you gain experience points from defeating enemies and can purchase superior weaponry or restorative power (medicine).

In some games you have to move quickly to adopt new technologies that come along, or they elude your grasp. In other games you may purchase or otherwise obtain advanced technologies, but you cannot use them before you have had certain experiences. In most games, you can lose the use of weapons, and so forth, when you are confronted by certain kinds of enemies.

CLASS

The research showed a definite class bias toward, or away from, certain of the game genres. The games have different price ranges, with the fantasy–adventure series being the most expensive; those modeled after cartoon series (not popular in my sample) and the spatial relations games and were the most inexpensive. The middle-class parents in my sample stressed games of the fantasy–odyssey type and avoided purchases of the urban-jungle and paramilitary sorts. They also bought the spatial relations types, like Marble Madness. The working class parents were more likely to buy the sports, ninja, and paramilitary adventure series and had not purchased the spatial relations games, except Pinball and Paper Boy. Only parents with sons had purchased sports games.

The class relations played out in the games are clearly hierarchical. There is no conception of questioning authority. The commando forces and military units are given instructions by an invisible officer corps: the game is how the men carry out their orders.

The fantasy–odyssey worlds are monarchies; the princess is to be saved, the hero is an ordinary man who becomes a warrior through experience and assistance by older people, faithful servants of the princess. The implication is that the warrior, when he succeeds, will either marry the princess or serve as regent/co-ruler.

In the play process as well, class relations determine life chances. Many of the games involve acquiring as well as using money, at least as one aspect of play. The fantasy–adventure series give the player the chance to earn money through skill. Accumulation is not the goal of any of the games, but it is helpful in all. Accumulating gold coins can buy you extra lives in some, or medicine to extend your lives in others. Survival sometimes depends on how much money you have, literally your money or your life.

GENDER

In my sample and in other studies done of home video games,[15] almost all the parents claimed to have bought the Nintendo sets for the children, particularly their sons. Judging from the themes in the games, preadolescent boys are obviously the targeted market.[16] This is reflects the gender orientation of the initial phase (early 1980s) of video game activity, which centered on arcade play, although the age range had dropped significantly.[17] The gender bias is often seen by researchers as a result, rather than a cause, of gender segregation in computer-related activities.[18] Other studies suggest social causation for a skewed interest in computers in general and video games in particular (Temple and

Lips, 215–226). One 1985 study found that kindergarten girls considered video games as a masculine province, although less so than kindergarten boys themselves considered the games (Wilder et al., 215–228). Interestingly, this study also found that the sex-typing of games in particular diminished after kindergarten. More in keeping with the latter results, my interviews showed no difference in either expressed interest or how much the girls and boys played.

I did find considerable gender differences in the kinds of games preferred by girls and boys, as well as class differences in the kinds of games played. The girls and boys in my sample showed similar patterns of interest and involvement in the fantasy–adventure games and the spatial relations games.[19] However, only boys played the sports games with any regularity, and only the two working class boys played urban-violence and paramilitary games.

Almost all of the fathers and a few of the mothers spent considerable leisure time playing the games, sometimes with the child(ren).[20] While two mothers played at least one of the games occasionally, two refused to participate and one was an avid player. These findings parallel those of Mitchell's study of families in the San Francisco area who purchased Atari game setups (Mitchell, 121–135).

With regard to the gender content of the games, the parallelism of play among the girls and boys was not matched by the characters in the games. A few early generation video arcade games showed gender parallelism, as in Pac Man and Ms. Pac Man. This level of acknowledging a female audience is all but absent in this generation of video games (a version of Ms. Pac Man is available for home use).[21] What is clear is that, even when a new game is developed for a young female audience, as Nintendo is currently doing, the dominant games show intense gender antagonism. In short, the depiction of women in today's games is consonant with a range of masculine (both boys' and men's) fantasies. In keeping with the preadolescent market, however, sexual themes are quite understated.

In the fantasy–odyssey games, for instance, there are no active female characters at all. Females, if they exist, are usually off-stage princesses and their handmaidens, who are rewards or goals for successfully navigating the particular adventure or level. In what I call the "urban-jungle" street-fighting games, women sometimes appear in minority roles as dangerous gang members whom the hero must beat up or kill through the same martial arts techniques used on male enemies. Occasionally a game will include a female ally as a co-player. Usually, however, active females are portrayed as dangerous competitors who must be dealt with violently.

Gender and class are intimately linked in the games. "Good" women are hierarchically organized and function as motivations and rewards for bravery—handmaidens will do at lower levels, but the higher status princess awaits only the most skillful and successful hero. "Good" women are shown as cute and unthreatening, usually sequestered invisibly in castles. In Mario, Zelda, and Link, there is a variation on the Sleeping Beauty theme. The princess waits for the warrior to work through the dangerous maze of the world to save her and to make the kingdom safe. In Link, other "good" women exist, dark haired beauties who wait passively in villages to assist the protagonist as he passes through. But women outside the home, even in villages, can be dangerous as well. As Link gains in experience, some of these raven-haired ladies turn into vampire bats when greeted.

Even in helping the protagonist, however, gender stereotyping is evident. Some of the pretty women help Link by asking him to do a favor for them (the helpless woman) and then reward him by leading him to their father, an older warrior, or some old wise man who then gives him advice, a new fighting skill, weapon, or protective device. Another kind of "good" woman waits outside her house and restores Link's life force when he follows her inside. The sexual overtones are striking: She is the woman who revitalizes the hero, presumably through sex. She stays in the village when he continues the game. It does not matter how long the hero stays inside with the woman, his life is restored fully even if he turns right around and leaves. It is particularly unnerving for a female player when she finds out that the structure of the game rewards such "quickies."

The urban jungle and paramilitary games explore the same turf with a different gender message, namely, that if women are going to go where men go in the world, they have to act like men, but not look like them. The implication, judging from the scarcity of female figures in the games, is that few women can/should do this. Most of the characters in these games are Rambo-type men, but most include at least one good and one bad woman. The good women are allies—busty and sexy, and as tough and disciplined as the hero. However, in terms of choosing the characters in a two person game, the female is generally the second choice.

The urban violence games imply that women in the streets are dangerous, lower-class and, like the males in these games, sexually mature. Good or bad women, like good and bad men, are shown as muscular, leather-garbed, and "tough." The women are subject to the same range of violence as the men, and they are capable of the same physical maneuvers. The implied message is that, if women are going to be in public (in the streets), they have to be like tough men and expect the hard knocks (literally) that men can deliver. Women in public are shown as dangerous; they are all right (as allies, not heroes) only if they become masculinized, including an athletically sexy body.

In all the games gender stereotyping is tinged with racial stereotyping as well: "Tough" women are rarely blond; "princesses" are rarely anything else. Dark-haired women can be good or bad, and there is no way of telling unless you have experience.

Some of the fantasy–odyssey series have older women characters. Zelda restricts older women and men to faces in caves, selling useful items; old women sell medicine. In Link, old women are shown as different from old men. Old men (wizards and wise men) are shown as holding canes or wands, but walking or standing upright. Old women are shown as stooped over and using canes. The crone figure is helpful, giving the hero advice when he talks to her, or magic when he visits her house in the village. She is a wise woman figure, but not as powerful as the old man/wizard figure.

Only boys played the urban-violence games. Some middle-class boys expressed distaste for the levels of violence in them: "Big deal: It's just fighting and killing people and that's really boring" was how one 9-year-old expressed it. The only middle-class boys I interviewed who liked to play Bad Dudes and similar games were from Upper Manhattan.

Girls were more likely to play fantasy–adventure and spatial relations games than any other genres. When asked if they would like to play Bad Dudes or Robocop/Robowarrior, the girls in the sample expressed distaste. When asked about the sports games, most of the girls said they had played the games their brothers had, but found them limited. "It's just reflexes and timing—you don't really have to think while you're playing them" was how one girl assessed the sports games. Her brother, in defense of his preferred genres, said, "They do too demand thinking!" When his sister said, "Oh, yeah, sure, like what?" he said, "You gotta really *think* [shouting while punching the air with his fist] when you play Mike Tyson's Punchout!" They both laughed at the silliness of his remark-plus-gesture. I then observed the girl playing a motorcycle race game while her brother watched; she did extremely well. All the girls in the sample said the urban jungle games were too violent and not sufficiently challenging to sustain interest.

The masculine bias of their preferred genre, the fantasy–odyssey games, creates a problem of identification for girls who play. Girls knew that the heroes were male, but they identified with the protagonist in all cases. Girls saw the hero-figures Link and Mario/Luigi as vaguely male, but not the same as *boys*. The graphics contributed to this split perception: Link is elf-like; Mario has a moustache; all heroes are little and vulnerable-looking. One girl said she saw herself sometimes as Link and sometimes as the princess: she said regardless of whether she saw herself as the princess or Link, the object of the game was "to get rid of the bad guys and get my kingdom back." Other girls resolved the active male/passive female dilemma through placing themselves in a management position. As one 11-year-old put it, "You're the brains behind Link's actions—you make him move the way you want him to. He's really sort of your puppet." An 8-year-old said, "I think the princess kind of wishes Link into coming and doing the things to save her kingdom; after all, he's not going to be the king, you are."

WORLD VIEW AND HUMAN NATURE

The prevailing world view embedded in the games is one of extreme caution, even paranoia. The world is fraught with danger; one must be prepared in terms of personal discipline and skill development to survive. Stated more positively, anyone can develop survival skills, but only if through practice, submitting yourself to repeated ordeals. Many people can harm you; certain types of people can be allies, but you have to be able to recognize them.

What is the view of human nature in the video games? In ways reminiscent of popular representations of Japanese culture, the games require that players develop emotional discipline.[22] At more challenging levels of play, the speed or complexity of action means that you cannot react emotionally or you risk disaster. Expressive gestures and the like must be limited to the times you make a mistake and "die," or the respite that comes when you successfully complete a level.[23]

Children (and adults) playing the games would shout"Yesss!" or "Gotcha!" and the like when they defeated a challenging enemy, lept a difficult chasm, or evaded a fireball, etc., or "Rats!" or "Shit!" when they made a mistake. But the concentration involved demanded that these outbursts be short and contained. Expansive or dramatic emotions, thus, inhibit success. Pleasure and pain can only be expressed fully at the conclusion of activity. During the process emotions cloud judgment; the mind must be focused.

In the fantasy–adventure and ninja/urban warrior games, this Zen quality is explicit. At the end of Link, for instance, after killing the last monster–guardian of the last and most dangerous palace, the hero must confront his own shadow before awakening the princess. The more reflective children, two preadolescent girls, said:

> You have to kill the shadow because the last monster is the one inside you. Then the shadow can be just a shadow again.
>
> After you kill so many enemies, you kind of get a little evil yourself. It's okay to kill them, because they're bad and kill other things, but you can't kill without being bad, too. The sword fight is to get the good you back.

In addition, the games replicate a major myth of human nature, namely, that we as a species are "man the hunter."[24] In the games, you literally cannot survive without killing. Evasion is rewarded in some circumstances, but not all.

The most that can be said is that killing is not always rewarded. Certain enemies should be avoided because either they are more powerful than you or, while they can be defeated, it is not worth the time it takes. While one might expect this of the urban-jungle games, even in the fantasy–odyssey games, most of the time killing enemies yields material benefits: In some cases you can only get extra lives by killing something.

Judging from what is expected of the player, human nature involves no altruism. The internal structure of these video games leaves no room for dulling the edge of competition. Participants can create cooperative settings for play, but even two-person game play does not demand it.

Some games require the player to perform good deeds, but these are instrumental—you cannot get a certain kind of power increase, for instance, without saving a kidnapped child, which involves slaying the evil guardians.

One difference between the urban-jungle and some of the fantasy–odyssey games lies in the frame in which the killing occurs. Both have an implicit structure of good guys versus bad guys, but the reasons for being considered good and bad are not explored in the urban-violence/paramilitary genre. In Zelda and Link, for example, defeating enemies is supposed to eventually free the kingdom from oppressive rule by the evil Ganon and his minions and restore Princess Zelda to the throne.

In keeping with the prevailing world view and image of human nature in the games, outsiders appear as dangerous, potentially deadly enemies. The only exceptions are some of the supernatural beings in fantasy–odyssey series, like the tiny fairies in Zelda, who restore the protagonist's lost lives. But even here, they only appear outside of their pond habitats when the player has killed a number of enemy creatures.

The differences in the genres have to do with whether or not the enemy is shown as a human being. In games pitched toward a working-class market, the enemy is always human: rival gang members, drug lords, terrorists, rival military men, and other generic evil-doers. Often this genre includes ethnic and racial stereotyping in the depiction of enemies.

The fantasy–adventure series have nonhuman enemies. There are stereotypic scary creatures (vampire bats, ghosts, dragons, and skeletons) and imaginary creatures (flying turtles, which reminded me of Japanese horror films from my youth), killer hedgehog creatures, and the like. But this genre is no less paranoia-inspiring than the more immediately violent genres. Indeed, the world is shown as a place where anything new is potentially dangerous; the new must be avoided or killed in order to survive or benefit from the world's hidden treasures.

The world, then, is certainly shown as a diverse place, but the diversity is threatening in most cases. In some of the working class game series, the diversity verges on racism: differences in color are linked with good and evil. In sum, the world view is neither uniquely Western or Asian; it is one associated with industrial capitalist societies.

IMPACT: ADULTS' AND CHILDREN'S VIEWS

Content analysis of the games presents a grim, even Hobbesian, picture of life, replete with sexism, racism, class hierarchy, competitive exclusion and other Social Darwinist notions. The room allowed for altruism and cooperation is limited. The dominant messages certainly uphold a corporate order, even if there are elements of romantic love and emotional balance to be seen. To what extent do children playing the games evince these qualities?

A youth Interviewed by anthropologist Surrey in his study of the Pac-Man arcade game was asked what he saw as the value of playing video games. He said, "It's, like, good training for life" (Surrey, 71). The basic issue, then, is what relationship game-playing has to social behavior. But the responses of girls to the gender imagery in the games, described above, should provide us with a sense of how children mediate messages through their own concerns and "kid-culture."

The first objection raised by people concerned with the impact of these video games is that they promote aggressive behavior. A number of studies of children and adolescents have been done, and there seems to be little or no evidence that the games increase aggressive behavior in players, even temporarily.[25] In one study parents complained that the games were too stimulating before bedtime, but this is not the same as stimulating aggression (Mitchell, 121–135). The same study found that noise levels—shouting, cheering, and talking—were far greater when family members were playing video games than when they were watching television, but this is a gauge of interaction, not aggression. The only study that seems disturbing in this regard evaluated the actions of children over time to playing aggressive and nonaggressive video games; the children habitually playing the aggressive games tended to give less to a schoolroom cannister labeled "For Poor Children" than those who did not, perhaps indicating a lower level of compassion (Chambers and Ascione, 499–505).

Sheingold raises another difficult issue.[26] While children experience increasing control over a game world, they could become increasingly frustrated and impatient with a real world they do not control. Greenfield also recognizes this potential, but argued that it could be offset by the positive sense of competence and predictability the games offer children who might not have such order in their everyday lives (Greenfield, 19–24). Of course, as indicated above, such control does not extend to determining the parameters of the game.

A third concern is raised by Kegan, namely, whether video games merely reinforce individualism and alienation: "Although we can seem to participate with others, the activity of playing (or watching) is individual and only apparently shared. Both are essentially valueless" (Keegan, 7). Based on watching children, and parents and children playing the games, I disagree. Among siblings or in adult-child relationships marked by competitive dynamics, the games replicated the pattern: teasing at failure, bragging at one's own success, and so on. Where intense rivalry was not characteristic of the players' relationships in general, as between some of the sibling pairs and some friends, the games involved a great deal of information-sharing, excitement and pleasure in others' successes, shared disappointment in failure, and notice of improving skills.

The degree of competition involved also was modified by the amount of discussion children engaged in about the games. Among the children I studied, Nintendo games were a frequent and intense topic of conversation when they were together—at school or daycare, at the pizza parlour, in the park, in each others' homes.[27] Children—siblings, friends, or schoolmates—shared information about dangers and rewards, gave advice, encouraged each other, and boasted about breakthroughs. These observations parallel comments by children and adults in Mitchell's study (Mitchell, 121–135).

Moreover, the children did not, in practice, accept the definition of the universe provided in the information packets accompanying the game. The games varied regarding the degree to which characters were named and plots described. But even where most items in the games were labeled in the information packet accompanying the game, children (and, to a lesser degree, adults) made up names for the various creatures. Only the hero(es) and the archvillain retained their given names. Some creatures and obstacles were close enough to animals or things in the real world to be called by those names (skeletons, ghosts, flying turtles, etc.). Children named more fanciful creatures by appearance and behavior—"killer helmet things," "spiny furballs," "mushroom guys," and the like. Even when the vocabulary was not shared, however, participants seemed to understand which creatures were which.

Do we need to be concerned with children absorbing objectionable messages in the games? Here it seems to depend on the child's wider environment. Children are not empty receptacles: They receive messages creatively. Like other people, children interpret what they experience—based on culture, class, social and community expectations, prior experience, and the fit or lack of fit between the message and their own milieu. The only consistent response children had to game-playing was they attempted to empower themselves, individually and as a group, through the process. In doing so, they redefined gender and other identities, or appropriated the dominant messages in ways that made sense to them, and thereby altered their meaning. In other words, mass culture is promoted in a predictable way in industrial capitalist societies, but it is received in a refracted way.

ENDNOTES

[1]See Sellnow (1987); Asimov (1983); and DeKoven (1982).
[2]See Price (1985); Skow (1982).
[3]See Wolpin (1989); McGough (1989); Roel (1989).
Nintendo's software licensing agreements have become controversial in the business community, and the center of antitrust suits brought by Atari and other video game manufacturers. (See Shao et al. [1989]; and Grimm [1989].
[4]For parents concerned with the idea of guns, there was reassurance from the children in the sample. They all said that "Duck Hunt" was "really boring" for anyone above the age of 4. None of the children used the pistol attachment for any other games.
[5]See McCabe (1986).
[6]See Dysart (1990).
[7]See Gailey (1989).
[8]See Price (1985) for a review of earlier social science research on arcade-type video games. Arcade games, of course, present differences in terms of social play process: See, for example, Cooper and Mackie (1986); Creasey and Myers (1986); Kaplan and Kaplan (1983); and Surrey

(1982). For case studies of home or school-based video game playing, see, inter alia, Baughman and Clagett (1983); Chambers (1987); Kubey and Larson (1990); Mitchell (1985); Schutte et al. (1988); and Silvern et al. (1983a; 1983b).

[9]On motivations for continued video game playing, see Harris and Williams (1985), and Morlock et al. (1985).

[10]Among the many discussions of the impact of video games on cognition and motor skills, see Griffith et al. (1983); Greenfield (1983; 1984); Clayson (1982); Miller (1983); Malone (1980; 1983); Perkins (1983); and Rebert and Low (1978).

[11]Greenfield (1983) and Malone (1980; 1983) are among many other researchers who have investigated the appeal of video games as a means of learning.

[12]See Anderson and Ford (1986).

[13]This is in keeping with the earlier findings of Creasey and Myers (1986).

[14]This parallels comments made to Sellnow (1984).

[15]See Mitchell (1983; 1985).

[16]See Chandler (1984).

[17]On gender influences on arcade game playing, see McClure (1985; 1984); see also Braun et al. (1986) and Morlock et al. (1985).

[18]See Kubey and Larson (1990: 126).

[19]The pilot study was done before the recent introduction of a Nintendo fantasy game pitched specifically at a girl's market, involving the adventures of a mermaid (see Horton 1990).

[20]See Dysart (1990).

[21]See Kegan (1983); Kubey and Larson (1990: 125-126).

[22]Kestenbaum and Weinstein (1985) and Graybill et al. (1985) discuss the venting or redirecting of aggression in adolescent males' and children's video game playing.

[23]This aspect of the games has made them valuable tools in training jet fighter pilots. The Air Force has used women's equivalent or superior performance in such training simulations as an argument in favor of allowing women to fly on combat missions.

[24]Popular even in academic circles in the late 1960s, this image of human origins has been roundly criticized; the more acceptable alternative today is that the human lineage emerged as gatherers of plants and scavengers of meat. Solid evidence of hunting is almost a million years later.

[25]See Anderson and Ford (1986); Cooper and Mackie (1986).

[26]Karen Sheingold's position is discussed in Greenfield (1983: 125).

[27]On the importance of Nintendo in children's culture, see Meltz (1991).

REFERENCES

Anderson, Craig and Catherine Ford (1986). "Affect of the Game Player: Short-Term Effects of Highly and Mildly Aggressive Video Games." *Personality and Social Psychology Bulletin* 12.4.

Asimov, Isaac (1983). "Video Games Are Dead: Long Live the Supergames of Tomorrow." *VideoReview* (May.)

Baughman, Susan and Patricia Clagett, eds. (1983). *Video Games and Human Development: Research Agenda for the '80s* Cambridge, MA: Monroe C. Gutman Library/Harvard Graduate School of Education.

Braun, Claude and Georgette Goupil, Josette Giroux, Yves Chagnon (1986). "Adolescents and Microcomputers: Sex Differences, Proxemics, Task and Stimulus Variables." *Journal of Psychology* Montreal.

Chambers, John and Frank Ascione (1987). "The Effects of Prosocial and Aggressive Video Games on Children's Donating and Helping." *Journal of Genetic Psychology* 148 Dec.

Chandler, D. (1984). *Young Learners and the Microcomputer.* London: Milton Keynes.

Clayson, James (1982). "Computer Games Teach Problem-Solving." *Impact of Science on Society* 32.

Cooper, Joel and Diane Mackie (1986). "Video Games and Aggression in Children." *Journal of Applied Social Psychology* 16.8.

Creasey, Gary and Barbara Myers (1986). "Video Games and Children: Effects on Leisure Activities, Schoolwork, and Peer Involvement." *Merrill-Palmer Quarterly* 32.3.

DeKoven, B. Video Games: The Future Present. *Personal Computing* 6 (1982).

Dysart, Joe (1990). "Nintendo Seeks Adult Market Niche." *Drug Topics* 134 (19 Feb.).

Gailey, Christine Ward (1989). " 'Rambo' in Tonga: Video Films and Cultural Resistance in the Tongan Islands." *Culture* 9.1.

Graybill, Daniel, Janis Kirsch, and Edward Esselman (1985). "Effects of Playing Violent versus Nonviolent Video Games on the Aggressive Ideation of Aggressive and Nonaggressive Children." *Child Study Journal* 15.3.

Greenfield, Patricia (1983). "Video Games and Cognitive Skills." *In Video Games and Human Development: Research Agenda for the '80s.* S. Baughman and P. Clagett, eds. Cambridge, MA: Monroe C. Gutman Library/Harvard Graduate School of Education.

———— (1984). "Video Games." *Mind and Media.* Cambridge, MA: Harvard UP.

Griffith, Jerry, Patricia Voloschin, and Gerald Gibb (1983). "Differences in Eye-Hand Coordination of Video-Game Users and Non-Users." *Perceptual and Motor Skills* 57.

Grimm, Matthew (1989). "Nintendo Gets a U.S. Justice Probe for Christmas." *Ad Week's Marketing Week* 30 (Dec. 11).

Harris, Mary B. and Randall Williams (1985). "Video Games and School Performance." *Education* 105.3.

Horton, Cleveland (1990). "Nintendo Wired for $ 95 Million Push." *Advertising Age* 61 (Jan. 15): 48.

Kaplan, Sidney and Shirley Kaplan (1983). "Video Games, Sex and Sex Differences." *Journal of Popular Culture* 17.

Kegan, Robert G. (1983). "Donkey Kong, Pac Man, and the Meaning of Life: Reflections in River City." In *Video Games and Human Development: Research Agenda for the '80s* Eds. S. Baughman and P. Clagett. Cambridge, MA: Monroe C. Gutman Library/Harvard Graduate School of Education.

Kubey, Robert and Reed Larson (1990). "The Use and Experience of the New Video Media among Children and Young Adolescents." *Communication Research* 17.

Malone, Thomas W. (1980). *What Makes Things Fun to Learn? A Study of Intrinsically Motivating Computer Games.* Palo Alto, CA: Xerox Corp., Palo Alto Research Center.

———— (1983). "What Makes Things Fun to Learn?" In *Video Games and Human Development: a Research Agenda for the '80s.* Eds. S. Baughman and P. Clagett. Cambridge, MA: Monroe C. Gutman Library/Harvard Graduate School of Education.

McCabe, Colin, ed. (1986). *High Theory/Low Culture: Analyzing Popular Television and Film.* New York: St. Martin's.

McClure, Robert (1984). "Age and Video Game Playing." *Perceptual and Motor Skills* 61 Aug. 1985.

————"Video Game Players: Personality Characteristics and Demographic Variables." *Psychological Reports* 55 Aug.

McGough, Robert (1989). "Passing Fancy? (Nintendo's Grip on Toys Unshaken)." *Financial World* 158 (28 Nov.).

Meltz, Barbara (1991). "Balancing Nintendo with the Rest of Life." *The Boston Globe* 5 April.

Miller, Inabetb (1983). "Video Games and Human Development." In *Video Games and Human Development: Research Agenda for the '80s* Eds. S. Baughman and P. Clagett. (Cambridge, MA: Monroe C. Gutman Library/Harvard Graduate School of Education).

Mitchell, Edna (1985). "The Dynamics of Family Interaction around Home Video Games." *Marriage and Family Review*, Special Issue: Personal Computers and the Family, 8.1-2.

———— (1983). "The Effects of Home Video Games on Children and Families." *Video Games and Human Development: Research Agenda for the '80s* S. Baughman and P. Clagett, eds. (Cambridge, MA: Monroe C. Gutman Library/Harvard Graduate School of Education).

Morlock, Henry and Todd Yando, Karen Nigolean (1985). "Motivation of Video Game Players." *Psychological Reports* 57.1.

Perkins, D.N. (1983). "Educational Heaven: Promises and Perils of Instruction by Video Games." In *Video Games and Human Development: Research Agenda for the '80s* S. Baughman and P. Clagett, eds. (Cambridge, MA: Monroe C. Gutman Library/Harvard Graduate School of Education).

Price, John A. (1985). "Social Science Research on Video Games." *Journal of Popular Culture* 18.

Rebert, C. & D. Low (1978). "Differential Hemispheric Activation during Complex Visuomotor Performance." *Electroencephalography and Clinical Neurophysiology* 44.

Roel, Raymond (1989). "The Power of Nintendo." *Direct Marketing* 52 (Sept.).

Schutte, Nicola and John Malouff, Joan Post-Gorden (1988). "Effects of Playing Videogames on Children's Aggressive and Other Behaviors." *Journal of Applied Social Psychology* 18 (April).

Sellnow, Gary (1987). "The Fall and Rise of Video Games." *Journal of Popular Culture* 21.

——— (1984). "Playing Videogames: The Electronic Friend." *Journal of Communication* 34.

Shao, Maria and Amy Dunkin, Patrick Cole (1989). "There's a Rumble in the Video Arcade." *Business Week* (Feb. 20).

Silvern, S.B., P.A. Williamson, and T.A. Countemmine (1983a). "Video Game Playing and Aggression in Young Children." Paper presented at the American Educational Research Association.

——— (1983b) "Video Game Play and Social Behavior: Preliminary Findings." Paper presented at the International Conference on Play and Play Environments.

Skow, John (1982). "Games that People Play." *Time* (Jan. 18).

Surrey, David (1982). "It's, Like, Good Training for Life." *Natural History* 91.11.

Temple, Linda and Hilary Lips (1989). "Gender Differences and Similarities in Attitudes toward Computers." *Computers in Human Behavior* 5.4. Winnipeg.

Wilder, Gita, Diane Mackie, and Joel Cooper (1985). "Gender and Computers: Two Surveys of Computer-Related Attitudes." *Sex Roles* 13.3-4.

Wolpin, Stewart (1989). "How Nintendo Revived a Dying Industry." *Marketing Communications* 14 May.

Chapter 3

Contextualizing Video Game Violence: From *Teenage Mutant Ninja Turtles 1* to *Mortal Kombat 2*[1]

MARSHA KINDER
School of Cinema–Television
University of Southern California

The year 1993 ended with a deluge of media coverage on video game violence from which very little information emerged.[2] Only two questions were repeatedly raised: Is there sufficient empirical evidence to establish a causative link between media violence and violent behavior, and should a system of ratings or censorship be imposed on the video game industry. Other issues were virtually ignored.

Within a three-month period, I personally received over fifty requests to address these two questions in interviews for radio, television, newspapers, and magazines, all stemming from a one-line quote in the September 27th cover story of *Time Magazine*, "Attack of the Video Games."[3] The most disturbing request came from a public defender who wanted me to serve as an expert witness in a San Diego murder case that involved a young man who, after playing the notoriously violent arcade game *Mortal Kombat* for three solid hours, impulsively stabbed a car salesman to death. The public defender was disappointed when I told her that I could not possibly testify that *Mortal Kombat* made him do it.

A few months later a similar scenario was dramatized in the season premiere of the NBC series "Homicide: Life on the Street" (broadcast on January 6, 1994) in which a "sensitive" African-American teenager (who as a child had witnessed the murder of his father) senselessly murders a woman during a mugging as soon as he takes a gun in hand, despite the fact that he had taken the weapon away from his accomplice to prevent any violence from occurring. Although the story is driven by the female detective's reluctance to believe that this sensitive young man was actually the shooter (a reluctance shared by his mother and aunt), he actually proves to be the killer. This anomaly is explained by two circumstances. First, the story suggests that the gun itself has special power for those who have previously felt powerless as its victim (a dynamic that is also experienced by the murdered woman's husband). Secondly, a flashback shows the young killer playing a violent arcade game just before the mugging, implying that this sensitive child has been transformed into an inadvertent killer by the simulated violence of the video game. The *L.A. Times* explained this twist in the plot by suggesting that the producers must have been hoping that the topicality of video game violence and gun control might help save the *Homicide* TV series from cancellation. Yet the plot could also be read as part of a larger cultural project to transfer some of the current heat about popular representations of violence from television to the newer medium of video games (the same way it had earlier been transferred from movies to TV).

Before any conclusions about the link between violence and video games can be reached, it may be useful to explore two closely related issues that thus far have tended to be ignored: What is unique about the representation of violence in an interactive medium (that is, what are its distinctive structures of identification, player positioning, and socialization) and how is the representation of violence contextualized in video games. To address these issues, we must take into account at least three levels of contextualization.

MEDIA SPECIFICITY

Since video games require active players who constantly push buttons or manipulate controls, they would seem to foster a different kind of identification than is found in more traditional popular media, such as television and movies, where the spectator is positioned to be more passive physically. Therefore, one might suspect that the representation of violence in video games is inherently more threatening than representations in television and cinema because (as one child I interviewed put it) "they let you control the moves . . . [instead of] only watch[ing] what happens."[4] Such interactivity provides an active sensori-motor experience that usually demands repetitive moves—that is, pushing the same buttons in various combinations and repeating the same sequences in a trial-and-error mode until victory is achieved. According to Piaget, this kind of "sensori-motor assimilation" is not only essential to perceptual intelligence but it also reveals "the affinity between habit and intelligence" (Piaget, 1960). If children's cognitive learning is accelerated by physical enactment as Piaget and other cognitive theorists have argued, then perhaps this means that the earlier they are exposed to violent video games, the more structural and habitual violent behavior is likely to become.

Yet, on the other hand, the threat of media violence is frequently assumed to be positively correlated with the realism of its representation. Since most existing video games have narrative content that is heavily dominated by fantasy and visual designs that are highly stylized and unrealistic, one might be tempted to conclude that their depictions of violence are therefore less threatening than those found in media such as television and movies that have a longer tradition and greater capacity for realistic representations[5] (Piaget, 1960). For example, in a recent poll prepared by Opinion Research Corporation for USA Today in April 1994, over 500 boys and girls between the ages of 8 to 12 from various parts of the nation (Northeast, Midwest, South and West), were asked whether they were "scared" or "upset" by violence they saw on a wide range of television shows. The tallies showed that children in virtually every category claimed they were most upset by the violence they saw in the news and in other realistic shows (such as *America's Most Wanted* and *Cops*) in contrast to animated shows (such as *Teenage Mutant Ninja Turtles, X-Men,* and *Tom & Jerry*) and unrealistic live-action adventure series (such as *Lois & Clark* and *Mighty Morphin Power Rangers*).[6] Even within the rating systems for video games (Sega's voluntary system as well as the new industry-wide system adopted in early 1995), realism functions as one criterion for evaluating the age-appropriateness of violent images and sounds (the more realistic the representation, the more threatening it is assumed to be). Although the lack of realism in most video games might lead players to conclude that their depictions of violence are rather harmless, this disavowal is frequently accompanied (both within the narrative and the player's reception) by a denial of the serious consequences and moral implications of violent behavior. It is this denial that is disturbing, especially when it occurs within a mode of sensori-motor interactivity that is linked to habitual action. It is the effects of this unique combination—of interactivity and lack of realism—that need empirical testing.

THE IMMEDIATE ENVIRONMENT WHERE
GAMES ARE PLAYED

This second context can be interpreted in at least two ways. First, it can refer to *the specific platform* (e.g., standard video game box, portable unit like Game Boy or Game Gear, computer, CD-ROM drive, Internet, or interactive broadcast television) and *particular commercial system* (Macintosh or IBM, Sega Genesis, Nintendo or SuperNintendo, Atari Jaguar or Lynx, Philips or 3DO) on which the game is played. These platforms and systems carry their own cultural connotations, especially on issues of violence and gender. For example, most kids know that the Sega version of *Mortal Kombat* is more violent than the Nintendo version, and they know which characters are omitted on the portable versions. It is like a film buff knowing the various versions of *Blade Runner.*

Secondly, the issue of immediate environment can also refer to whether the game is being played *in private or public space*—that is, playing at home on your own equipment with your intimates, or in the promiscuous public space of the arcade, theater lobby, or airport where you have less control over picking your playmates. On-line games offer a combination of public and private realms, for you are playing with strangers in your own domestic space, and have the choice of whether to reveal your "true" identity, adopt a false persona, or remain anonymous.

THE LARGER CULTURAL ENVIRONMENT

This third context involves *cultural and historical specificity,*—the distinctive conventions in the way a particular culture represents violence, a question explored within the context of Spain in *Blood Cinema: The Reconstruction of National Identity in Spain* (Kinder 1993). This issue leads us to consider the broader cultural implications of the way violence is narrativized within video games at a particular moment in history, the way it is represented formally, the way it positions players, and the way it functions within the political economy—issues I began to address in *Playing with Power in Movies, Television and Video Games* (1991). In *Violence and the Sacred*, René Girard argues that the sole purpose of all sacrificial violence (whether in art, myth, ritual, or religion) is the prevention of recurrent reciprocal violence—a theory that makes violence essential to civilization. Girard claims that most societies perform this protective function by creating a distinction between an official violence that is authorized by the law and an anarchic violence that threatens to undermine the dominant social order and its structuring oppositions. Girard's theory is useful because it encourages us to ask what set of values any specific act of violence is designed to enforce or subvert. Thus, it helps us understand how violence is actually used in various settings at specific moments of history. Although most of Girard's examples were taken from so-called primitive societies, he claimed that his theory was also applicable to modern cultures, particularly when they were undergoing "sacrificial crises" that threatened the prevailing system of values. It would be easy to apply his theory to our own post-cold war era where we are currently experiencing a restructuring of values on many different registers and to read the representation of violence in video games as a way of negotiating those changes.

In many current video games (such as *Desert Strike, Lethal Enforcers, Robocop vs. Terminator, Street Fighter,* and *Blood Bath*), the narrative premise sets up an obviously arbitrary distinction between lawful and unlawful violence, which the action quickly undermines. Players are positioned to control the moves of good guys who are authorized to kill anything that moves. As if to strike an ironic balance between manichean morality and total nihilism, characterization and plot remain minimal. The only moral justification that appears essential are the rules of the game.

I do not mean to suggest that all video games fit this paradigm. Rather, I am interested in examining subtle historical shifts within the action genre. Thus, I want to compare how these three contexts function within two specific games: *Teenage Mutant Ninja Turtles 1*, the Konami arcade game that was the rage in 1990, and the Sega version of *Mortal Kombat 2*, a popular arcade game that invaded the home market on what the product advertisers called "Mortal Friday" (September 9, 1994) and promptly grossed a record $50 million during its first weekend in the stores.

NINJA TURTLES VERSUS MORTAL KOMBAT

In July 1990 while I was writing *Playing with Power in Movies, Television and Video Games*, my research team made a video tape (shot and edited by Walter Morton) of the children we were interviewing at the Playland Arcade on the Santa Monica Pier. We were there for a 5-hour period, interviewing kids (ranging in age from 6 to 14) who were playing *Teenage Mutant Ninja Turtle 1*. Since no girls were playing this particular game, we interviewed the only girl in the arcade who was playing video games, an 8-year-old African-American girl, and also a 10-year-old Hispanic girl wearing a TMNT t-shirt who was walking by the arcade. Following that session, we taped three of the boys (whom I will call J, E, and V) whom we had earlier interviewed now playing video games at the home of one of the children. We observed a dramatic contrast in how these three boys played video games in the two different settings. The video tape shows that within the arcade, all three boys stood tensely at the machine, seeming to use their whole body as they played and making grimacing facial expressions (which were most extreme in J). In one shot E turns to the young observers beside him (whom he did not know and who are trying to get a better view of the screen), and angrily shouts, "One person, okay!" Later in the tape the same three boys are seen quietly seated in front of a TV monitor playing another "action" game. Although this game also allowed two players to play at the same time, only one of the boys (E, who was the most skillful of the three) was actually playing while the other two (J and V) watched and commented. The boy who had made the most extreme grimaces (J) in the arcade now remained silent and almost immobile, his face impassive.

When players go from their own video game setup at home to the arcade, the competitive field frequently broadens and the excitement intensifies. The arcade presents a safe version of urban encounters where players can compete with others of all ages and of all racial, ethnic and class backgrounds. The particular game helps to structure these relations. For example, in *Teenage Mutant Ninja Turtles 1* players are positioned as allies fighting against the villains to save the city. This camaraderie seemed important to the kids we interviewed, and at one point in the tape we see four boys (who do not know each other) playing side by side with little sign of conflict—a 7-year-old Mexican-American, a 12-year-old African-American, a 7-year-old Euro-American, and a 6-year-old Asian-American.

This mode is very different from games of one-on-one serial combat like the *Street Fighter* and *Mortal Kombat* series where a player fights either against the game or against another player (frequently of a different race, ethnicity, or class) while others watch the competition. Frequently a player seems embarrassed when beaten in front of friends, especially when a teenager is beaten by a younger kid or a boy is beaten by a girl.

As players await their turn, they can cruise other players, observing their playing strategy for possible future encounters. Many games use ominous urban settings as backgrounds for serial encounters with waves of dangerous strangers—scenarios that are strangely evocative of promiscuous sex in public places like piers and parks. Ironically this analogy with the public sex arena was explicit in a bill [#126] proposed by California Assemblyman Polanco, which would require arcade owners to enforce a rating system for any games deemed "harmful" to minors, as with magazine racks displaying X-rated images and in adult video establishments featuring porn.

Like the public sex arena, the arcade is gendered primarily as a male space. In our five hours at the Santa Monica arcade, not only did we find only one female videogame player, but I was the only mother present in this part of the arcade—it was mainly buddies, brothers, and fathers and sons. One striking pair was a burly father in bermudas steadily feeding quarters to his four-year-old son, who had a toy sword fastened to his waist and who was literally (and compulsively) licking his lips as he played. We also noticed that in order to play the game, he had to stand on a box so that he could reach the controls of the game, which were obviously designed for bigger players.

In 1990 what was most innovative about the *Teenage Mutant Ninja Turtles* arcade game was that it allowed four kids to play at the same time—quadrupling the income as well as the degree of socialization. Like the turtles, players were positioned as members of a team, which was structured around male bonding. But in games of one-on-one serial combat like *Mortal Kombat*, no matter whether you come to the arcade alone or with a companion, the game positions you as a loner. If you do have a playmate, he or she is necessarily positioned as an opponent. Not only does *Mortal Kombat* provide immediate gratification through quick victories but it also maximizes profit by multiplying the ways in which you can win the game—defeating all the other characters with each of the fighters as well as beating an unlimited number of players, a structure that motivates each player to play as long as possible.

Mortal Kombat encourages competition at every level and this spiraling rivalry escalates the violence: *Mortal Kombat 2* is more violent than *Mortal Kombat 1*, the *Mortal Kombat* series is more violent than the *Streetfighter* series (a point stressed in the TV ads), the Sega version of *Mortal Kombat* is more violent than the Nintendo version, the arcade version has better graphics (and hence gorier representations of violence) than the home version, the Super Nintendo version has more combatants than the Game Boy version, etc. No wonder *Teenage Mutant Ninja Turtles* now looks so dated.

In *Teenage Mutant Ninja Turtles* players are positioned to identify only with the turtles, who are teenage males. Their status as fantasy mutants helps children perceive their violent behavior as unrealistic, and their multinationalism and green color make them an easy object of identification for all races. (In fact, when I asked children in a daycare center why they thought the game was so popular, one little African-American girl said, "Because they're green!") Players are not allowed to identify with the turtles's Japanese rat guru Splinter nor with their human Irish-American friend April O'Neill, who are merely captives. Not only are issues of gender and age emphasized over those of race, ethnicity and class but masculinity and adolescence are clearly privileged, for they represent either what the target audience already is or what younger kids and females presumably aspire to become. Despite April's androgynous jumpsuit and her characterization (in the *Teenage Mutant Ninja Turtles* comic books, TV series, and movies) as a feisty Hawksian female who wants to be one of the boys, the arcade game doubly codes her (both through its software and hardware) as a static object of desire. Yet none of the children we interviewed mentioned those provocative April pin-ups painted on the machine.

In contrast to *Teenage Mutant Ninja Turtles*, many games of one-on-one combat provide at least one active female character who is usually an androgynous twin. For example, in *Mortal Kombat 1* Sonya Blade is literally fighting to avenge her dead twin brother, and in *Mortal Kombat 2* she is replaced by two Asian twin sisters, Kitana and Mileena. These games also usually include characters of color—*Mortal Kombat 1* has several Asian characters, and *Mortal Kombat 2* adds Jax, an African-American fighter. But we cannot assume that this greater diversity represents a more progressive identity politics, for one could argue that it merely increases the racist and sexist potential of the individual fights.

In *Teenage Mutant Ninja Turtles* the violence is positioned within a moralistic narrative of good versus evil, and players can identify only with good guys. Since this narrative premise becomes a means of justifying the violence, players are frequently reminded of it within the game, especially through kudos and kisses from the captives and comical threats from the villains that function as rewards and punishments for fighting on the "right" side.

It is very different in *Mortal Kombat 1 and 2*, where a player can choose to identify either with a good guy or villain. The booklet that comes with the game gives the backstories of the various characters, including their moral status. But most players of *Mortal Kombat* I have spoken with claim they do not bother to read the booklet and this moralizing dimension is not apparent in the game. All the characters are equally brutal, and their amoral performance is applauded by crowds or praised as a "flawless victory" merely on the basis of pragmatics.

We also must consider the basis on which players decide which character to choose for identification. In *Teenage Mutant Ninja Turtles 1* most boys we interviewed chose on the basis of the weapons or physical powers (e.g., reach or the ability to roll), characteristics that distinguished the unique style of violent behavior performed by each of the individual turtles. In contrast, the girls responded with a more general adjective that expressed their own judgment or emotional reaction to the character ("he's cool, he's fresh and neato") but had nothing to do with violence. Perhaps this difference can be attributed to the fact that these girls were not really playing the game and therefore did not know the moves and weapons as well as the boys, but I found a similar pattern (of only boys referring to weapons as a reason for preferring a turtle) in another study where I questioned a number of children about the turtles after they had watched an episode of the animated TV series (see Appendix 2 in Kinder, 1990). These choices of identification are not arbitrary; they are partially structured by the game through what it chooses as the "functional difference" (color, personality, weapons). I found that the boys we interviewed seemed to take greater pleasure than the girls in demonstrating they had mastered these codes.

In *Mortal Kombat 2* most players choose on the basis of the fighter's strategy and final "fatality" moves (e.g., decapitation, dismemberment, ripping the torso in two, bisecting the opponent vertically with a buzzsaw, sucking in the opponent and spitting out the bones), which actually require a secret code to access—codes that players learn from video game magazines like *Nintendo Power* and *GamePro*, hot lines, friends, or from watching others play in the arcades. These fatality moves are the "functional difference" not only between fighters but also between the Sega *Mortal Kombat* and the less violent Nintendo version. They are what made *Mortal Kombat 1* so notorious and popular and what distinguished it from other violent games in this genre.

A new feature in *Mortal Kombat 2* (as opposed to *Mortal Kombat 1*) is that players have two other alternative non-violent options for the final move. Instead of inflicting a "fatality," they can also choose either an individualized Friendship move that helps to stereotype the particular fighter (e.g., Jax makes paper cutouts, Kung Lao pulls a rabbit out of a hat, Johnny Cage signs an autograph, Kitana bakes a cake, and Mileena demonstrates her green thumb) or "Babality" (where their opponent is transformed into a helpless baby). For the arcade crowd, this humiliating infantilization may be a fate worse than death, especially in a medium that is so coded with a generational discourse that fetishizes adolescence, as we have aleady seen in *Teenage Mutant Ninja Turtles*.

CULTURAL SPECIFICITY

In exploring the cultural specificity of the violence in these two games, we see it consistently linked with seven related concepts—a pattern that can also be found in other contemporary American mass media. First and foremost, is *humor*. The juxtaposition of violence and humor goes back to slapstick farce, American silent comedy and animated cartoons, but it became a politicized form of comic hysteria through a wide range of popular genres in the 1960s with a road movie like *Bonnie and Clyde*, a satire like *A Clockwork Orange*, and a revisionist western like *The Wild Bunch* (where nervous laughter preceded orgasmic outbursts of violence, frequently substituting for sexuality). This fusion of violence and humor reached new levels of excess in the 1980s and 1990s in a diverse array of films like *Who Framed Roger Rabbit, Reservoir Dogs, Total Recall, Last Action Hero, The Mask, True Lies, Natural Born Killers,* and *Pulp Fiction*, where humor frequently functioned to sever the connection with "the real" and to disavow any guilt that might be associated with watching violent behavior, a dynamic that was satirically turned against the spectator in the satirical gangsterfilm, *Goodfellas*. This tradition helps explain why the violent excesses in *Mortal Kombat 2* often generate laughter rather than outrage.

Secondly, violence (like humor) functions as a source of *empowerment* in American media—particularly for those spectators who feel powerless like kids, which helps explain the phenomenal box office success of the *Home Alone* movies. More specifically, this empowerment is linked to *transformability* (our third concept)—not being locked into a fixed identity but being able to function like a violent transformer toy or shapeshifter, which helps explain the tremendous success not only of the Ninja Turtles but also their successors, Fox's *Might Morphin Power Rangers* (a popular television series that has generated phenomenally successful action figures, a videogame, and a movie). What distinguishes the Ninja Turtles and Power Rangers from other more traditional protean superheroes (such as *Batman, Superman,* and *Wonder Woman*) is that they provide a choice of several characters for identification so that spectators can move fluidly from one to another and thereby quadruple their own transformative power. Similarly, the power to transform enemies is one of the features that has made the violent action game *Doom* so popular with adult players. This empowering plasticity is appealing not only to youngsters as a commodified form of growth but also to adults as a means of survival in a global culture that is rapidly being restructured by economic and technological changes and that increasingly puts a high premium on transformative processes like recycling, retraining and masquerade. Even high-tech multinational corporations must adopt these transformative strategies to survive in the global economy. As Akio Morita, the founding chairman of Sony, said shortly after his company's 1989 purchase of Columbia Pictures: "We are more willing to act in the U.S. like a U.S. company, in Europe like a European company, and in Japan like a Japanese company. That's the only way a global company like Sony can truly become a significant player in each of the world's major markets."

Within our culture, empowerment through violence is also linked to *technical mastery* (our fourth concept), usually over hardware—whether it is weapons, joysticks, or generators of special effects. This pattern, which can be found in popular works from Roadrunner cartoons to *Jurassic Park*, is pivotal and all-pervasive in a cutting-edge medium like electronic games, which frequently function as an introduction to computers (a connection that is sometimes used to justify their social value). If we compare the "mutation" of the Ninja Turtles with the "morphing" of the Power Rangers, we can see how even the concept of transformation shifts from a natural process that alters the heroes to a technical process that they themselves control. Since it is identified with a specific computer-generated process, morphing is also very photogenic and therefore provides a ready source for the recurrent visual spectacle that has become one of the most popular features of the show and that is simulated in several of the Power Ranger toys.

Fifth, violence in our culture is frequently represented formally through extravagant visual spectacle and loud explosive sounds—usually generated by complex special effects that require potent hardware and that arouse excitement and pleasure. Paradoxically, this sensory extravagance helps violence become synonymous with *action* (our sixth related concept).

As *action* games become the dominant genre, there is a continuing rapid acceleration in violence to make them more exciting. If a game is not violent, it is considered boring. For example, several kids we interviewed said they liked the violence in *Teenage Mutant Ninja Turtles* because it was action! Violence provides the main pivots or climaxes in the video game narrative, and thus paradoxically it both interrupts and drives the plot forward. It functions like the production number in the musical and the sex scene in pornography, whose structural similarities have been noted by Linda Williams (1989) and which also serve this dual narrative function of suspension and propulsion.

Finally, violence is associated with *masculinity*. In these game narratives, violence is frequently narrativized as the primary testbed of male competence. Most of the violence is inflicted by males while females are usually victims or captives. Even when females are formidable fighters like Mileena and Kitana in *Mortal Kombat 2*, their bodies and moves are highly eroticized. As the proverbial castrating woman, Kitana decapitates her opponents with her deceptively feminine razor-sharp fan. She also uses a mortal kiss to inflate her opponent and blow him to bits. Conversely, her sister Mileena (whom *Nintendo Power* calls a "man eater") sucks in her opponent's body and spits out the bones—a high powered kiss that evokes *vagina dentata*. To devour their opponents, these twin sisters do not have to be transformed into dragons (like one of their male rivals Liu Kang) because *all* aggressive women in this video game genre are depicted as dragon ladies bent on destroying phallic power. Thus the violence is always related to the issue of masculinity, even when performed by a woman. No wonder, then, her triple decapitation is repeated three times in the game's most extreme instance of excess.

Moreoever, whether the winner is male or female, the disembodied voice-over authorizing the murderous moves is always the voice of the patriarchy, which sounds very much like Darth Vader. Players are positioned not only to please and obey this voice of violence but also to internalize it (Daddy made me do it!).

If violent games are culturally gendered male and if violence becomes synonymous with action, then it is assumed that games specially targeted at girls will lack any action at all (violent or otherwise) and therefore be boring, as in fact, most of them are.[7] Some examples are *Kiss* and *The Girls' Club* by Philips and the games based on Barbie, Little Mermaid, and Beauty and the Beast, none of which has been a big commercial success.

The gendering of games occurs not only through narrative content but also through formal means, such as direct address and point of view. In the notoriously misognyist *Night Trap*, not only do male vampires with high-tech phallic drills drain the blood out of scantily clad coeds, but the coding of direct address helps gender the player male. Whereas male characters use direct address to command the players, supervising their participation on a male rescue team, female characters use it to plead for help. They move close to the camera as if looking directly into the player's eyes, and then pathetically (or flirtatiously) make an appeal to their rescuer whom they presume is male. Thus, even if the player is female, she is expected to occupy a player position and to play a role that has been gendered male by the behaviors of the characters in the game.

In *Prize Fighter* (another adult game like *Night Trap* using digitized live-action footage of real actors), you are positioned to identify with a new boxer called The Kid through subjective point-of-view shots. This illusion is intensified as you control his moves because your own performance in the ring determines the behavior of other characters and how they address you as The Kid— whether your manager praises or insults you, and whether sexy groupies proposition or heckle you.

The gendering of games is also transmitted through advertising, promotion and packaging. Most television ads show only boys playing video games. For example, the television ad for *Mortal Kombat 1* shows a crowd of young boys running through the urban streets to play (or buy) the game. If you look very carefully in the crowd, you might spot a couple of girls dressed like boys, but the victorious kid in the foreground is definitely male. Eugene Provenzo (1991) has analyzed covers of 47 top Nintendo games and found that 90% show no females at all—on these covers he found 155 males and only nine females.

The ancillary products are also targeted at boys. There are at least six large-circulation magazines addressed to video game players, whose readership is at least 90% male (e.g. *Game Pro* has 1 million readers per month, 95% of whom are male).

One finds a similar approach in the promotions for Sega and Nintendo, whose platform systems are now widely perceived by children to be essentially masculine, a process of gendering that has accelerated over the last couple of years along with the proliferation of "violent action" games.[8] According to their own figures, 30% of Nintendo owners are female, whereas only 15% of Super Nintendo users (the 16-bit model) are female, which is around the same percentage Sega cites for female users of its Genesis system. Apparently the more high powered the hardware, the more male oriented it is assumed to be; the portable systems (Game Boy and Game Gear) are perceived as more user friendly to females.

An interesting case is the popular educational game *Where in the World is Carmen Sandiego?*, which has a female villain and was designed to appeal to players of both genders. While this game was very popular with female players as a computer game, the Sega version was not. It was as if female players assumed that the Sega version of the game (like most other Sega products) must be targeted at boys, even if it had essentially the same content as the computer game. This strange discrepancy suggests that both the software and the hardware can be separately gendered. The gendering of commercial systems like

Sega and Nintendo is particularly disturbing since they function like genres or cognitive schema—that is, as ways of categorizing perceptual data or mapping the world beyond the games.[9] Many people fear that this masculine gendering of video game hardware is being generalized to all computers. In emphasizing media specificity in the representation of violence, I do not mean to essentialize video games, which, like all forms of cultural production, are always subject to historical change, not only in their technology, form, and content but also in their modes of reception and socialization. As video games increasingly absorb movie technology and incorporate the latest developments in virtual reality, their powers of realistic representation and modes of interactivity will undoubtedly be transformed. Such changes will provide all the more reason to continue expanding the discourse on video game violence—to keep asking new questions and to continue seeking answers in a broader range of contexts.

ENDNOTES

[1] This chapter is based on a paper that was presented at the Console-ing Passions Conference on Television, Video and Feminism in Tucson, AZ, April 1994.

[2] For example, in December 1994, the *Los Angeles Times* daily featured stories on this topic headlined, "Video Games Will Be the Next Venue for Debate on Violence" (December 9); "Most Say TV Violence Begets Real Violence" (December 18); "Tracking the Media-Violence Explosion"(December 26); "Fears Cloud Search for Genetic Roots of Violence" (December 30); and "Nipping Violence in the Bud" (December 31). On December 3, 1994, Mediascope, a southern California nonprofit organization, mobilized a phalange of experts drawn from 200,000 members of the American Psychological Association, the American Academy of Pediatrics, the American Psychiatric Association, and the Society for Adolescent Medicine to send a letter to 125 leaders in the entertainment industry offering "their assistance in lessening the harmful effects of violence in films, television, music, and video games."

[3] The quoted line read: "It's worse than TV or a movie. It communicates the message that the only way to be empowered is through violence."

[4] These interviews were conducted in July 1990 in conjunction with the writing of *Playing with Power in Movies, Television, and Video Games: From Muppet Babies to Teenage Mutant Ninja Turtles* (1991) and are described at length in the appendices.

[5] For a fuller discussion of this issue in the context of television, see Luke (1990).

[6] "Violence on Television Poll of Youths," ORC Study 31084. Out of 255 males (from age 8-12), 58.1% said they even were "scared" or "upset" when "someone gets hurt on" the news; 53.4% on *America's Most Wanted* or *Cops*; 15% on *Power Rangers* or *Lois & Clark*; 7.8% on *X-Men* or *Tom & Jerry*. Out of 245 females of the same age, 70.6% said they even were "scared" or "upset" "when someone gets hurt on the news; 74.5% on *America's Most Wanted* or *Cops*; 27.2% on *Power Rangers* or *Lois & Clark*; and 14.4% on *X-Men* or *Tom & Jerry*.

[7] One exception is *Hawaii High, The Mystery of the Tiki*, distributed by Sanctuary Woods, a Nancy Drew type adventure game targeted at girls over the age of eight, which was developed as a CD-ROM interactive comic book drawn by Trina Robbins (the first woman in comic book history to write and draw *Wonder Woman*).

[8] To change this perception, Sega produced a new television commercial in June 1995 that was specifically targeted at girls.

[9] No wonder then that kids from an early age see videogames as "boy toys." One of the most comprehensive studies from the 1980s (Wilder, et al., 1985) surveyed almost 2,000 students from kindergarten through college freshmen and concluded that "as early as kindergarten, boys and girls viewed videogames as more appropriate to boys."

REFERENCES

Kinder, M. (1993). *Blood cinema: The reconstruction of national identity in Spain.* Los Angeles and Berkeley: University of California Press.

Kinder, M. (1991). *Playing with power in movies, television, and video games: From Muppet Babies to Teenage Mutant Ninja Turtles.* Berkeley and Los Angeles: University of California Press.

Girard, R. (1970). *Violence and the sacred* (translated by Patrick Gregory). Baltimore: Johns Hopkins University Press, p. 134.

Luke, C. (1990). *Constructing the child viewer: A history of the American discourse on television and children, 1950-1980.* New York: Praeger.

Piaget, J. (1960). *The psychology of intelligence.* Totowa, NJ: Littlefield, Adams, & Co.

Provenzo, E. F., Jr. (1991). *Video kids: Making sense of Nintendo.* Cambridge: Harvard University Press.

Wilder, G., Mackie, D., & Cooper, J. (1985). Gender and computers: Two surveys of computer-related attitudes. *Sex Roles, 13* (3 & 4), 215–228.

Williams, L. (1989). *Hard core: Power, pleasure, and the "frenzy of the visible."* Berkeley and Los Angeles: University of California Press.

Chapter 4

Gender Differences in Children's Constructions of Video Games*

YASMIN B. KAFAI

School of Education & Information Studies
University of California, Los Angeles

Playing video games has become a common activity among American children. Many research approaches have focused on explaining why children love playing these games and what effects video game playing have on children's social, cognitive and emotional well-being. Here I propose to discuss video games from a different perspective—when children are *making* their own video games instead of *playing* them. In designing such games, which features of commercially available video games would children choose to include in their own designs? Concerning the male-oriented gender stereotyping found in many video games, what kind of games would girls choose to design? The results indicate significant gender differences in game character development and game feedback. Similar trends could be observed in the choice of the game genre and the design of game worlds. The gender-related choices and the emergence of narrative game forms are discussed in more detail. Conclusions address the potential of game-making environments in light of the study's results.

Children's culture of the late 20th century—their toys, games and activities has been marked by the advent of information technologies. Video games more than any other medium have brought interactive technologies into children's homes and hearts, and they have been received enthusiastically. In contrast to most adults, most children do not feel threatened by computational media and other programmable devices. They seem to embrace the new media readily. With good reason, children have been dubbed media enthusiasts (Papert, 1991).

---

*A similar version of this paper has been presented at the The Association for the Study of Play meeting in Atlanta, April 1994. Many thanks to Patricia Greenfield, Mitchel Resnick, Uri Wilensky, and Greg Kimberly for their reviews. The results are based on my thesis research. I wish to thank my thesis committee members, David Perkins, Seymour Papert, Idit Harel and Terry Tivnan for their help and insightful comments. I also wish to thank Joanne Ronkin and her students for their collaboration and their great contribution to this work. Without them, this research would not have been possible. The research reported here was conducted at Project Headlight's Model School of the Future and was supported by the IBM Corporation (Grant #OSP95952), the National Science Founda-tion (Grant #851031-0195), the McArthur Foundation (Grant #874304), the LEGO Company, Fukatake, and the Apple Computer, Inc. The preparation of this paper was supported by the National Science Foundation (Grant #MDR 8751190) and Nintendo Inc., Japan. The ideas expressed here do not necessarily reflect the positions of the supporting agencies.

This increasing presence of computer and video games in homes has initiated many discussions in the media and educational circles about, the games' value and influence on children's affective, social, and cognitive well-being (Baughman & Clagett, 1983; Provenzo, 1991). Most of the research efforts have focused on studying the effects on social behavior and cognitive skills of children playing video games (Greenfield & Cocking, 1994; Loftus & Loftus, 1983; Selnow, 1984). Discussions in cultural studies have centered around the issues of which particular messages are promoted in video games and in which ways they are received by children (Gailey, 1992; Kinder, 1991). As important as these findings are, researchers always look at children as consumers of games and try to induce from children's game-playing interests and behaviors what impact and attractions video games hold.

In the present study, I address some of these issues from a different perspective by placing children in the role of producers rather than consumers of video games. In a six-month-long project, called the Game Design Project (Kafai, 1993, 1995), 16 ten-year-old children were in charge of creating imaginary worlds, characters and stories in the context of video game design. My intention was to explore to what extent the activity of making games revealed something about children's likes and dislikes, their motivation and interest in playing games. One question was whether children would import features such as the violence and male-oriented gender stereotyping embedded in commercially available video games into their own designs. A related issue concerned the relationship between girls and video games. Given the choice, what kind of video games would girls produce if the design of all the features—genre, place, characters, and interactions—was left to them? I used the process of video game design to allow children to visualize and implement their fantasies and ideas. A general goal of this study was to investigate whether constructive activities such as game-making offer rich and playful opportunities for an ethnically diverse group of players.

In the following sections, I describe the research context and methodologies used to gather the data in the Game Design Project. I present the games developed by the children and analyze them in regard to their features, themes and interactions. In the discussion, I raise issues concerning to what extent these choices were gender-related and which particular cultural values they reflected, if any. Based upon the results, the conclusions address the potential of different game-making activities, tools and contexts with more powerful computational technologies. Before I enter the empirical arena, however, I briefly review what is known about video games in the research literature.

REVIEW OF RESEARCH

The prominence and social significance of video games in children's lives has not been matched by research efforts. Most of what we know about video games, which is little, comes from research on the effects of video game-playing. Many research efforts have focused on identifying the psychological processes involved while playing video games (Dominick, 1984; Morlock, Yando, & Nigolean, 1985; Silvern & Williamson, 1987) and discussing the pros and cons of game-playing (Harris & Williams, 1984; Selnow, 1984). Other research has focused on the development of children's spatial and attentional skills while or because of playing video games (Greenfield, Brannon & Lohr, 1994; Greenfield, deWinstanley, Kilpatrick, & Kaye, 1994; Okagaki & French, 1994; Subrahmanyam & Greenfield, 1994). Many of these studies point out gender differences in spatial skills, which sometimes disappear after extended exposure.

Other studies have investigated the relationships among video game playing, representational competence in various media, and impact of cultural factors (Greenfield, 1993; Greenfield, Camaioni, Ercolani, Weiss, Lauber & Perruchini, 1994). Some other research has addressed the gender differences found in game-playing interests (Inkpen et al., 1993; Lawry, 1994) and the promotion of cultural values such as violence and sexism in video games (Gailey, 1992; Kinder, 1991). Researchers, such as Gailey, have questioned to what extent these messages are received as transmitted. She analyzed what values video games convey, how children as players interpret the play process, and what children get out of the games. One of her findings was that children did not accept the universals provided in video games; they made up their own descriptions. Irrespective of the considerable gender stereotyping found in many video games (portraying women as victims or prizes), girls seem to resolve the dilemma by redefining their roles in placing themselves in managerial roles. In contrast, Kinder (1991) argued that the values embedded in movies, toys, television and video games provide powerful stereotypes for children's thinking.

Irrespective of the research focus, children's attraction to video and computer games has not changed. Children love playing these games as the multi-billion dollar game industry indicates. The reasons for the attractiveness of video games have been investigated from different perspectives such as psychoanalysis (Turkle, 1984) and cognitive psychology (Malone, 1981; Malone & Lepper, 1987; Lepper & Malone, 1987). Lepper and Malone investigated the intrinsic motivational value of computer games. They asked students to play a number of different computer games, then to rate the games according to attractiveness and to name their outstanding features. In the presentations of their results, these investigators distinguished between the following factors: individual motivations (such as challenge, fantasy, curiosity, and control) and interpersonal motivations (such as cooperation, competition, and recognition) as the main attracting features of games.

A different view has been provided by Turkle (1984) who not only analyzed several video game players and their interests in games but also investigated the attractions of programming. Pertinent in her interpretations of the players' motivation is what she calls the "holding power" of video games. Part of the holding power comes from the role playing and fantasy aspects included in video games. Turkle characterized video games as a:

window onto a new kind of intimacy with machines that is characteristic of the nascent computer culture. The special relationship that players form with video games has elements that are common to interactions with other kinds of computers. The holding power of video games, their almost hypnotic fascination, is computer holding power and something else as well. At the heart of the computer culture is the idea of constructed, "rule-governed" worlds. (p. 66)

This holding power is not the same for all players. One of Turkle's cases, Marty, played video games to be in control. In contrast, David liked to play video games because it allowed him to concentrate fully in a relaxed way and to be in the "perfect contest." One can conclude from these observations that playing video games resonated with different aspects of the players' personalities.

The research I am reporting here does not investigate the effects of or reasons for game playing. Instead it looks at the process of game *making* as a way of examining children's interest in games. My analysis must be preceded by the recognition that we do not know very much about children's making games. A search through the psychological and educational databases of the last 10 years showed not one entry on making games. Incidentally, Turkle saw a parallel between the attractions of playing games and of programming computers:

When you play a video game, you are a player in a game programmed by someone else. When children begin to do their own programming they are not deciphering someone else's mystery. They become players in their own game, makers of their own mysteries, and enter in a new relationship with the computer, one in which they begin to experience it as a kind of second self. (1984, p. 92)

There seems to be a common denominator between why people love to play video games and what gets them involved in programming. Making games could combine attractions from both playing games and programming in that players not only explore worlds but also build them. The "holding power" of playing games—moving in rule-governed worlds with determined boundaries—may also apply to the "holding power" of making games, in which the rules and boundaries governing the world are determined by the designer. This parallel provides the rationale for investigating game-making as an avenue into children's minds to explore the features of game-playing.

Of particular interest are gender differences as they might appear in the design of the video games. We know little about girls' interest and playing of video games because the majority of video game players are boys. One obvious reason for this situation is that most commercial video games aim predominantly at the male player with their emphasis on fighting and sports. Furthermore, the principal game characters almost always are male; women are assigned the roles of victims and prizes (Gailey, 1992; Rushbrook, 1986). It seems worthwhile to ask how video games that appeal to girls would look.

Hence, the process of game-making might give us a window into girls' likes and dislikes of particular video game features. Of interest are the design of the game worlds and the creation of characters as well as the interaction structure, the control and the feedback given into the hands of the player.

RESEARCH CONTEXT AND METHODOLOGY

The Game Design Project provided the research context (Kafai, 1993, 1995). The project was conducted with a class of 16 fourth-grade students who were programming games in Logo to teach fractions to third graders. The class was divided evenly between girls and boys, from mixed ethnic backgrounds and ranging in age from 9 to 10. The children met every day and transformed their classroom into a game design studio for six months, learning programming, writing stories and dialogues, constructing representations of fractions, creating package designs and advertisements, considering interface design issues, and devising teaching strategies.[1]

The following scene captures the first 20 minutes of one day in the project where two students discuss their games, design ideas, and programming issues as they work at the computer:

On a Wednesday morning, 10 weeks into the project, two students, Amy[2] and Trevor, sit next to each other at the computers while working on their games. The computers are arranged outside of their classroom in two circles, with 16 computers each. The notebooks in which the students write every day about their ideas, plans, and designs are stacked between their computers. Trevor sits with both his legs folded on the chair and types in the name of a Logo procedure to start his game. The introduction to his game, called "The Island of the Goon," reads: "You are a monkey. You are going to Island Snow. There are blue birds at a lake and a mountain. First go to the lake, then to the mountain. and last to the GOLDEN MOUNTAIN. You have to get the Golden Snow from the GOLDEN MOUNTAIN to cure the king monkey, Contrae, because he is sick. At the island, you will meet the monkey you just saw turned into a goon by the evil wizard. Use the arrow keys to move. He will ask you a fraction problem. If you get it wrong, you will become mentally deformed. Good Luck!!!"

While the turtle begins drawing on the screen, Trevor looks over to Amy's computer screen, which displays a page full of turtle shapes. He points to one of her shapes and asks, "Why do you have a question mark?" then leans back waiting for Amy's answer.

Amy replies, "It's for my game. What do you have done so far in your game?"

On Trevor's screen, the turtle draws the outlines of a circle and fills the background with color. Trevor responds, "I have an island."

Amy retorts: "That's it?! Why don't you tell what's going on?" She then comments on the player figure placed on the bottom of the Trevor's screen: "You can't see that's you."

"How do you know?" Trevor asks.

Amy replies, "Because I can read it, if I look very close. It just doesn't look good because it lies on top of the line." Pointing to Trevor's screen, she suggests a new place: "I'd just put YOU ARE here."

Even though Trevor challenges Amy's observation—"So? It works for me— he selects the page with all his shapes. He starts working on the player shape by moving a cursor over a grid of squares. By deleting some of the squares, he changes the outline of his player's shape and explains: "I'm cleaning him up, so you can see the line."

When Trevor returns to his page with the island map, the new shape appears in the player's place. Amy congratulates Trevor on his improvement: "See, very good."

After Trevor has completed the revisions of his player figure, he looks again at Amy's screen and points to one of her shapes that shows six small squares, three of which are shaded in and comments, "This is one half."

Amy replies, "No, three sixths. I can't make them [the third graders] reduce. You know, I can't make them reduce it."

"Why can't you make them reduce it?"

"Because they don't know how to do it." Amy then starts playing her own game. She reads aloud the introduction: "You want to go to the home of Zeus but the map was ripped up by the Greek God Hades. All of the Greek Gods and Goddesses have a fraction of the map. You are to go to the Gods and Goddesses one at a time and they will ask you a fraction problem. If you get it right you will get a fraction of the map. When you get the whole map you will be at the gate of Zeus' home. The bull at the gate will ask you three hard fraction problems. If you get them right you will go inside Zeus' home and get to become the God or Goddess of fractions and meet Zeus!"

As Amy continues to play her game, she answers one fraction question after the other and collects the different parts of the map. After she has correctly answered the third fraction question, she realizes that the third quarter of the map is not in the right place; it partially covers other parts. "This isn't right. This is messed up," she complains. She stops her program by pressing the control and S keys, then flips to the page where she can see all her procedures. She reads aloud the Logo code while scrolling down the page: "There is something wrong with SETSHAPE. SETPOSITION 60 50. It has to be 60 10."

Meanwhile, Trevor has been working on a new shape. Several times, he tries to get Amy's attention: "Now, does this look like a stick figure? Does this look like a stick figure? Answer me! Does this look like a stick figure?"

Amy briefly turns her head and says: "Yes. Shhh, I am trying to figure something out! SETSHAPE 11. SETPOSITION 75 10. Oh Oh." She slaps herself on the head: "75 10. I am on the wrong page! That's it! Heh, it worked." Amy and Trevor continue working on their games.

The previous description provided an snapshot of the actual game design process; in the context of their game design, students dealt on a daily basis with issues such as story telling, character creation, and graphics during the six-month-long project. The collaborative structure of the project provided opportunities for the game designers to discuss their project with their classmates, and to show it to their potential users and to a wider public. Several "focus sessions" presented opportunities for the teacher and researcher to initiate discussions around issues and ideas relevant to all game designers. For example, issues about games, students' experiences playing games, what they learned, and programming ideas were among the issues discussed at these occasions.

The research took place in an inner-city public elementary school in Boston. One part of the school is an experimental site of the MIT Media Laboratory, which was established nine years ago and investigates on a large scale the implementation and rituals of a computer culture. The school houses 15 classrooms with approximately 250 students and has 110 networked computers. The computers are arranged in four circles in the open areas that are surrounded by the classrooms with additional computers. While this feature distinguishes the school from the usual types of classrooms, the student population is characteristic of an inner-city school with a high percentage of Hispanic and African-American students. The most distinctive features of the regular classroom activities are that all the students have daily access to the computer and that they use mostly the programming language Logo to create their own software in contrast to using pre-designed program packages.

A combination of qualitative methods was used to document the students' ideas, thoughts, and progress in game development. Pre- and post-interviews were conducted to gather information on students' interest, knowledge and evaluation of video games. During the project, the students participated in research activities by keeping notebook entries, saving log files, and interviewing to provide additional information for the researcher. In the interviews that I conducted individually with each student before the project began, I found that all students knew about and had played video games. However, the extent of the video game-playing experience varied considerably. The major difference was between girls and boys; most boys played actively and consistently video games, whereas only two girls said that they did so. In a few cases, the students also explained that their lack of video game playing experience was due to their parents' resistance to purchasing a game system and they were limited to playing at friends' or relatives' homes. Furthermore, most girls also stated that they had no particular interest in pursuing video game-playing because they did not like their themes and violence. To summarize, the girls' and boys' knowledge of video games was not comparable. But this result is not surprising considering that the majority of commercial video games are played by boys (e.g., Greenfield, Brannon, & Lohr, 1994; Provenzo, 1991).

RESULTS

Sixteen students were involved in designing and implementing a video game. Each of them completed at least one game in the course of the project; some students started or completed more than one game. The children's games were analyzed in regard to the following features: (1) the game genre; (2) the game worlds and places created; (3) the game characters and supporting cast of actors developed by students; (4) the interaction modes and feedback provided for the player; and (5) the narrative development in the game structure. To highlight potential gender differences in the design of the games, the results are arranged by gender groups: girls' and boys' games.

Game Genres

There are various kinds of video games which can be divided into the following categories: adventure, sports/skills, teaching context, and simulation. This categorization is by no means exhaustive and exclusive as many games actually fall in serveral categories at the same time. For example, an adventure game may also be a skill game as the player has to overcome many obstacles demonstrating considerable athletic skills. Or, a simulation game of city building may as well have educational purposes as the player deals with the complexity of dynamic networked systems. Nevertheless, this general categorization may serve as a starting point. For the analysis of the designed games, the category adventure has been used when the player experienced extraordinary events or was sent to unknown places to be explored. The category skill has been used for games of an athletic nature such as basketball or skiing. A third category was games that used the teaching context in an explicit fashion.

The majority of games used the adventure-travel-exploration genres (10 out of 18 games). Figure 1 provides an overview of all game genres and their distribution among boys and girls.

Almost all of the boys created adventure hunts and explorations whereas the girls' games were more evenly-divided among adventure, skill/sport or teaching games. The sports theme was selected by a few students (two boys, skating and basketball, and one girl, skiing) who focused on skill aspects such as navigating a maze or a spider web, or dunking basketballs. Only two students (girls) choose an educational format, a teaching game, to incorporate the content to be learned.

The sharpest thematic difference between boys and girls concerned the morality issue—the contest between good and evil. The player is on the good side fighting off the bad guys in order to achieve the goal. In the boys' games the goal of the player is to recover a "stolen fraction wand" (Shaun) or "a stolen jewel" (Jero), to "defeat demons, evil fraction aliens, globe ghosts or mash Martians" (Albert) in order to receive a "bucket full of gold, a trip to Orlandoville, a wedding to a princess" (Sid) or "tickets to a summer water park" (Shaun). In contrast, there are few evil characters in the girls' games (e.g., the sun in Miriam's skiing game, the spider in Gaby's spider game). In some of the girls' games, the player has to "go down the mountain without falling" (Miriam),

Girls	Game Places &Worlds	Game Genre	Presence of Evil
Amy	fair, mount Olympus	adventure-mythology	no
Gaby	spider web	skill	no
Gloria	classroom	teaching	no
Miriam	ski slope	skill	no
Rosy	basement, castle	adventure-travel	no
Shanice	airport	skill	no
Sina	classroom	teaching	no
Tyree	space city	adventure-travel	no

Boys	Game Places &Worlds	Game Genre	Presence of Evil
Albert	haunted house	adventure-exploration	yes
Barney	city, ocean, forest, airport	adventure-travel	no
Darvin	surfing maze	skill	no
Jero	Hect Village	adventure-travel	yes
Juan	Funland	adventure	no
Shaun	space station	adventure	yes
Sid	basketball court/obstacle course/Peaceville	skill/skill/adventure	yes
Trevor	coin grid/island	adventure-exploration	yes

Figure 1. Overview of game places and genres, and the presence of evil as they were designed and implemented by students. (The greater number of places and genres than actual students is due to some students who started and implemented more than one game. Some students used more than one world or place in their games; those places are separated by commas. The hyphen in game genre denotes the special nature of the game. The slash distinguishes between the different genres and places for students who created more than one game in the project.)

"avoid a spider" (Gaby), "land a helicopter" (Shanice) or answer fraction questions (Gloria, Sina). Then the player can receive an unspecified "treasure"

(Rosy), "prize" (Gloria), "avoid French" (Sina), or "become the God or Goddess of fractions" (Amy). Not one girl incorporated the conquest of evil in her game whereas five boys chose to do so. This difference proved to be significant at the .025 level (Fisher's Test).

In all games, the player's success depends on figuring out the correct answer to the fraction questions in order to continue or finish the game. Fractions have become the obstacle to be overcome. This emphasizes an interesting relation with fractions. It might express the negative feelings many children have toward fractions. Or, it could just be that fractions are always positioned as "problems to be solved" in the classroom, and this carries over in the game. One could say that, at least in the beginning, the game designers were not able to decenter from and to develop positive feelings about fractions.

Game Worlds
The diversity of genre and gender differences was also reflected in the design of the game world. All game designs centered around the construction of physical spaces. Many students had quite original ideas for their games: Gaby's spider web and Trevor's coin grid (Figure 2), Jero's map game and Shaun's street scene (Figure 3) are just a few examples.

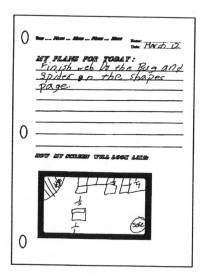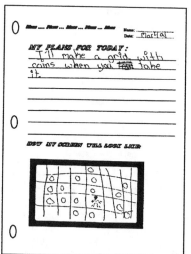

Figure 2. Designer Notebook entries—Gaby's and Trevor's game designs. Gaby's game describes a spider web in which the player moves around as a fly away from the spider and turns on fraction blocks where questions are posed. Trevor shows the coin grid and a figure that represents the player.

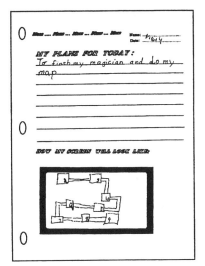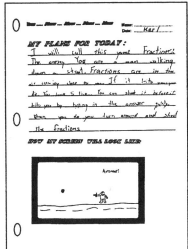

Figure 3. Designer Notebook entries—Jero and Shaun's game designs. Jero's map shows the different stations or levels of the world that the player has to pass. Shaun's street scene is the context in which the fraction questions will be posed.

Yet there was an interesting difference in the reality aspect of the game world. In many instances, game worlds could be described as fantasy places because they were imaginary worlds for the younger players to learn about fractions. The majority of students created fantasy places such as imaginary cities, islands or countries, (e.g., Funland and Peaceville). In contrast, a number of other games featured more well-known places such as the classroom, ski slope, airport, and a spider web. Six out of eight girls confined their game places and worlds to real-life settings, whereas only one boy did so. In contrast, the games of seven out of eight boys included fantasy places. According to a Fisher Test, this difference is significant at the 0.025 level. In a few situations, the players started out in familiar places such as the home, neighborhood or street before adventuring into more distant places such as schools, castles, mount Olympus or encounters with spaceships. These were also counted as fantasy places if the major part of the game-playing took place in them.

Many games made reference to commercially available games from systems such as Nintendo. For example, Jero's different warp zones are reminiscent of Mario Brother's tunnel system. Oscar made explicit reference to the PacMan game, but eating fractions instead of dots. In Tyree's game, the player could earn fractions of a magic potion as a reward, incorporating a feature found in the Nintendo game Super Mario Brothers. Sid's basketball game is available in various video game versions. Gaby took an educational game she had used in her previous school, the spider web, and adapted it to frac-

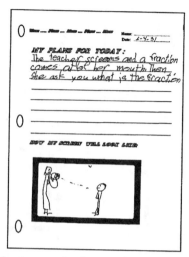

Figure 4. Designer Notebook entry—Sina's game design. Sina shows the two protagonists of the game, the teacher and the player.

tions. Some of the students used the school situation when choosing a game theme. For example, Sina's outline of her teacher game shows a teacher asking, or more accurately "screamin" a fraction. Gloria came up with a similar idea (see Figure 4).

Development of Game Characters
The places or worlds in which the games were situated were populated with an interesting cast of characters. One group concerned the game character assigned to the player, the other describes the supporting cast of game actors (see Figure 5).

What is apparent in the figures assigned to the game player is that all the boys (except for one) chose fantasy figures or assigned a specific gender to the player. In the case of fantasy figures, the students created an artificial game player persona such as a surfer (Darvin's game) or Gemini (Sid's game). Most of the boys also assumed that the player would be male too. The fictive game player was called Mike, Jose, Tommy, or Alex. Some of them had fantasy names where the gender was more difficult to detect. Darvin was the only boy who addressed the player as both "dude" or "dudette." In contrast, most girls left the player's gender or age open: the player simply was addressed by a generic "you" without any further specifications. One might interpret this choice also as involving a more personal identification: the player and the character are one and the same. This analysis revealed a strong and significant gen-

Girls	Player Character	Supporting Cast
Amy	you	Greek Gods and Godesses, snake, Zeus
Gaby	you	spider
Gloria	fly	teacher
Miriam	you	evil sun
Rosy	Plum, a cat	mouse, rich man
Shanice	you	—
Sina	Tom, a student	teacher
Tyree	you	martians

Boys	Player Character	Supporting Cast
Albert	you, a kid	demon from underworld, aliens from Planet Zork, leader of the Zorks
Barney	Jose, a third grader	Marley, the magician, man in balloon, shark, lion, man robbing money
Darvin	surfer	seven ghosts
Jero	Alex	King Martian
Juan	Tommy	Funland people
Shaun	Mike, a third grader	Zarcon
Sid	Gemini (with Swartz)	Garvin, the magician, Sparzi, dragon, soldier from loft
Trevor	monkey	evil wizard, goon, princess

Figure 5. Overview on students' choices for game players and game actors. For students who created more than one game, only the last game was included in the analyses because it was the most developed game.

der difference: whereas five girls chose a genderless or more personally identified player, only one boy adopted the same approach for his player choice
(Fisher Exact Test, $p < 0.01$).

The cast of supporting game actors emphasized this result even more: most
boys created several characters (e.g., demons, aliens from planet zork, magi-
cians, dragons, soldiers from loft, goons) with fantasy names (e.g., Zork,
Zarcon, Garvin, Sparzi, Marley) for the game world in which the player had to
interact. Albert's thoughts are a good example of character development. In four
weeks, he considered a whole cast before he settled on the demon figure. The
following excerpts are taken from his notebook entries and reflect his ongoing
considerations (see Figure 6).

In contrast, most girls choose one or two figures for their supporting cast (see
Figure 5). It is apparent in this comparison that the girls had a significantly different take on the role the player and actors have in the game. Whereas seven
out of eight girls created between zero and two supporting characters, six out
of the eight boys created three or more (Fisher Exact Test, $p < 0.025$).

One could argue that commercial video game figures provided the inspiration for the game figures designed by the boys in the Game Design Project.
This argument gains support if one considers the abundance of available video
games and their focus on a male audience (Provenzo, 1991; Kinder 1991). For
the girls, on the other hand, there are fewer examples to draw from because of
the lack of gender-appropriate video games.

The choice of familiar and personal figures provides room for the interpretation that girls grounded their designs in what they knew and liked: Rosy liked
cats hence a cat plays a major role in her game; Miriam used a skier because
she liked skiing; Gloria and Sina used a teacher in their games. Another possibility is that the small number of supporting characters reflected preferred social
groupings: Girls are known to play in smaller groups than boys.

Design of Game Interactions and Feedback

Another difference became clear in the interactions that children designed for
their players. One distinction can be drawn between the guided interaction mode
and the manipulation mode. In the first mode, the player follows the game
process as it has been determined by the designer. Most interactions between
the player and the game consist of answering questions by pressing a key or
typing an answer. Actions and animations of the game figures on the screen are
preprogrammed by the designer; the player has no impact on their development.
In contrast, in the manipulation mode, the player has to manipulate keys and
move a figure around to certain designated places. The distinction between the
two game interaction modes revealed no significant gender differences: four
girls adopted the guided interaction mode whereas six boys chose this mode for

On March 12, Albert wrote that "I made one change. I am going to make creatures ask you problems and if you don't solve them you die." He continued March 13 with "I will make a guy on shapes and make him do something." Then on March 26, he wrote, "I am going to make a bully and his gang on shapes and they'll ask you a fraction question and if you get it right, you quit or chicken out." He announced on March 27 that "I need to make a gang of punks and they will ask you a question and if the answer is wrong they kill you." At the end of that day, he wrote, "I need to finish the gang and make them ask you a question. I have to finish the outcome of what happens when you get the right answer and wrong answer."

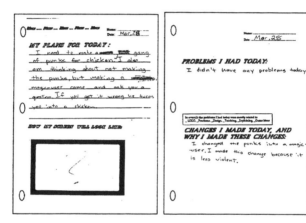

On March 28, he changed the characters of the game again: "I need to make a gang of punks for chicken. I also am thinking about not making the punks but making a magic user come and ask you a question. If you get it wrong he turns you into a chicken." At the end of the day, he decided that "I changed the punks into a magic-user. I made this change because it is less violent." His plans for the next day confirmed this decision: "I am planning to work on the question that the magic user asked. If you get it wrong he turns you into a chicken." After the month of March, Albert setted on the demon figure.

Figure 6. Albert's game-character development during the month of March and notebook designs from March 28. Note that he did not actually implement any of these ideas except for the demon figure.

their games. Two of those girls, Amy and Miriam, adopted the guided interaction mode only in the last scene of their game (see Figure 7). For that reason their interaction mode was counted as manipulation.

This trend in girls' preference for the manipulation mode has to be interpreted with care since the guided mode was much easier to implement than the

Girls	Interaction Mode	Feedback (in case of wrong answer)
Amy	manipulation mode (some guided interaction) player moves figure to Gods	non violent player does not get part of the map
Gaby	manipulation mode player moves fly around	non violent player gets correct answer
Gloria	guided interaction player answers questions	non violent no reward
Miriam	manipulation mode player moves skier down slope	non violent back to top of ski slope
Rosy	guided interaction (with some manipulation)	non violent doesn't get home
Shanice	manipulation mode player maneuvers helicopter	violent helicopter crashes
Sina	guided interaction player answers questions	non violent player has to take French
Tyree	guided interaction player answers question	non violent player can try again and does not get magic potion

Boys	Interaction Mode	Feedback (in case of wrong answer)
Albert	guided interaction player is given choices and answers questions	violent player is killed and sent to underworld
Barney	guided interaction playerpresses keys and answers questions	violent player disappears, gets kicked to moon, eaten by shark
Darvin	manipulation mode player moves figure around maze	non violent insults player verbally
Jero	guided interaction player answers questions to continue	violent game over
Juan	guided interaction player answers questions	violent game over
Shaun	guided interaction player presses keys and answers questions	violent freezes to ice cube; game over
Sid	guided interaction player answers questions	violent game over
Trevor	manipulation mode player moves figure on island to different places	violent player becomes mentally deformed

Figure 7. Overview on game interaction modes and dominant type of feedback.

manipulation mode. Yet, interestingly enough, most girls preferred to handle a more complicated programming task. It could be that the girls intended to give the player more control by having her or him manipulate the principal game figure. This fits with the girls' construction of greater identification between the player and game character, noted earlier. For the boys, in contrast, the programming of animations was more interesting (as documented by their interest in developing characters; see previous section) which forced them to keep more control over the game-playing process.

The feedback that was provided as a result of the interaction between the player and the game differed as well: in case of a wrong answer, most boys chose to end the game in a violent fashion. 'Game Over' by itself would not constitute a violent feedback if it were not in connection with loosing one's life or suffering harm. Game actors either loose their lives before the game is over or as a result of it. For example, game actors on the screen were "kicked to the moon" (Barney's game), "turned into an ice cube" (Shaun's game), "sent frying to the underworld" (Albert's game), or "mentally transformed" (Trevor's game). Darvin made his surfer character insult the players' intelligence: "Let me see how smart you are, Dude or Dudette" and "So you are telling me you're dumb" when they gave a wrong answer. The harm here is psychological rather than physical, but it is still a harm.

In contrast, almost all girls (7 out of 8) programmed different kinds of feedback for a wrong answer most of the time (Fisher Exact Test, $p < 0.01$). In case of a wrong answer, the player continued but did not receive a piece of the map (Amy), had to start again from the top of the ski slope (Miriam), take French (Sina), or did not receive a fraction of the magic power (Tyree). One exception was Shanice who ended her game end with a helicopter crash in case the player did not give the right answer. Miriam's game experienced a change in the course of its development. In the major part of her game, the skier went down a slope and was sent up back to the top in case of a wrong answer. However, in last two scenes of her game, when the player is on the way back home, Miriam decided to end the game. I do not know the reason for her change of mind but it is possible that she was influenced by the other games in her class. Furthermore, she might have tried to experiment with a new form of feedback as she also changed the narrative mode in her game structure (see next section). To summarize, in case of feedback for the player, there are again significant gender differences: Boys' feedback modes are overwhelmingly violent, girls' feedback overwhelmingly nonviolent.

Game Narrative

As students continued developing their games, defined their characters, and outlined the scenes in the subsequent weeks of the Game Design Project, they also created a story that situated the actors in a fantasy yet meaningful context. One of the most prominent examples for the development of the story or narrative in games can be found in Barney's game. I could see his impact on many other students as they were playing his game or talking about it. To emphasize the narrative stream in his game, I extracted the text from his Logo program code, excluding the fractions exchanges (see Figure 8).

Barney's game starts with the story of Jose who gets lost and experiences a series of adventures over several days and nights. His story is driven by the plot that Jose tries to find his way home. The story has several dialogues accompanying the graphics: sometimes his text is direct speech, other times it

You are Jose, a third grade kid who gets lost and must find his way home. You will go on many different adventures. Along the way, people (or beasts, creatures, etc.) will ask you questions about fractions, (you will type A, B or C, remember to press enter.) If you get the question right, you will go on safely, but beware! Danger lurks if you get the question wrong. Have fun if you dare! Type play and press enter.

"Where am I?" "I have to get home!"

A mysterious man approaches you. "Hey kid, I'm Marley the Magician and I'm going to make you disappear if you don't tell me how much of this square is colored!, says the man.

A. THREE FOURTHS   B. TWO-FOURTHS   C. FOUR-TWELTHS

What is it?

NO! "Dumb Kid" GAME OVER

YES! Go free says the man.

A man comes out of a hot air balloon and approaches you. "I'm going to take you prisoner in my balloon if you don't tell me which one of these fractions is equal to two-thirds." says the man.

A. two-fourths   B. eighth-twelfths   C. one-third.

No! You idiot! let's go GAME OVER

Yes! See Ya'

I'm tired," you say "I'll look for home in the morning."

While you are sleeping, a robber comes and takes the $33 dollars you have in your pocket.

"MONEY!"

Morning comes. You get up and realize you have no money in your pocket. "OH NO!" "I'll just have to do without it."

You see a man coming towards you. You need some money so you kindly say "Excuse me sir, could you please give me a few dollars, a robber robbed me broke!" It doesn't look hopeful. After a minute the man says "I'll give you $30 dollars if you tell me what one-half of $30 dollars is, otherwise I kick you to the moon!

A. $15   B. $ 20   C. $11   What is it?

NO! Whoa! THE MOON GAME OVER AND YOU WERE NEVER SEEN AGAIN

"Here kid, 30 dollars, don't spend it all in one place.

It gets a bit darker. You thought you would take a walk on the beach.

"I'll take a swim," you say.

Onder the water .....

A fish swims with you. You see a shark. You are too terrified to move but the fish swims away.

"You'll be makin' me a fine meal, lil' one."

Who said that?

It was you the shark! You can talk!

"Boy, kid, you're a regular Einstein!"

You are very scared.

"I'll just want to leave, please don't eat me!" you say.

"I'm hungry! But if you tell me what four-twenty-fourths is in lowest terms you can go."

A. one third   B. two sixths   C. one sixths   What is it?

SUPPER TIME CHOMP! MUNCH! MUNCH!......... BURRRPPPPPP! GAME OVER

I guess I'll go and eat that dumb old fish.

You get out.

Meanwhile at home ..... "Where's Jose, I'm so worried!"

It's getting late again. You walk around for a place to sleep. You walk into a jungle. You see a lion.

The lion is looking for supper when he comes upon you. Just as the lion is about to lunge forward

and eat you, you dodge him. "You look like a nice little kid, I'll let you free if ....

A talking shark, a talking lion! This is getting wiered!

The lion says "As I was about to say, you can go free if you tell me which one of these decimals is

equal to one-tenth."

A .1   B. 1.5   C .7

Sorry kid! GAME OVER

Well, you're allright, see ya' later.

You go to sleep and when you wake up you walk back into the city.

AIRPORT

I don't even know where I am, I'll go into the airport to find out.

INSIDE THE AIRPORT TICKET BOOTH

Figure 8 Barney's game Jose in the Fraction World. Barney's game was never finished because he left class after the summer and moved to another school. (Note that the spelling mistakes are Barney's.).

57

gives information, and still other times, the text becomes the running inner thoughts of Jose or of other actors in the game. The text essentially has an explanatory function as it sets the mood and annotates the events on the screen for the player.

The narrative format was not present in many games from the beginning. To document the shift toward the narrative in the students' game formats, I analyzed the game development of all 16 students and compiled the results (see Figure 9). Some students, such as Barney, Albert, Gloria, Juan, Rosy, and Sina, started early on incorporating narrative elements in their game design. Several students stayed with their game format: Gaby's Spider web; Shaun's Fraction Killer; Darvin's Maze; Gloria's Teacher; Sina's Teacher; and Shanice's Helicopter Madness. But the number of students who used the narrative format increased (from 6 to 12) in the course of the game development. Twice as many boys as girls made the shift from game to narrative format. No student moved from narrative to game format. By the end, 12 of the 16 children were using the narrative format. This predominance of the narrative format was statistically significant, according to a binomial test ($p < 0.05$).

This change had different forms. Some of the students changed their game on the surface without having to redo a lot of previous programming: Amy retained her map idea but changed the content of the game to Greek myths; Albert's haunted house turned into a game called Mission Town; Rosy's game first took place around the world and then changed to a travel story. In all these cases, the change of the story plot, as some students called it, did not affect the programming done prior to the change, but for another group of students, it meant that they started a new game. For example, Sid's third game is a fractions journey of two characters, Gemini and Swartz. Trevor's second game, after he finished his first, involved adventures on the Island of the Goon. The characteristic of this conversion to the narrative is that students designed scenes not solely for instructional purposes. They included additional scenes in which the different actors spoke to each other. The graphics were accompanied by text and the fraction questions were asked in the context of dialogue. There is no logic for fractions learning to take place in Greek myths, spaceships, and mazes that the students created, except that it made sense to the students themselves.

A possible explanation for the popularity of the narrative game format is that it could be considered as a form of problem-solving. It reconciled two seemingly adverse domains in a more coherent framework. Designing an educational game is a complex task. The programming of animations and concurrent actions—as they are found in many commercial video games—is difficult to accomplish in Logo, especially with the game designers' beginning programming skills. In the games, the narrative provides the glue or sugar-coating that connects the different scenes or places *and* the instructional content.

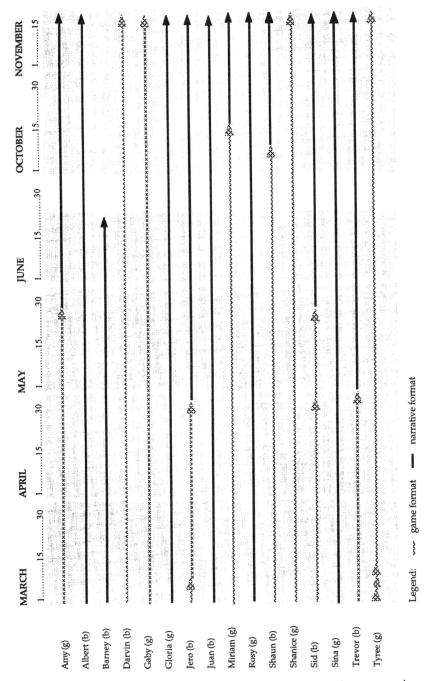

Figure 9. Overview of changes in the games and narrative format. The arrows indicate the beginnings of a new game. Some student used the new game beginning also to change the format. [g = girl; b = boy]

59

Furthermore, it allowed students to incorporate fantasy and to decorate their worlds in a more attractive way. This was also one of the features that the children in Malone and Lepper's study (1987) identified as appealing in playing games.

DISCUSSION

Sixteen children were involved in making video games, which resulted in sixteen different products. All games included sophisticated graphics, animations, and interactions in their programming. Although boys' and girls' games were similar in many aspects, it was obvious that students chose themes that facilitated their entry into the design task and allowed them to personalize their game. Analyses of games made by the children in regard to their choices of game genre, worlds, characters, interactions, feedback and narrative revealed the following:

- The adventure genre was the most popular game format, more so for boys than for girls. Some boys and girls chose skill game formats in which the player had to navigate an obstacle course such as a ski slope, or basketball court. Girls were the only ones to create a teaching context.
- Games were organized around different spaces. Most of the girls chose familiar places such as classrooms, a fair or a ski slope. The boys organized their games more around fantasy spaces such as imaginary islands and countries.
- Many students designed and developed fantasy game characters. Most boys preferred to assign the player a fantasy character persona whereas most girls addressed the player with a generic and more personal "You."
- The player controlled the game in different ways. In some games, the players manipulated the game actors by pressing keys whereas in other games the player was guided through the game by providing well-defined intervention opportunities. Girls preferred the manipulation mode in the design of their games.
- The feedback provided to the player was of a different nature for boys and girls. In the games programmed by girls, this feedback was of a non-violent nature and allowed most players to continue the game. Violent feedback such as killing the player and terminating the game in case of a wrong answer was chosen mostly by boys.
- Narrative emerged as an increasingly popular element in both girls' and boys' games.

There is a clear trend in these results: the video games made by girls differ in several features from those made by boys. The most striking, and significant, differences could be observed in the character development and the design of the feedback. But even within the construction of their game worlds, places and interaction modes, boys and girls chose different pathways. The prevalence of these gender differences begs for an explanation.

A simple answer would refer to the girls' lack of game playing exposure and experience. It is well-documented that the majority of video game players are boys (Provenzo, 1991). In the interviews of the game designers I found that the extent of the video game playing experience varied considerably. Most boys actively and consistently played video games over the week, whereas only two girls said that they did so. One could argue then that the observed gender differences would disappear by simply providing more opportunities for girls to play video games.

This lack of game-playing experience also might be influenced by girls' less successful video game play. There is an abundance of research that documents gender differences in spatial skills that are crucial to successful video game play (e.g., Loftus & Loftus, 1983). This could lead to the argument that girls are not interested in playing video games because they are not successful, due to their lack of spatial skills. New research points out that these observed gender differences disappear after extended exposure (Subrahmanyam & Greenfield, 1994). It seems therefore that girls could overcome their shortcomings in spatial skills if they only would play video games more often.

There is some appeal to these explanations; yet they all assume that the currently available commercial video games are models to emulate for all children, girls as well as boys. Popular media have a strong foothold in children's lives because they allow for the integration of the "affective, cognitive, and social" as Kinder (1991, p. 20) argued. The narrative of these different media formulates and highlights the children's understanding of their own position and place in the social context, and provides examples for children to draw from. Commercial video games make strong use of narrative. Many video games take the eternal conflict between evil and good from adventure and fairy tales. The main game figure usually is a male hero whose function it is to save the princess or to obtain a treasure. One could argue that the game designers transferred these narratives into their games because of the impact and presence of popular models.

The influence of commercially available games was especially strong in the case of boys' games. Many game designers started out with ideas taken from popular video games such as "Super Mario Brothers" or "Pac Man." Many of the boys' game implementations included violent aspects as documented in the design of their feedback to player interactions. The violence is one of the most prominent features in commercial video games (Provenzo, 1991). Hence, popular media offered models on how to organize the game design (at least for the boys). This might offer an explanation of why more boys chose in the end the narrative form compared to girls even though in the beginning an equal number of boys and girls started using narrative.

Yet popular media do not provide similar models to emulate for girls. Female game figures rarely are cast in the main role. The thematic embedding of video games in hunts and adventures are not necessarily to girls' taste. In the interviews, many girls also stated that they had no particular interest in pursuing video game-playing because they did not like the games, their content and their violent aspects. Because of this lack of popular models, girls chose as the starting point of their narrative a familiar and likeable figure (i.e., Rosy's cat) or a familiar place (i.e., Sina's classroom or Miriam's ski slope). In many ways, girls created their own worlds and characters while making their games, compensating for the sexism and violence found in many video games (Gailey, this volume).

Furthermore, in the design of their games girls renounced the use of violent feedback. Another feature, game player control, was more often included in girls' games than in boys' games. Providing the player with control to manipulate the principal game actor allows the player also to control the pace of the game. A recent study conducted in a museum setting seems to confirm this interpretation (Inkpen et al., 1993). Girls are interested in playing those electronic games that do not favor quick paced interactions.

These results allow some conjectures about why girls lack involvement in video game play. It simply seems that most commercially available video games do not appeal to girls. In spite of gender differences, game design offered for both girls and boys a framework in which to situate their preferred ideas and fantasies. In their choices of game themes and their programming of animations and interactions, the students offered a glimpse into what they found appealing and unappealing in the games and stories they experience through other media. Making a game and its rules allowed the game designers to be in charge and to determine the player's place and role in the world with all the consequences.

CONCLUSIONS

One of the conclusions to be drawn from these results is that most commercially available video games do not reflect the interests and tastes of half of the potential game-playing population, namely girls. Many girls are not attracted to the "kill features" that dominate most video game interactions. Instead they prefer less violent features to guide the game play process and different kinds of game characters and worlds. One solution is for manufacturers to create video games that address these issues and incorporate those features in their design. Furthermore, one could suggest employing female game designers, as in the past this profession has been dominated by men.

A different solution is found in the activity of game making and suggests further constructive activities. The energy and motivation that the children dedicated to the task of game making led me to believe that this is a promising avenue to pursue. In the following sections I outline briefly three different routes that children's game making/playing can take into the future: (a) tool kits for game construction, (b) physical game construction with computational elements, and (c) collaborative game construction. All of these approaches emphasize game making and games to play.

Tool Kits for Video Game Construction

There have been some early attempts in this direction such as the Pinball Construction Set (see Greenfield, 1984), which provides users with a blank board and all the necessary tools and parts to install flippers, backgrounds, controllers for their own pinball game. The user can design innumerable versions of pinball games. Eventually the user can play her or his own game alone or with others.[3] The present study suggests developing an environment that provides children with a video-game-design tool kit. Here children could create their own characters, design their own environments or worlds, and determine the rules of the game. Children could be provided with primitives in terms of rules and actions, and could adapt the parameters according to the game's needs and their desires. A first example of such a game construction tool kit is LiveWorld (Travers, 1994) in which the player can create so-called animate systems. The sharing of ideas and strategies that is already an essential part of the existing video game culture could continue in such an environment, in which children could invite each other to play their designed games (Gailey, 1992).

Physical Game Construction With Computational Elements

A different version of game making would move game design from the two-dimensional space of the computer screen back into the three- dimensional space of the real world while retaining the valuable connection to the computational domain. A first step into this direction is a construction kit that includes LEGO bricks as well as sensors and motors that can be connected via wires and controlled through programs written in Logo (Resnick, & Ocko, 1991). In this process, children would not only build mechanical objects such as cars or robots but also environments such as houses, gardens, or mazes. Children would then program the interactions between the environment and the mechanical objects. An extension of LEGO/Logo, called the programmable brick (see also Resnick & Sargent, 1994), allows one to control motors and sensors without being tethered to a personal computer and to construct objects that can interact independently with the world. One could imagine then a game world consisting of dozens of these bricks, each carrying their own programs and interacting with each other.

Collaborative Game Construction

Network developments can add collaborative dimensions to game playing and making. Multi-user environments, also called MUDS (i.e., multi-user dungeons), and collaborative simulations take advantage of these features. MUDs are text-based virtual reality environments on the Internet that can be accessed by users from all over the world (Curtis, 1992). MUDs are organized around metaphors of physical spaces such as space stations, buildings and so on. When users log into a MUD they usually assume characters of their own choice and then explore the space by typing in commands and programming objects that can be used and manipulated by other users. One example of such a MUD is MOOSE (i.e., Multi Object Oriented Scripting Environment), a multi-user environment that is being developed for children (Bruckman & Resnick, 1994). In this enviromnent, children can create their own worlds with different places, objects, features, and activities. The children use a specially developed language to describe and define their creations.

Whereas MUDs and MOOSE allow game-making in a text-based world, CitySpace (Conn, 1994) is an example for game-making with graphical features. Here children can build a virtual city with images, text, sounds and models sent across the Internet using commercially available graphics software and real-time video conferencing for communication. In contrast to MUDs, objects built in CitySpace do not have behaviors. The goal of this environment is to have children construct collaboratively a living habitat and negotiate together its constraints and features. With reference to that goal, CitySpace picks up on existing simulation games such as SimCity and SimEarth, where players can design and govern cities and ecological habitats according to their own choices.

Children making games provided us with a window into their minds. By placing children in the roles of producers rather than consumers of video games, we allowed them to express their ideas and fantasies. It was more than obvious that gender differences permeated all aspects of the game designs. One conclusion is that today's commercial video games do not address girls' interests and concerns, if one takes the games girls construct as an expression of what they wish to see and play with. Another, important conclusion of this study is that making video games, as opposed to playing them, clearly engaged girls' and boys' minds and fantasies for a long period of time. When the tables are turned, video games become a medium for children's personal and creative expression.

ENDNOTES

[1]One of the primary purposes of this project was to investigate game making as a context for learning Logo programming and fractions among other things (see also Harel, 1991). For that reason, the games designed by the students are a special breed of games, called educational games. Yet, as my analyses will indicate, it was this particular constellation that emphasized game aspects as students had to think about how to create games that were educational and entertaining at the same time. In the following analysis, I focus more on the game aspects than on the learning aspects which are discussed more extensively in other publications (e.g., Kafai, 1993).

[2]All student names are pseudonyms.

[3]One of the drawbacks of designing pinball games is that certain feelings and sensations from the mechanical world (such as the tilting of the machine) cannot be replicated in the computational environment. A further limitation is that the designer must work with a given set of parts.

REFERENCES

Baugham, S. S., & Clagett, P. D. (1983) (Eds.). *Video games & human development. Research agenda for the '80s*. Cambridge, MA: Harvard Graduate School of Education.

Bruckman, A., & Resnick, M. (1994). Virtual professional community. In Y. Kafai & M. Resnick, (Eds.), Constructionism in practice (pp. 133–146). Cambridge, MA: MIT Media Laboratory.

Bruner, J. (1987). Life as narrative. *Social Research, 54*, 11–32.

Conn, C. (1994). Coco's Channel. Connie Guglielmo. In *Wired*, 2(4), 58–60.

Curtis, P. (1992). *Mudding: Social Phenomena in Text-Based Virtual Realities*. Proceedings of DIAC 1992.

Dominick, J. R. (1984). Videogames, television violence, and aggression in teenagers. *Journal of Communication, 34*, 136–147.

Fennell, F., Houser, L. L., McPartland, D., & Parker, S. (1984, February). Ideas. *Arithmetic Teacher, 31*, 27–33.

Gailey, C. (1992). Mediated messages: Gender, class, and cosmos in home video games. *Journal of Popular Culture, 15*(2), 5–25.

Greenfield, P. M. (1984). *Mind and media. The effects of television, video games, and computers*. Cambridge, MA: Harvard University Press.

Greenfield, P. M. (1993). Respresentational competence in shared symbol systems: Electronic media from radio to video games. In R. R. Cocking & A. Renninger (Eds.), *The Development and Meaning of Psychological Distance* (pp. 161–183). Hillsdale, NJ: Lawrence Erlbaum Associates.

Greenfield, P. M., & R. R. Cocking (1994) (Eds.). Effects of interactive entertainment technology on development. *Journal of Applied Developmental Psychology, 15*(1), 1–2.

Greenfield, P. M. (1994). Video games as cultural artifacts. *Journal of Applied Developmental Psychology, 15*(1), 3–12.

Greenfied, P. M., Brannon, G., & Lohr, D. (1994). Two-dimensional representation of movement through three-dimensional space: The role of video game expertise. *Journal of Applied Developmental Psychology, 15*(1), 87–104.

Greenfield, P. M., deWinstanley, P., Kilpatrick, & Kaye, D. (1994). Action video games and informal education: Effects on strategies for dividing visual attention. *Journal of Applied Developmental Psychology, 15*(1), 105–124.

Greenfield, P. M., Camaioni, L., Ercolani, P., Weiss, L., Lauber, B. A., & Perucchini, P. (1994). Cognitive socialization by computer games in two cultures: Inductive discovery or mastery of an iconic code? *Journal of Applied Developmental Psychology, 15*(1), 59–86.

Harel, I. (1991). *Children designers*. Norwood, NJ: Ablex Publishing Corporation.

Harris, M. B., & Williams, R. (1984). Video games and school performance. *Education, 105*(3), 306–309.

Inkpen, K., Upitis, R., Klawe, M., Anderson, A, Ndunda, M., Sedighian, K., Leroux, S., & Hsu, D. (1993, December). "We have never-forgetful flowers in our garden": Girls' responses to electronic games. Technical Report 93–47, Department of Computer Science, University of British Columbia, Vancouver BC V6T 1Z4, Canada.

Inkpen, K., Booth, K., & Klawe, M. (1993). Cooperative learning in the classroom: The importance of a collaborative environment for computer-based education. Technical Report, Department of Computer Science, University of British Columbia, Vancouver BC V6T 1Z4, Canada.

Kafai, Y. (1995). *Minds in play: Computer game design as a context for children's learning*. Hillsdale, NJ: Lawrence Erlbaum Associates.

Kafai, Y. (1993). Minds in Play. Computer Game Design as a Context for Children's Learning. Unpublished Doctoral Dissertation, Harvard University Graduate School of Education, Cambridge , MA.

Kinder, M. (1991). *Playing with Power*. Berkeley: University of California Press.

Lawry, J., Upitis, R., Klawe, M., Anderson, A., Inkpen, K., Ndunda, M., Hsu, D., Leroux, S., & Sedighian, K., (1994, January). Technical Report 94–1, Department of Computer Science, University of British Columbia, Vancouver BC V6T 1Z4, Canada.

Lepper, M. R., & Malone, T. W. (1987). Intrinsic motivation and instructional effectiveness in computer-based education. In R. E. Snow & M. J. Farr (Eds.). *Aptitude, Learning and Instruction. Volume 3: Conative and Affective Process Analyses* (pp. 255–285). Hillsdale, NJ: Erlbaum.

Loftus, G. R., & Loftus, E. F. (1983). *Minds at play*. New York: Basic Books.

Malone, T. W. (1981). What makes computer games fun? *BYTE, 6*(12), 258–277.

Malone, T. W., & Lepper, M. R. (1987). Making learning fun: A taxonomy of intrinsic motivations for learning. In R. E. Snow & M. J. Farr (Eds.). *Aptitude, Learning and Instruction. Volume 3: Conative and Affective Process Analyses* (pp. 223–253). Hillsdale, NJ: Erlbaum.

Morlock, H., Yando, T., & Nigolean, K. (1985). Motivation of video game players. *Psychological Reports, 57*, 247–250.

Okagaki, L., & French, P. (1994). Effects of video game playing on measures of spatial performance: Gender effects in late adolescence. *Journal of Applied Developmental Psychology, 15*(1), 33–58.

Papert, S. (1991). *New images of programming: In search of an educational powerful concept of technological fluency*. National Science Foundation Proposal. Cambridge, MA: MIT Media Laboratory.

Papert, S. (1980). *Mindstorms*. New York: Basic Books.

Provenzo, E. F. (1991). *Video Kids: Making sense of Nintendo*. Cambridge, MA: Harvard University Press.

Resnick, M., & Ocko, S. (1991). LEGO/Logo: Learning through and about design. In I. Harel and S. Papert (Eds.), *Constructionism*, (pp. 141–150). Norwood, NJ: Ablex.

Rushbrook, S. (1986). *Messages of video games: Socialization implications*. Unpublished doctoral thesis. University of California, Los Angeles.

Sargent, R., & Resnick, M. (1994). Programmable bricks: Ubiquitous computing for kids. In Y. Kafai & M. Resnick, (Eds.). *Constructionism in practice* (pp. 101–108). Cambridge, MA: MIT Media Laboratory.

Selnow, G. W. (1984). Playing videogames: The electronic friend. *Journal of Communication, 34*, 148–156.

Silvern, S. B., & Williamson, P. A. (1987). The effects of videogame play on young children's aggression, fantasy and prosocial behavior. *Journal of Applied Developmental Psychology, 8*, 453–462.

Subrahmanyam, K., & Greenfield, P. M. (1994). Effects of video game practice on spatial skills in girls and boys. *Journal of Applied Developmental Psychology, 15*(1), 13–32.

Travers, M. (1994, April). LiveWorld. In *Proceedings of the Computer Human Interaction Conference* (pp. 341–350). Boston, MA: Addison-Wesley.

Turkle, S. (1984). *The second self: Computers and the human spirit*. New York: Simon & Schuster.

Wilensky, U. (1991). Abstract mediations on the concrete and concrete implications for mathematics education. In I. Harel and S. Papert (Eds.), *Constructionism*, (pp. 193–204). Norwood, NJ: Ablex.

Chapter 5

Impact of Virtual Reality on Young Adults' Physiological Arousal and Aggressive Thoughts: Interaction Versus Observation

SANDRA L. CALVERT
SIU-LAN TAN
Georgetown University

The information age has brought about opportunities for symbolically mediated experiences that affect human behavior. Viewing televised violence, for example, has been implicated as one causal agent in the acquisition and performance of aggressive actions (Friedrich-Cofer & Huston, 1986). Nevertheless, one can learn aggressive content from television without translating that knowledge into one's personal behavior (Bandura, 1965).

The heir apparent to the action–violence formula, which is already the staple of television programs and video games (Greenfield, 1984), is the *virtual reality* game. Virtual reality is defined as a three-dimensional computer-simulated scenario in which a person can look, move around in, and experience an imaginary world (Pimentel & Teixeira, 1993). The perception of this artificial world is accomplished by wearing special virtual reality goggles and other gear to immerse the perceptual systems within the virtual reality simulation. The more a computer simulation submerges a person's sensory systems, the more immersed he or she feels in that world (Biocca, 1992).

This research was conducted while Sandra L. Calvert was a Senior Research Associate for the National Research Council.

Appreciation is expressed to the U.S. Army Research Institute for the Behavioral and Social Sciences and Dr. Joseph Psotka, Chief of Smart Technology, for hosting this work. The position presented here is that of the authors and does not represent the position of the U.S. Army Research Institute or the National Research Council. The following people provided assistance in completing this project: Dr. Daniel O'Connell, Dr. Daniel Robinson, Dr. Aletha Huston, Katherine Hinke, Kevin Weinfurt, Marc Shepanek, Darren Metzger, Marsha Berg, Angela Norman, Brian Cho, Raymond Soh, Christopher McBride, and the students of Georgetown University. We also thank Dean Ivy Broder for allowing us to collect data on the campus of American University.

Correspondence and requests for reprints should be sent to Sandra L. Calvert, Department of Psychology, Georgetown University, 37th & O Streets, NW, Washington, DC 20057.

Unlike television, video games and virtual reality require direct action for a game to continue. In the case of aggressive content in the virtual reality game used in this study, a person must *kill* or *be killed* in this life-like, computer-simulated reality. Consequently, aggressive action is incorporated directly into a person's behavioral repertoire when virtual reality games are played. Bruner, Olver, and Greenfield (1966) advanced the idea that people can represent information at three levels: (1) enactive (e.g., with the body), (2) iconic (e.g., with the visual system), or (3) symbolic (e.g., with words). Video game play cultivates iconic, visual–spatial representational skills (Greenfield, Camaioni, et al., 1994; Subrahmanyam & Greenfield, 1994). Interactions with an aggressive virtual reality game may well cultivate enactive, bodily representations (e.g., firing a gun) that may then be easily recoded into subsequent aggressive behavior in future situations.

It is the shift from observational to interactive, immersive technologies that is the focus of the inquiry here. Specifically, we examine the impact of acting upon versus observing aggressive content in a virtual reality environment.

Theoretical Models in Relation to Aggression

Various theoretical models have been used to examine the impact of violence on a person's aggressive behavior. According to the *arousal theory,* physiological responses to aggression should initially increase as one engages in a threatening experience. For example, a person's blood pressure, a measure of the autonomic nervous system, increases when he or she is exposed to an aggressive situation. Physiological arousal can then be channeled into the activities that one is exposed to—aggressive ones in this instance.

As stated in the *social cognitive theory* (previously known as the social learning theory), a person can become more aggressive after observing and then imitating a model who is acting aggressively. Observational learning is regulated by attention, retention, production, and motivation (Bandura, 1986). Once attended to, aggressive content can be retained in memory to be reproduced when a person is motivated to do so. According to social cognitive theory, a second way that aggressive behavior can occur is by disinhibition. With age and development, internal impulse controls are created to inhibit aggressive actions. As stated by Bandura, these controls can be disinhibited, or weakened, when one observes another act aggressively, thereby resulting in more personal aggression.

Finally, according to the *psychoanalytic theory* (Hall, 1954), a subsequent decrease in aggression should occur through catharsis as one releases aggressive drives safely in symbolic games rather than actual experiences. Hall suggested that drive reduction should occur when a person participates in fantasy experiences that allow him or her to "drain off" dangerous aggressive impulses, a primary human drive. In a game, one can kill another person symbolically.

Impact of Information Technologies on Aggressiveness

Over the past two decades, a significant body of research has been gathered which indicates that viewing television violence increases aggressive behavior (Friedrich-Cofer & Huston, 1986). Children who observe aggressive television models sometimes imitate those behaviors or have the internal controls disinhibited that prevent aggressive action (Stein & Friedrich, 1972; Steur, Applefield, & Smith, 1971). Blood pressure increases after viewing sexual or aggressive content, providing support for the arousal theory (Zillmann, 1971). However, children rarely act less aggressively after viewing televised violence as would be predicted by a drive-reduction hypothesis via the psychoanalytic theory (Friedrich-Cofer & Huston, 1986).

In a seminal study for the social cognitive theory, Bandura (1965) drew a distinction between acquisition and performance. Children viewed a violent film. After viewing the program, some children, particularly boys, spontaneously incorporated those aggressive actions in their play. Other children, primarily girls, did not spontaneously imitate the observed aggression. However, when offered incentives to do so, most children were quite capable of depicting the aggression they had viewed which indicated that the actions had been learned even if not performed. This finding suggests that girls may think about the aggressive actions that they view, even if they do not necessarily act aggressively.

Games created for new technologies often require aggressive performance by participants. In many video games, players must shoot or harm their symbolic opponents in order to win. Consistent with television studies on observed aggression, children who played aggressive video games subsequently became more aggressive in their social play, supporting both the social cognitive and arousal theories (Silvern & Williamson, 1987). Similarly, children who interacted with a violent video game were found to imitate those aggressive behaviors in their later free play (Schutte, Malouff, Post-Garden, & Rodasta, 1988). Prosocial behavior that benefits others can also be inhibited for those who play violent video games (Chambers & Ascione, 1987). Hostile feelings increased for young adults who played violent video games (Anderson & Ford, 1986), supporting the arousal theory. Although video game play is associated with increased hostility, the effect is smaller than that produced by television or darts (Favaro, 1983).

There is also a set of studies that suggest catharsis or tension release from video game play (Brooks, 1983; Egli & Meyers, 1984; Graybill, Kirsch, & Esselman, 1985). For instance, aggressive ideation was lower for children who played an aggressive rather than a nonaggressive video game, suggesting a discharge of aggression in a socially acceptable way (Graybill et al., 1985). However, Graybill, Strawniak, Hunter, and O'Leary (1987) found no differences in the aggressive behavior of children who played a violent versus a nonviolent video game.

In summary, as in the television area, imitation (Schutte et al., 1988), disinhibition (Silvern & Williamson, 1987), and arousal (Anderson & Ford, 1986; Silvern & Williamson, 1987) are viable constructs for explaining the impact of aggression on children. To the extent that girls become active participants in these aggressive games, one might expect a closer link between acquisition and performance than has been reported in the television literature. However, drive reduction via catharsis has received more support in the video game literature than in the television literature (Brooks, 1983; Egli & Meyers, 1984; Graybill et al., 1985).

Appearing now in video arcades, a male haven (Greenfield, 1984), virtual reality interfaces can create the illusion that a person is part of the game. Player movements control the virtual reality game. For instance, turning one's head to the right yields one visual perspective; turning it to the left yields a different one. No screen boundaries are seen, as in the case of a television screen, because the goggles provide a continuous, peripheral view. Actions within this setting may be more realistic than those encountered in previous technologies because information is presented in a three-dimensional form that is responsive to player movements. As in video game play, the person is now the character, not an observer as in television viewing (Shapiro & McDonald, 1992).

In the case of aggression, the virtual reality game player has the personal experience of being pursued by or shooting an opponent. As in video games, aggressive performance is required for successful performance; in this way, aggressive action may be incorporated directly into a person's behavioral repertoire. The immersive quality of the technology may increase both arousal levels and aggression more than previous formats because people feel they are directly and personally experiencing violent events. Involuntary emotional responses may be influenced by such immersive, life-like experiences (Shapiro & McDonald, 1992).

Person Characteristics

Characteristics of people also impact the ways that technologies influence them. In the case of aggression, we considered two primary personal attributes: gender and aggressive traits. Men have long been identified as demonstrating more aggressive behavior than women (Huston, 1983; Maccoby, 1980). Some argue that differences in aggression between men and women, as well as within a particular gender group, are based on biologically based traits (Maccoby, 1980) and thus certain people are simply inherently more aggressive than others. Other theorists approach aggressive behavior as a state at a given point in time (Huston, 1983). From the latter perspective, aggression is learned just like any other behavior: through reinforcement and punishment.

Regardless of the origins, aggression is clearly stable within people of both genders for many years (Maccoby, 1980). Aggressive youth are likely to become aggressive adults. Consequently, we included a priori trait measures of aggression in order to control for initial differences in aggression. After treatments, we also examined two temporary state measures of aggressiveness in feelings and thoughts, respectively.

The Present Study

The purpose of this study was to compare the impact of participation versus observing an aggressive virtual reality game on young adults' arousal levels, feelings of hostility, and aggressive thoughts. The major hypothesis was that physiological arousal and aggressive thoughts would increase more for those who participated directly in the virtual reality experience than for those who observed it. The arousal and social cognitive theories were expected to provide the best fit for explaining how virtual reality impacts adults' aggressive behaviors. No support was expected for a tension-reduction hypothesis, indexed by hostile feelings, as would be predicted by the psychoanalytic theory. Gender and aggressive traits were included in order to examine differential effects of aggressive exposure on different kinds of people.

The following five hypotheses were made: (1) physiological arousal and aggressive thoughts were predicted to be higher in the virtual reality immersion condition than in the virtual reality observation and control conditions; (2) subjects in the virtual reality observation condition were predicted to report more aggressive thoughts than were those in the control condition; (3) hostile feelings were not expected to decrease from baseline to treatment in the virtual reality or observation conditions, as would be predicted via a drive-reduction hypothesis; (4) because one aggresses directly in the virtual reality immersion condition, gender differences in aggressive thoughts were not predicted within this condition; and (5) as aggression is more in keeping with male rather than female roles, men were expected to report more aggressive thoughts than were women in the observation condition.

METHOD

Subjects

Subjects were 36 middle-class college students (*M* age = 20 years, 6 months), equally distributed by gender, who attended a private university in a large metropolitan area. Few had ever seen or played a virtual reality game or even knew what it was.

Procedure

Pretest. Subjects initially came for a 5 to 10 min pretest in the 2-week period prior to the experimental conditions. Each subject completed three subtests of the

Buss and Durkee (1957) personality trait measure assessing hostility. The sub-tests measured assault ($n = 10$ items), verbal hostility ($n = 13$ items), and irritability ($n = 11$ items). Subjects circled either *true* or *false* for each item. An example of an assault item is, "Once in a while, I cannot control my urge to harm others." A verbal item is, "When people yell at me, I yell back." An example of an irritable item is, "I often feel like a powder keg ready to explode." Test–retest correlations were .78 for assault, .72 for verbal hostility, and .65 for irritability (Buss, 1961). Using factor analysis techniques, Buss and Durkee clustered these three subscales into a *motor* component of hostility.

On the day of the study, a physiological measure of pulse rate was taken in the virtual reality setting. This pretest pulse rate was taken manually by an experimenter by placing her fingers on a subject's left wrist. She then counted the number of heart beats for 15 s and multiplied by four. At a later time, reliability was assessed for 6 subjects. To do so, two experimenters simultaneously took the pulse rate of individual subjects. One experimenter placed her fingers on a subject's left wrist and counted heart beats for 15 s while the other experimenter placed her fingers on the subject's right wrist and counted heart beats during that same 15-s time frame. Each score was then multiplied by four. Interobserver reliability for pulse rate, computed as two times the number of agreements divided by the total number of scores for both experimenters, averaged 98% for the six protocols where each beat was counted as a judgment.

Treatment Conditions. On a Saturday afternoon, subjects assembled outside a building at their home university. Within gender groups, each randomly signed one of three lists, thereby determining their respective treatment condition. Sub-jects were then transported by one van in groups of 12 (i.e., by treatment condition) to another university campus that was hosting a fair. Transportation time was about 10 min. The virtual reality game was located outside on campus grounds at this fair.

Upon arrival, the pretest pulse rates were taken individually for the first group: the *virtual reality condition.* They then joined a line and waited 30 to 45 min to play a virtual reality game. A research assistant, who waited with them, told them not to watch the monitors. Subjects were given a virtual reality pass instead of money to play the $5 game.

Subjects in the virtual reality condition played Dactyl Nightmare. In this game, two opponents stand on raised platforms called pods. Each wears a set of goggles and a belt and holds a pistol-action device to control the perception of bodily movement through space and of shooting a gun. The goggles provide visual images of the game: by turning one's head to the left or to the right, one alters the visual images appearing through the goggles. The belt controls the direction of movement, and one pushes the top of the hand-held device to move. It is analogous to turning one's body to face a particular direction (controlled by the belt) and then walking in that direction (controlled by pushing the top of the hand-held device). To fire the gun, one pulls the trigger.

The 4-min virtual reality game, much like a video game in content, consists of two players whose physical bodies are represented as a green or yellow cartoon-stick figures inside a three-dimensional animated world. Unlike a video game where you see both players, in a virtual reality game the player is one of the characters, and thus, sees only the represented opponent. The players are adversaries of one another. Several black-and-white checkerboard platforms appear in a multilevel acropolis. Stairs connect the platforms and columns appear in various parts of the platforms. The edge of the platforms end in black space. However, one can jump onto a small disc and ride to other levels of the platforms by pushing the forward position of the hand-held device. A pterodactyl, an additional adversary of both players, flies overhead. Players can shoot the pterodactyl; the pterodactyl can also pick up the players, lift them into the sky, and then drop them. The object of the game is to move through the platforms and shoot both the opponent and the pterodactyl. Whenever a player is dropped by the pterodactyl or shot by the other player, his or her character explodes and is then reassembled at another point on the platforms. Points are scored every time an opponent is shot. To win, a player must shoot his or her opponent more times than being hit by his or her opponent. Scores are kept mechanically.

While the first group was waiting to play, the van returned with the second group: the *observation condition*. Upon their arrival, the observation group had their pulses taken. Same-gender groups of three then watched another person's 4-min virtual reality game on a 3 ft × 3 ft video monitor.

The *control group* arrived last. Pulses were taken, and a research assistant led them as a group in the motions that are used when playing the virtual reality game. For example, subjects moved their heads and torsos 180° from side to side while keeping their feet in a constrained space. They did not see or interact with the virtual reality game. They were told to dodge the pterodactyl, one property of the virtual reality game, but aggression was not mentioned. The 4-min simulation controlled for possible arousal effects from movement per se.[1]

Posttest. The 10-min posttest consisted of three measures: (1) pulse rate, (2) the Multiple Affective Adjective Check List, and (3) a thought-listing questionnaire.

After their respective treatment conditions, each subject's pulse was immediately taken, as described in pretest procedures.

Next, subjects selected adjectives from the revised Multiple Affective Adjective Check List that described how they felt at that moment. Following the procedure of Bushman and Geen (1990), the state version of the hostility sub-

---

[1]The authors thank Daniel N. Robinson for this suggestion.

scale was used with filler items. Hostility was operationally defined as the number of hostile adjectives, such as *aggressive, angry, annoyed, complaining, critical, cross, cruel, disagreeable, disgusted, enraged, furious, hostile, incensed, irritated, mad,* and *mean,* that a subject chose. *Dizzy* and *nauseous* were added to the list because some players report motion sickness after virtual reality experiences (e.g., Biocca, 1992; Psotka, Davison, & Lewis, 1993).

Subjects also completed a questionnaire about their thoughts during the 4 min when they played, observed, or simulated the virtual reality game. Subjects were told to write about their thoughts without concern for grammar or spelling (Cacioppo & Petty, 1981). A research assistant timed them in this 4-min task. The protocols were evaluated following procedures developed by Bushman and Geen (1990) for words having aggressive meanings, such as *kill, hit, shoot, shot,* and *blow up.* In the present study, two raters later scored all 36 protocols for both aggressive thoughts and for the total number of thoughts, the latter measure reflecting general arousal. The reliability coefficient was $r = .78, p < .0001$ for aggressive thoughts, and $r = .94, p < .0001$ for total thoughts.

At the end of the study, subjects in the observation and control conditions were given the option of playing the virtual reality game. The treatment procedure, from the time subjects were picked up until they returned to their university, lasted about 3 hr.

RESULTS

Pretest Scores

Condition was assigned to subjects on the day that the experiment was conducted. We then examined the pretest information to ensure that subjects were initially equivalent on various measures. Specifically, arousal scores and hostile personality scores were examined as dependent variables with condition and gender as independent variables.

Arousal Scores. The 3 (Condition) × 2 (Gender) between-subjects analysis of variance (ANOVA) computed on pretest arousal scores yielded no effects for condition or gender. Thus, subjects were initially equivalent across groups in arousal on the day of the study.

Hostile Personality Scores. The Buss and Durkee (1957) subscales of assault, verbal aggression, and irritability were summed to create a total hostile personality score. A 3 (Condition) × 2 (Gender) between-subjects ANOVA was run on pretest hostile personality scores. No differences were found for condition or gender. Thus, there were no pretest differences in hostile personality scores across groups. However, a two-factor ANOVA computed on the three respective subtests of Buss and Durkee did yield a main effect of gender for assaultive personality, $F(1, 30) = 4.30, p < .05$. Specifically, men reported more assaultive personalities than did women ($M = 4.17$, $SD = 2.48$ vs. $M = 2.67$, $SD = 1.50$, respectively). There were no gender differences reported for personality traits like verbal aggression or irritability. There were also no condition effects on the subtests.

Posttest Scores

The analysis strategy for the posttest was to examine arousal and aggression as dependent variables as a function of condition and gender. One dependent measure examined only arousal (i.e., pulse rate), one measured hostile feelings (i.e., revised Multiple Affective Adjective Check List), and one examined both arousal (measured as total number of thoughts) and aggressive thoughts. Pretest scores were used as covariates. When a significant F ratio was found, Duncan's (1955) multiple-range follow-up contrast was used for post-hoc comparisons.

Pulse Rate Scores. A 3 (Condition) × 2 (Gender) analysis of covariance (ANCOVA) was run on posttest pulse rate scores with pretest pulse rate scores as the covariate. The two-factor ANCOVA computed on posttest pulse scores yielded a main effect of condition, $F(1, 29) < 3.35$, $p < .05$; pretest pulse scores were also significant as a covariate, $F(1, 29) = 10.23$, $p < .01$. As seen in Table 1, subjects in the virtual reality immersion condition increased in arousal more than those in either the control (i.e., the virtual reality movement simulation condition) or the observation condition.

Responses of Nausea and Dizziness to Virtual Reality. Participation in a virtual reality game could increase arousal by disrupting a person's sense of equilibrium. Therefore, we asked subjects if they felt dizzy or nauseated after their treatment conditions. Dizziness scores for the three conditions were submitted to a chi-square analysis. As seen in Table 2, subjects in the virtual reality immersion condition reported feeling dizzy or nauseated more often than those in the observation or control conditions, $\chi^2(2, N = 36) = 16.89$, $p < .001$.

TABLE 1
Mean Pretest and Posttest Pulse Rate Scores for the Control,
Observation, and Virtual Reality Conditions

Condition	Pretest Pulse Rate		Posttest Pulse Rate	
Control	74.67[b]	(7.69)	79.67[b]	(9.57)
Observation	75.67[b]	(15.39)	78.00[b]	(15.49)
Virtual Reality	81.00[b]	(12.24)	92.33[a]	(11.11)

[a,b]Means are significantly different from pretest to posttest at $p < .05$. Standard deviations are presented in parentheses. Cell means are based on 12 subjects.

TABLE 2
Frequency of Subjects Reporting Dizziness
by Condition

Condition	No Dizziness	Dizziness
Control	12	0
Observation	11	1
Virtual Reality	4	8

$N = 36$.

Within the virtual reality immersion condition, partial correlations were computed between dizziness/nausea scores and pulse rate scores after participating in the game; pretest pulse rate scores were partialled out of the equation. The partial correlation was not significant (two-tailed, $p > .10$).

Multiple Affective Adjective Check List Scores. The number of adjectives reflecting hostile feelings was summed for each subject (range 0–4). Hostility scores were submitted to a 3 (Condition) × 2 (Gender) ANCOVA with pretest scores of hostile personality traits as the covariate. The two-factor ANCOVA computed on hostile feelings yielded a main effect of gender, $F(1, 29) = 7.80$, $p < .01$. Men reported more hostile feelings during the posttest than did women ($M = 1.06$, $SD = 1.16$ vs. $M = .17$, $SD = .38$, respectively). Contrary to prediction, neither condition nor hostile personality covariate scores were significant.

Aggressive Thoughts. The next analysis examined the content of subjects' thoughts as they participated, observed, or simulated virtual reality movements. The number of aggressive thoughts was submitted to a 3 (Condition) × 2 (Gender) ANCOVA with pretest scores of hostile personality traits as the covariate. The two-factor ANCOVA computed on aggressive thoughts yielded a main effect of condition, $F(1, 29) = 6.18$, $p < .01$. As predicted, aggressive thoughts were reported more often by subjects in the virtual reality immersion condition ($M = 1.42$) than by those in the observation ($M = .17$) or control ($M = .33$) conditions. As expected, men and women reported similar frequencies of aggressive thoughts in the virtual reality condition ($M = 1.50$ vs. $M = 1.33$, respectively). Contrary to prediction, men did not report more aggressive thoughts than did women either in the observation condition ($M = .17$ vs. $M = .17$, respectively) or in the control condition ($M = 0$ vs. $M = .67$, respectively). The hostile personality trait covariate score was not significant.

Total Number of Thoughts. To test for overall arousal effects, an analysis strategy developed by Bushman and Geen (1990) was adapted. Specifically, the total number of thoughts was submitted to a 3 (Condition) × 2 (Gender)

ANOVA. As expected, there were no significant differences in the number of thoughts in varying conditions. Thus, the type of thought (i.e., aggressive) was affected by playing the virtual reality game, not the quantity of thoughts as would be predicted by the arousal theory.

DISCUSSION

The purpose of this study was to examine the impact of participating in versus observing aggressive acts, as represented in a virtual reality game, on young adults' physiological arousal, feelings of hostility, and aggressive thoughts. Individual variations were considered by including both gender and a priori levels of hostile personality traits.

As expected, subjects' heart rates increased after participation in the virtual reality game. Physiological arousal was a function of the virtual reality experience rather than of movement per se because the control condition moved in ways that paralleled the virtual reality group. This finding provides support for the arousal theory.

Those who played the virtual reality game also reported more dizziness and nausea than did those in either the observation or control conditions. Physiological arousal, however, was unrelated to motion sickness. This suggests that other factors were causing their arousal to increase.

As expected, aggressive thoughts increased more for those who played than for those who observed the virtual reality game or simulated game movements, providing support for the social cognitive theory over the arousal theory. More specifically, the aggressive content of thoughts separated virtual reality game players from those in other conditions. In contrast, the total number of thoughts, as would be expected from a straight arousal effect, did not distinguish the three conditions. One implication is that immersion has a more profound impact on thoughts than does observation.

In contrast, no differences were found between participants versus observers of a violent video game (Cooper & Mackie, 1986; Silvern & Williamson, 1987). In the Silvern and Williamson study, young children who viewed a Road Runner cartoon or who played a Space Invaders video game increased in their subsequent aggressive interpersonal behavior. Thus, participants and observers were affected similarly by exposure to a violent television program or video game. Our virtual reality study differed from both of these studies in several respects. First, we studied young adults rather than children. Second, arousal, thoughts, feelings, and personality traits were the focus of our inquiry; aggressive behavior was the focus of the television and video game studies. Third, immersion may potentially be a more powerful perceptual experience than video game play, thus increasing the impact of interactive over observational experiences. Fourth, one child at a time played the video game whereas two adults played the virtual reality game.

Minimal observer involvement was apparent in another aspect of our study.

Those who observed the aggressive virtual reality game did not report more aggressive thoughts than did those in the control condition. Based on the social cognitive theory (Bandura, 1986), differences should also have occurred between these groups.

Parallel to most television studies (Friedrich-Cofer & Huston, 1986) but unlike the video game literature where the results are more diverse (Egli & Meyers, 1984; Graybill et al., 1985; Silvern & Williamson, 1987), no support was found for catharsis for virtual reality participants. Specifically, neither aggressive ideation nor hostile feelings decreased from baseline to treatment for young adults who played an aggressive virtual reality game, as would be predicted by the psychoanalytic theory's drive-reduction hypothesis. However, hostile feelings did not increase for virtual reality participants either, as would be predicted by the arousal theory.

Personal characteristics seemed to provide the best explanation for hostility. In particular, men reported more hostile feelings on the posttest and had a more assaultive personality on the pretest than did women. These findings provide further support for gender differences in aggression (Huston, 1983; Maccoby, 1980).

Even so, men and women had similar levels of aggressive thoughts when they interacted with violent content. When aggressive action is represented directly in a person's behavioral repertoire (e.g., Bruner et al., 1966), aggressive thoughts are generated and available for action. Bandura (1965) demonstrated that gender differences occurred in children's spontaneous aggressive behaviors after viewing a violent film, but there were no gender differences in aggressive learning. Moreover, this learning could easily be translated into action, given motivational incentives to reproduce the observed aggression. Consistent with Bandura's findings concerning learning, the number of aggressive thoughts was similar for men and women who played a violent virtual reality game. Repeated participation in this type of virtual reality game could eventually reduce gender differences in aggressive behavior, but only if women are motivated to play violent games. Given the appearance of virtual reality games in video arcade contexts, where men outnumber women and play more games than women do (Greenfield, 1984), it seems that aggressive differences may actually be accentuated in natural environments.

The study of behavior in everyday situations, such as playing a virtual reality game at a fair, provides an example of the ways that people act in naturalistic rather than laboratory settings. This kind of study allows us to observe behavior in context as well as to analyze context and behavior interactions. Video games and virtual reality games, as cultural artifacts, have the potential for exploring the roles that situations play in the initiation, maintenance, termination, and constraint of human behaviors.

In summary, young adults who played an aggressive virtual reality game exhibited increased physiological arousal and increases in aggressive thoughts more so than those who observed another person play the game or who simulated virtual reality game movements. Increases in heart rate provided support for the arousal theory, and increases in aggressive thoughts provided support for the social cognitive theory. However, the observational condition did not produce more aggression, as would be predicted by the social cognitive theory. Drive-reduction via a decrease in hostile feelings, as would be predicted by the psycho-analytic theory, was not found; nor did hostile feelings increase, as would be predicted by the arousal theory. Hence, the arousal and social cognitive theories received the most support in this study, but no one theory adequately described the impact of virtual reality game play on aggression.

In general, violent virtual reality interactions override personal characteristics like gender and prior levels of hostile personality traits, resulting in similar aggressive effects for all players. These results suggest that virtual reality is an even more potent purveyor of aggression than are historical villains like television.

The symbolic nature of this interaction suggests that participants may not generalize these actions to real-life situations. However, the long history of television research suggests the opposite (Friedrich-Cofer & Huston, 1986). Interactive behaviors with violent video games can also result in interpersonal aggression (Schutte et al., 1988; Silvern & Williamson, 1987), and now we have an even more realistic medium: one in which a person can actually be percep-tually immersed in a world of violent activities.

Shifts from observational to interactive technologies provide tools that allow researchers to link emotion, behavior, and ideation. Such developments can be used to challenge and modify theoretical positions by providing direct links between symbolic media, thinking, and behavior. Personal and societal levels of aggression may well increase when participants become actively immersed in these violence-laden forms of entertainment. Research in this area can provide guidance to policymakers about the potential behavioral consequences of these new interactive technologies.

REFERENCES

Anderson, C.A., & Ford, C.M. (1986). Affect of the game player: short-term effects of highly and mildly aggressive video games. *Personality and Social Psychology Bulletin, 12,* 390–402.

Bandura, A. (1965). Influence of models' reinforcement contingencies on the acquisition and perfor-mance of imitative responses. *Journal of Personality and Social Psychology, 1,* 589–595.

Bandura, A. (1986). *Social foundation of thought and action: A social cognitive theory.* New York: Lieber-Atherton.

Biocca, F. (1992). Communication within virtual reality: Creating a space for research. *Journal of Communication, 42,* 5–22.

Brooks, B.D. (1983). *Video games and social behavior.* Symposium on video games and human development, Harvard Graduate School of Education.

Bruner, J.S., Olver, R.R., & Greenfield, P.M. (1966). *Studies in cognitive growth*. New York: Wiley.

Bushman, B.J., & Geen, R.G. (1990). Role of cognitive–emotional mediators and individual differences in the effects of media violence on aggression. *Journal of Personality and Social Psychology, 58,* 156–163.

Buss, A.H. (1961). *The psychology of aggression*. New York: Wiley.

Buss, A.H., & Durkee, A. (1957). An inventory for assessing different kinds of hostility. *Journal of Consulting Psychology, 21,* 343–349.

Cacioppo, J.T., & Petty, R.E. (1981). Social psychological procedures for cognitive response assessment: The thought listing technique. In T. Merluzzi, C. Glass, & M. Genest (Eds.), *Cognitive assessment*. New York: Guilford Press.

Chambers, J., & Ascione, F. (1987). The effects of prosocial and aggressive videogames on children's donating and helping. *Journal of Genetic Psychology, 148,* 499–505.

Cooper, J., & Mackie, D. (1986). Video games and aggression in children. *Journal of Applied Social Psychology, 16,* 726–744.

Duncan, D. (1955). Multiple range and multiple *F* tests. *Biometrics, 11,* 1–42.

Egli, E.A., & Meyers, L.S. (1984). The role of video game playing in adolescent life: Is there reason to be concerned? *Bulletin of the Psychonomics Society, 22,* 309–312.

Favaro, P.J. (1983). The effects of video game play on mood, physiological arousal and psychomotor performance. Unpublished doctoral dissertation, Hofstra University, Hempstead, NY.

Friedrich-Cofer, L., & Huston, A.H. (1986). Television violence and aggression: The debate continues. *Psychological Bulletin, 100,* 364–371.

Graybill, D., Kirsch, J., & Esselman, E. (1985). Effects of playing violent versus nonviolent video games on the aggressive ideation of aggressive and nonaggressive children. *Child Study Journal, 15,* 199–205.

Graybill, D., Strawniak, M., Hunter, T., & O'Leary, M. (1987). Effects of playing versus observing violent versus nonviolent video games on children's aggression. *Psychology: A Quarterly Journal of Human Behavior, 24,* 1–8.

Greenfield, P.M. (1984). *Mind and media: The effects of television, video games, and computers*. Cambridge, MA: Harvard University Press.

Greenfield, P.M. (1994). Video games as cultural artifacts: *Journal of Applied Developmental Psychology, 15,* 3–11.

Greenfield, P.M., Camaioni, L., Ercolani, P., Weiss, L., Lauber, B.A., & Perrucchini, P. (1994). Cognitive socialization by computer games in two cultures: Inductive discovery or mastery of an iconic code? *Journal of Applied Developmental Psychology, 15,* 59–85.

Hall, C. (1954). *A primer of Freudian psychology*. New York: World.

Huston, A.C. (1983). Sex typing. In P. Mussen (Ed.), *Handbook of child psychology: Vol. 4. Socialization, personality, and social behavior* (4th ed.). New York: Wiley.

Maccoby, E.E. (1980). *Social development*. New York: Harcourt, Brace & Jovanovich.

Pimentel, K., & Teixeira, K. (1993). *Virtual reality: Through the new looking glass*. New York: McGraw Hill.

Psotka, J., Davison, S.A., & Lewis, S. (1993). Exploring immersion in virtual space. *Virtual Reality Magazine, 2,* 70–92.

Schutte, N., Malouff, J., Post-Garden, J., & Rodasta, A. (1988). Effects of playing videogames on children's aggressive and other behaviors. *Journal of Applied Social Psychology, 18,* 454–460.

Shapiro, M., & McDonald, D. (1992). I'm not a real doctor, but I play one in virtual reality: Implications of virtual reality for judgments about reality. *Journal of Communication, 42,* 94–114.

Silvern, S.B., & Williamson, P.A. (1987). The effects of video game play on young children's aggression. *Journal of Applied Developmental Psychology, 8,* 453–462.

Stein, A.H., & Friedrich, L.K. (1972). Television content and young children's behavior. In J.P. Murray, E.A. Rubenstein, & G.A. Comstock (Eds.), *Television and social behavior: Vol. II. Television and social learning* (pp. 202–317). Washington, DC: U.S. Government Printing Office.

Steur, F.B., Applefield, J.M., & Smith, R. (1971). Televised aggression and the interpersonal aggression of preschool children. *Journal of Experimental Child Psychology, 11,* 442–447.

Subrahmanyam, K., & Greenfield, P.M. (1994). Effect of video game practice on spatial skills in girls and boys. *Journal of Applied Developmental Psychology, 15,* 13–32.

Zillmann, D. (1971). Excitation transfer in communication-mediated aggressive behavior. *Journal of Experimental Social Psychology, 7,* 153–159.

Part II

Cognitive Effects of Video Games

Chapter 6
Video Games as Cultural Artifacts

PATRICIA M. GREENFIELD

University of California, Los Angeles

Everyday cognition (Rogoff & Lave, 1984) refers to the cognitive processes that are used in real-world situations, as opposed to the psychological laboratory. Everyday cognition is embedded in a particular social and cultural setting. Although psychologists often think of cognition as being something that goes on inside the head of an isolated individual, cognitive processes most often depend on interaction either with other people (e.g., Cole & Traupmann, 1981; Gauvain, 1993; Greenfield, 1984b; Rogoff, 1990; Wood, Bruner, & Ross, 1976) or with cultural artifacts (Gauvain, 1993; Greenfield, 1984a; Lave, 1988; Saxe, 1991; Scribner & Cole, 1981). The study of the cognitive processes elicited or stimulated by video games is the study of one particular example of everyday cognition that depends upon interaction with one particular class of cultural artifact: the action video game (Greenfield, 1983; Greenfield, 1984a; Greenfield, 1993; Turkle, 1984).

Often a cultural artifact will embody a particular symbol system, the use of which involves its own sort of representational competence. Representational competence (a term coined by Sigel & Cocking, 1977) is concerned with the means, modes, and modalities by which we take in, transform, and transmit information. Bruner (1965, 1966) developed a theory of three modes of representation and their role in development. In essence, this was a theory of the development of representational competence. The three modes of representation were the enactive, the iconic, and the symbolic. The essence of representation is a relationship between signifier and signified. In enactive representation, motor action serves as a signifier; in iconic representation, an analogue image serves as the signifier; and in symbolic representation, an arbitrary sign such as a word serves as the signifier.

For each mode, according to Bruner, there are amplifiers. An amplifier is a cultural artifact that expands the range of motor, sensory, or thinking processes associated with a particular mode of representation. With his studies of the cultivation of mental skills through the symbolic forms of film, Salomon (1979) was the first to apply this notion to the audiovisual media.

I would like to thank Sandra Calvert for carefully and insightfully reviewing all of the manuscripts in this section.

Correspondence and requests for reprints should be sent to Patricia M. Greenfield, Department of Psychology, University of California, Los Angeles, 405 Hilgard Avenue, Los Angeles, CA 90024–1563.

A major theme of the studies that follow is that video games are cultural artifacts that both depend on and develop the iconic mode of representation, particularly one important aspect of iconic representation: the dynamic representation of space. As a group, the studies by Subrahmanyam and Greenfield (1994), Okagaki and Frensch (1994), and Greenfield, Brannon, and Lohr (1994) show that video game experience and expertise require and develop skills in the dynamic representation of space. In the study by Greenfield, Camaioni, et al. (1994), computer games are shown to use and develop skills using the iconic code of computer graphics. Finally, the study by Greenfield, deWinstanley, Kilpatrick, and Kaye (1994) demonstrates the effects of video game experience on the attentional skills required to process the quickly moving multiple iconic images that constitute the visual stimuli of action video games.

Video games not only embody particular symbol systems; they do so in a context of goal-directed activity with instantaneous feedback. Activity theory, elaborated by Leont'ev (1981), emphasizes the importance of goal-directed activity in cognitive development (Gauvain, 1993). The goal-directed activity involved in video games is certainly a reason for their popularity (Malone, 1981) and may well be a reason for their power in exercising and stimulating cognitive skills, as demonstrated by the articles in this special issue.

Goal-directed activity has content as well as form. In principle, content and form are independent dimensions of video games, as of any other medium. In practice, however, the violent nature of much video game activity has been an ongoing cause for concern, as it has been in the older medium of television (e.g., Greenfield, 1984a). The effects of video game violence on social behavior (cf. Silvern & Williamson, 1987) and attitudes is an area that demands much more research, particularly because of the increasingly graphic violence in popular video games such as Mortal Kombat.

However, the articles in this section deal with the cognitive effects of video games as interactive symbol systems and not with the social effects of their thematic content. In principle, the cognitive effects of video games are independent of any particular content. Therefore, in reading the articles that follow, the reader should keep in mind that the same cognitive effects should generally be obtained from games with similar symbolic design features (e.g., representation of three-dimensional space) but dissimilar content. In practice, however, the cognitive effects of action video games may not be totally independent of thematic content. In fact, the findings as a whole are suggestive concerning an interactive relation between violent video game content, gender, game mastery, and cognitive skill building.

Video games as a cultural or cognitive artifact have tremendous social importance because of their nature as a mass medium. For most children, video games are their introduction to the world of computer technology. As an example of the diffusion of video games, in December of 1991 there were more than 45 million Nintendo game sets in the U.S., representing 34% of all homes. In

1991, the home video game industry had $4.4 billion worth of sales (of which Nintendo had $3.5 million). The primary age range of Nintendo game players is 6 to 11 years, with 12- to 17-year-olds in second place (Berkhemer Kline Golin/Harris Communications, 1992). With this degree of market penetration, the video game has gone beyond a relationship with individual children to become a part of child and adolescent culture in the U.S. (Kinder, 1991; Provenzo, 1991).

The set of studies in this section indicates that video games are cultural artifacts that require and develop a particular set of cognitive skills; they are a cultural instrument of cognitive socialization. A major theme is that, just as different kinds of games have, in the past, prepared children and youth for the varying adult skills required by different societies around the world (Roberts & Sutton-Smith, 1962), so too do video games prepare children and youth for a future in which computer skills will become ever more crucial to thriving in a technological world. As writer Donald Katz put it, Nintendo (and other video games) hails "from a world in which the grown-up games of shopping, banking, moneymaking, and even war really are played out on video screens" (Katz, 1990, p. 50).

Video games are part of a trend in cultural history that started 20,000 years ago, as the number and types of symbolic codes external to the individual mind went from none to few to many (Donald, 1993). In a world in which devices for external memory storage have become increasingly important (Donald, 1993), video games socialize the minds of players to deal with the symbolic systems of the computer, society's latest form of external memory storage. As will become clear later, the spatial and iconic skills developed by video games are important for all sorts of computer applications from word processing (Gomez, Egan, & Bowers, 1986) to spreadsheets, programming, desktop publishing, databases, multimedia (Tierney et al., 1992), and scientific/technical simulations (Greenfield, Camaioni, et al., 1994). The games are revolutionary in that they socialize children to interact with artificial intelligence[1] on a mass scale and from a very early point in their development.

But video games are a cultural artifact that have greater appeal to some groups than to others (e.g., the special appeal of action video games for the military, discussed in Greenfield, deWinstanley, et al., 1994). Most pervasive and important for the topic of selective appeal, gender was an issue that could not be avoided as the study of the relationship between action video games and cognitive skills began. In several of the studies (Greenfield, Camaioni, et al., 1994; Subrahmanyam & Greenfield, 1994), it was clear that, relative to boys, girls lacked motivation to participate in a video game study. In Greenfield, Camaioni, et al. (1994), male university students in Rome and Los Angeles showed more

---

[1]Rick Sinatra, a computer programmer, originated the idea that video games are revolutionary because they involve human interaction with artificial intelligence.

skill on the average at the video game, both initially and after several hours of practice, than did female university students. The rates of improvement were, however, roughly comparable. In the study by Greenfield, Brannon, and Lohr (1994), female subjects were recruited without advance knowledge that the study involved video games. In addition, the experimental task was to learn a violent action game (The Empire Strikes Back). In that study, the male subjects generally mastered the game whereas the female subjects did not, even though they played more games in their attempts to reach criterion.

It seemed quite possible that the problem of female mastery in the Greenfield, Brannon, and Lohr research might have arisen from the violence in the particular game that was used. Research on video game tastes indicates that whereas boys are turned on by a violent game theme, girls are turned off (Malone, 1981). Studies of children and adult television preferences confirm this finding: Boys and men are much more attracted to violent action themes than are girls and women (Condry, 1989; Korich & Waddell, 1986). With this in mind, a study was designed to explore gender issues using a nonviolent action game, Marble Madness (Subrahmanyam & Greenfield, 1994). In that study, fifth-grade boys and girls were not significantly different in video game skill at the outset of game play. After a few hours of practice, however, the average boy performed better in the game than did the average girl.

However, action per se is recognized by children as a male characteristic, according to research on responses to television commercials with different formal features (Welch, Huston-Stein, Wright, & Plehal, 1979). Hence, the genre of action video game could by its very nature have greater appeal for boys than for girls. Contrary to this explanation, in the Subrahmanyam and Greenfield study it was informally observed that children of both genders preferred the action game Marble Madness to the control condition, a nonaction computer word game called Conjecture. For whatever reason, however, it is clear that males do have more video game experience than females, both in childhood (Subrahmanyam & Greenfield, 1994) and adulthood (Greenfield, Brannon, & Lohr, 1994; Greenfield, Camaioni, et al., 1994). Through this experience, they may have "learned how to learn" video games, therefore benefiting more from video game practice. Myers's (1984) extensive ethnographic study in a computer store confirmed the development of such learning strategies.

Another factor in better average male performance on video games could be that the average male may take a more experimental (trial and error) approach to the games than the average female. That is, the average male may be more willing than the average female to learn by acting before he understands all of the rules and patterns of the game. Smith and Stander (1981) found this to be the case with anthropology students who were first-time users of a computer system. This gender difference in being willing to act without full understanding could be related to the possible link between male gender and physical action noted earlier. Given an interactive medium in which experimentation yields instant feedback, an experimental approach logically has to be of great advantage.

Gender differences in the application of logical and strategic planning skills to game playing may also be a factor in gender differences in learning to play video games. Mandinach and Corno (1985) found that boys used these processes more than girls and were more successful at playing a computer adventure game called Hunt the Wumpus. These differences showed up despite equal experience with computers in general and equal liking for the game.

Another factor in gender differences in video game skill could be differences in the requisite spatial skills; such skills were a major focus of the studies that follow. All three of the articles that measured spatial skills (Greenfield, Brannon, & Lohr, 1994; Okagaki & Frensch, 1994; Subrahmanyam & Greenfield, 1994) found gender differences in favor of males at the outset of the studies, whether the participants were children (Subrahmanyam & Greenfield, 1994) or university students (Greenfield, Brannon, & Lohr, 1994; Okagaki & Frensch, 1994) and whether spatial skills were measured using paper-and-pencil stimuli (Greenfield, Brannon, & Lohr, 1994; Okagaki & Frensch, 1994) or computer stimuli (Okagaki & Frensch, 1994; Subrahmanyam & Greenfield, 1994). Nonetheless, it should be noted that under some conditions and with some tasks, gender differences did not appear (e.g., the perceptual speed test given by Okagaki & Frensch). It is also clear from the results that spatial skills are related to video game performance (Greenfield, Brannon, & Lohr, 1994; Okagaki & Frensch, 1994; Subrahmanyam & Greenfield, 1994).

Nonetheless, Okagaki and Frensch (1994) found that gender differences in performance on the nonviolent game of Tetris remained even when spatial skills, as measured by their tests, were partialed out. These remaining differences could reflect males' greater overall experience with video games, as found in many surveys (e.g., Berkhemer Kline Golin/Harris Communications, 1992; Rushbrook, 1986) as well as in the studies in this issue (Greenfield, Brannon, & Lohr, 1994; Greenfield, Camaioni, et al., 1994; Subrahmanyam & Greenfield, 1994).

There is also evidence (Ferrini-Mundy, 1987; Lowery & Knirk, 1982–1983) that spatial skills exert a positive influence on math and science performance in addition to their positive influence on the use of various computer applications. We must remember that average gender differences hide both important variability within each gender group and a large overlap between the genders. Nevertheless, even average differences in video game experience and mastery must be of concern, given the pervasiveness of the games in the early socialization of spatial and other skills of iconic representation important to developing facility with computers, math, science, and technology in general (Ferguson, 1977).

A concerted effort needs to be made to develop games that appeal to girls. Clearly this involves the development of more nonviolent games (Malone, 1981), which is socially desirable for other reasons as well. The effort should also involve developing games with more female characters that take an active role

(Provenzo, 1991; Rushbrook, 1986). Other design features, such as music (Malone, 1981), could enhance the appeal of video games to girls. Greater thematic emphasis on the drama of human relationships might make video games more appealing to girls, by analogy with female tastes in television programs (e.g., Korich & Waddell, 1986). Games designed by females are part of the answer (Kafai, in press). But there are also types of television programs (notably comedy) that appeal equally to males and females (e.g., Korich & Waddell, 1986). There must be possible video game themes that would have equal appeal for boys and girls.

The studies in this section cover a range of arcade-style action games that reflect the constant change in software from the more primitive graphics of Evolution (Greenfield, Camaioni, et al., 1994) to the more sophisticated three-dimensional representations of Marble Madness (Subrahmanyam & Greenfield, 1994). This trend toward more sophisticated graphics has continued and will continue into the foreseeable future. The games also range from arcade games (The Empire Strikes Back used by Greenfield, Brannon, & Lohr, 1994; Robotron used by Greenfield, deWinstanley, et al., 1994) to home computer games (Evolution used by Greenfield, Camaioni, et al., 1994; Robot Battle used by Greenfield, deWinstanley, et al., 1994) to games that are available for varying combinations of arcade machines, home computers, and home game sets (Marble Madness used by Subrahmanyam & Greenfield, 1994; Tetris used by Okagaki & Frensch, 1994). The studies also include other kinds of computer games in comparison conditions (a computer memory game in Greenfield, Camaioni, et al., 1994, and a computer word game in Subrahmanyam & Greenfield, 1994).

It should not be assumed that every computer game or even every action video game develops all of the skills assessed in the studies as a whole. Each game was selected to relate to the specific skill assessments used in that particular study. Indeed, earlier research by Gagnon (1985) showed that skill in each of two video games, Targ and Battlezone, was related to an overlapping but not identical set of spatial skills. However, the nature of the technology is such that skill in reading iconic and spatial representations will, in some form, come into every video game just as it comes into every computer application. As the graphics of games become ever more realistic, the particular nature of the iconic and spatial representations changes but remains central to the medium.

One reason for the predominance of spatial skills in action video games is that spatial strategies can be carried out more quickly than verbal-analytic strategies (Lowery & Knirk, 1982–1983). Neural research (Goffinet, De Volder, Bol, & Michel, 1990) indicates that action video games hyperactivate the visual cortex while depressing activity in the prefrontal cortex, the part of the brain responsible for complex linguistic grammar and sequential motor planning (Greenfield, 1991).

There is a tendency for people to use a verbal-analytic approach to visual-spatial tasks when given sufficient time to do so (Lowery & Knirk, 1982–1983). As Harris (1992) pointed out, home video games, unlike arcade games where time is money, often permit stopping time for reflection. It will be interesting to see whether nonspatial symbolic approaches to this genre, termed the adventure game, are more successful than they are to speed-based arcade-style action games, the focus of the research presented in this section.

However, as Harris pointed out, even nonspeed-based adventure games elicit iconic as well as symbolic strategies, insofar as players consult complex maps which are forms of iconic representation. The use of printed maps should add a more conceptual knowledge of space to the procedural knowledge developed by navigation through a game, if navigation through the two-dimensional representational space of a video game is cognitively similar to navigation through the real three-dimensional world studied by Thorndyke and Hayes-Roth (1982).

Video games make it possible for the first time to actively navigate through representational space. How does this experience relate to skills in navigating real-world space such as those studied by Hazen, Lockman, and Pick (1978)? How does this experience with a dynamic two-dimensional spatial representation relate to skills in dealing with static spatial representation such as map reading (Liben & Downs, 1989; Uttal & Wellman, 1989) or map making (Spencer, Harrison, & Darvizeh, 1980)? How does it relate to skills in utilizing three-dimensional models of real-world space such as those studied by DeLoache (1989)? How does navigating through a two-dimensional external representation affect internal mental representations of space such as those studied by Somerville and Bryant (1985)? A case study by Coty (1985) indicated that navigating through the representational space of linked video screens leads to the rapid development of a mental map, but more extensive research is needed. Finally, is there a connection between navigational activity in the two-dimensional representational space of video games and the communication of spatial information studied by Gauvain and Rogoff (1989)? These are important questions for future research.

Harris (1992) pointed out that home video game players consult elaborate reference manuals (which include symbolic words as well as iconic maps and other iconic images), and use the Nintendo telephone hot line (a more purely symbolic form of communication). Some statistics put these communication media and representational tools in social perspective: Nintendo of America received more than 7.2 million calls and letters from players in 1991 and its magazine *Nintendo Power* has the largest subscription base of any child- and youth-directed magazine in the U.S. with a circulation of 1.2 million.

The relatively new Super Nintendo gives an idea of the way the technology is moving: It allows players to become creators, as they produce their own animation, complete with music and sound effects. Complex simulation games, such as Sim City (the player builds a functional city) and Sim Ant (the player constructs a functional ant colony), have also become very popular. Future study of video games and their cognitive effects will have to take account of this multimedia and multimodal set of representational tools surrounding the increasingly fertile marriage of television and the computer.[2]

---

[2]Credit for the phrase "the marriage of television and the computer" belongs to Gardner (1983).

REFERENCES

Berkhemer Kline Golin/Harris Communications. (1992). *Nintendo of America: Comprehensive statistics.* Los Angeles: Author.

Bruner, J.S. (1965). The growth of mind. *American Psychologist, 20,* 1007–1017.

Bruner, J.S. (1966). On cognitive growth. In J.S. Bruner, R.R. Olver, & P.M. Greenfield et al. (Eds.), *Studies in cognitive growth* (pp. 1–67). New York: Wiley.

Cole, M., & Traupmann, K. (1981). Comparative cognitive research: Learning from a learning disabled child. In W.A. Collins, (Ed.), *Minnesota Symposium on Child Development* (Vol. 14, pp. 125–154). Hillsdale, NJ: Erlbaum.

Condry, J. (1989). *The psychology of television.* Hillsdale, NJ: Erlbaum.

Coty, B. (1985). *Class project for Analysis of Communication Effects.* Unpublished manuscript, University of California, Los Angeles.

DeLoache, J.S. (1989). Young children's understanding of the correspondence between a scale model and a larger space. *Cognitive Development, 4,* 121–129.

Donald, M. (1993). Human cognitive evolution: What we were, what we are becoming. *Social Research, 60,* 143–170.

Ferguson, E.S. (1977). The mind's eye: Nonverbal thought in technology. *Science, 197,* 827–836.

Ferrini-Mundy, J. (1987). Spatial training for calculus students. *Journal for Research in Mathematics Education, 18,* 126–140.

Gagnon, D. (1985). Videogames and spatial skills: An exploratory study. *Educational Communication and Technology Journal, 33,* 263–275.

Gardner, H. (1983, March 27). When television marries computers [Review of *Pilgrim in the microworld* by Michael Sudnow]. *New York Times,* p. 12.

Gauvain, M. (1993). The development of spatial thinking in everyday activity. *Developmental Review, 13,* 92–121.

Gauvain, M., & Rogoff, B. (1989). Ways of speaking about space: The development of children's skill in communicating spatial knowledge. *Cognitive Development, 4,* 295–307.

Goffinet, A.M., De Volder, A.G., Bol, A., & Michel, C. (1990). Brain glucose utilization under high sensory activation: Hypoactivation of prefrontal cortex. *Aviation, Space, and Environmental Medicine, 61,* 338–342.

Gomez, L.M. & Egan, D.E. (1986). Learning to use a text editor: Some learner characteristics that predict success. *Human–Computer Interaction, 2,* 1–23.

Greenfield, P.M. (1983). Video games and cognitive skills. In *Video games and human development: Research agenda for the '80s* (pp. 19–24). Cambridge, MA: Monroe C. Gutman Library, Harvard Graduate School of Education.

Greenfield, P.M. (1984a). *Mind and media: The effects of television, video games, and computers.* Cambridge, MA: Harvard University Press.

Greenfield, P.M. (1984b). A theory of the teacher in the learning activities of everyday life. In B. Rogoff & J. Lave (Eds.), *Everyday cognition: Its development in social context* (pp. 117–138). Cambridge, MA: Harvard University Press.

Greenfield, P.M. (1991). Language, tools, and brain: The ontogeny and phylogeny of hierarchically organized sequential behavior. *Behavioral and Brain Sciences, 14,* 531–551.

Greenfield, P.M. (1993). Representational competence in shared symbol systems: Electronic media from radio to video games. In R.R. Cocking & K.A. Renninger (Eds.), *The development and meaning of psychological distance* (pp. 161–183). Hillsdale, NJ: Erlbaum.

Greenfield, P.M., Brannon, C., & Lohr, D. (1994). Two-dimensional representation of movement through three-dimensional space: The role of video game expertise. *Journal of Applied Developmental Psychology, 15,* 87–103.

Greenfield, P.M., Camaioni, L., Ercolani, P., Weiss, L., Lauber, B.A. & Perrucchini, P. (1994). Cognitive socialization by computer games in two cultures: Inductive discovery or mastery of an iconic code? *Journal of Applied Developmental Psychology, 15,* 59–85.

Greenfield, P.M., deWinstanley, P., Kilpatrick, H., & Kaye, D. (1994). Action video games as informal education: Effects on strategies for dividing visual attention. *Journal of Applied Developmental Psychology, 15,* 105–123.

Harris, S. (1992). *Media influences on cognitive development.* Unpublished manuscript, University of California, Los Angeles.

Hazen, N.L., Lockman, J.J., & Pick, H.L., Jr. (1978). The development of children's representation of large-scale environments. *Child Development, 49,* 623–636.

Kafai, Y.B. (in press). *Minds in play: Computer game design as a context for children's learning.* Hillsdale, NJ: Erlbaum.

Katz, D.R. (1990, February). The new generation gap. *Esquire,* pp. 49–50.

Kinder, M. (1991). *Playing with power in movies, television and video games: From Muppet Babies to Teenage Mutant Ninja Turtles.* Berkeley, CA: University of California Press.

Korich, M., & Waddell, H. (1986). *A comparative study of age and gender influences on television taste.* Unpublished manuscript, University of California, Los Angeles.

Lave, J. (1988). *Cognition in practice.* New York: Cambridge University Press.

Leont'ev, A.N. (1981). The problem of activity in psychology. In J.V. Wertsch (Ed.), *The concept of activity in Soviet psychology* (pp. 37–71). Armonk, NY: Sharpe.

Liben, L.S., & Downs, R.M. (1989). Understanding maps as symbols: The development of map concepts in children. In H.W. Reese (Ed.), *Advances in child development and behavior.* (Vol. 22, pp. 145–201). San Diego, CA: Academic.

Lowery, B.R., & Knirk, F.G. (1982–1983). Micro-computer video games and spatial visualization acquisition. *Journal of Educational Technology Systems, 11,* 155–166.

Malone, T.W. (1981). Toward a theory of intrinsically motivating instruction. *Cognitive Science, 5,* 333–370.

Mandinach, E.B., & Corno, L. (1985). Cognitive engagement variations among students of different ability level and sex in a computer problem solving game. *Sex Roles, 13,* 241–251.

Myers, D. (1984). The patterns of player-game relationships: A study of computer game players. *Simulation and Games, 15,* 159–185.

Okagaki, L., & Frensch, P.A. (1994). Effects of video game playing on measures of spatial performance: Gender effects in late adolescence. *Journal of Applied Developmental Psychology, 15,* 33–58.

Provenzo, E.F., Jr., (1991). *Video kids: Making sense of Nintendo.* Cambridge, MA: Harvard University Press.

Roberts, J.M., & Sutton-Smith, B. (1962). Child training and game involvement. *Ethnology, 1,* 166–185.

Rogoff, B. (1990). *Apprenticeship in thinking: Cognitive development in social context.* New York: Oxford University Press.

Rogoff, B., & Lave, J. (Eds.). (1984). *Everyday cognition: Its development in social context.* Cambridge, MA: Harvard University Press.

Rushbrook, S. (1986). *"Messages" of video games: Socialization implications.* Unpublished doctoral dissertation, University of California, Los Angeles.

Salomon, G. (1979). *Interaction of media, cognition, and learning.* San Francisco: Jossey-Bass.

Saxe, G.B. (1991). *Culture and cognitive development: Studies in mathematical understanding.* Hillsdale, NJ: Erlbaum.

Scribner, S., & Cole, M. (1981). *The psychology of literacy.* Cambridge, MA: Harvard University Press.

Sigel, I.E., & Cocking, R.R. (1977). Cognition and communication: A dialectic paradigm for development. In M. Lewis & L.A. Rosenblum (Eds.), *Interaction, conversation, and the development of language: The origins of behavior* (Vol. 5, pp. 207–226). New York: Academic.

Silvern, S.B. & Williamson, P.W. (1987). The effects of video game play on young children's aggression, fantasy, and prosocial behavior. *Journal of Applied Developmental Psychology, 8,* 453–462.

Smith, C.L., & Stander, J.M. (1981). Human interaction with computer simulation: Sex roles and group size. *Simulation and Games, 12,* 345–360.

Somerville, S.C., & Bryant, P.E. (1985). Young children's use of spatial coordinates. *Child Development, 56,* 604–613.

Spencer, C.P., Harrison, N., & Darvizeh, Z. (1980). The development of iconic mapping ability in young children. *International Journal of Early Childhood, 12,* 57–64.

Subrahmanyam, K., & Greenfield, P.M. (1994). Effect of video game practice on spatial skills in girls and boys. *Journal of Applied Developmental Psychology, 15,* 13–32.

Thorndyke, P.W., & Hayes-Roth, B. (1982). Differences in spatial knowledge acquired from maps and navigation. *Cognitive Psychology, 14,* 560–589.

Tierney, R.J., Kieffer, R., Stowell, L., Desai, L.E., Whalin, K., & Moss, A.G. (1992). Computer acquisition: A longitudinal study of the influence of high computer access on students' thinking, learning, and interactions. *Apple classrooms of tomorrow* (Research Rep. No. 16). Cupertino, CA: Apple Computer, Inc.

Turkle, S. (1984). *The second self: Computers and the human spirit.* New York: Simon & Schuster.

Uttal, D.H., & Wellman, H.M. (1989). Young children's representations of spatial information acquired from maps. *Developmental Psychology, 25,* 128–138.

Welch, R.L., Huston-Stein, A., Wright, J.C., & Plehal, R. (1979). Subtle sex-role cues in children's commercials. *Journal of Communication, 29,* 202–209.

Wood, D. Bruner, J.S., & Ross, G. (1976). The role of tutoring in problem-solving. *Journal of Child Psychology and Psychiatry, 17,* 89–100.

Chapter *7*

Effect of Video Game Practice on Spatial Skills in Girls and Boys

KAVERI SUBRAHMANYAM
PATRICIA M. GREENFIELD
University of California, Los Angeles

In recent years there has been increasing recognition that, on the one hand, education is not limited to formal schooling and, on the other hand, cognitive processes are broader than those taught and tested in school (Greenfield & Childs, 1991; Greenfield & Lave, 1982; Guberman & Greenfield, 1991; Rogoff & Lave, 1984; Saxe, 1991; Scribner, 1986; Scribner & Cole, 1981). This has led to the study of both informal education and everyday cognition.

Informal education takes place by means of a host of cultural tools (Vygotsky, 1978), among which the electronic media have become increasingly important. The computer is the newest such medium. Whereas the impact of explicitly educational computer formats has been amply studied (e.g., Pea, 1985; Salomon, Perkins, & Globerson, 1988), recreational forms of computer use have been relatively ignored as a means of informal education. Chief among these is the action video game.

We would like to thank Harold Chipman of the College for Developmental Studies; Lois Levy, coordinator; Sheila Camden and Scott Rice, computer teachers; and the children at the Center for Early Education in West Hollywood, Los Angeles, without whose cooperation this research would not have been possible. Thanks also to Mitzi Fong, Lisa Kendig, Jennifer Kim, Sterling Kim, Debbie Land, Sabrina Lu, Brian Printz, and Ralph Vogel for their help in different stages of the research and manuscript preparation. We are indebted to Nancy Henley for comments on an earlier draft of this article. This research was supported by a grant from the Spencer Foundation to Patricia Greenfield.

Correspondence and requests for reprints should be sent to Kaveri Subrahmanyam, Department of Psychology, University of California, Los Angeles, 405 Hilgard Avenue, Los Angeles, CA 90024–1563.

The pervasive nature of these games is evident from a 1982 Gallup poll, which indicated that more than 93% of the nation's youth have at least played video games at some time or another (Alperowicz, 1983). Furthermore, in a random sample of 748 of the 1,274 respondents in a high school survey near Stanford University, it was found that students reported playing an average of 1.25 hours per week in a video arcade and 0.93 hours per week at home (Rogers, Vale, & Sood, 1984). Thus, the action video game has the potential to be a significant tool of cognitive socialization.

Whereas there has been considerable public concern about the possible deleterious effects of video games (e.g., Mayfield, 1982), there are relatively few data regarding their impact. A number of studies have investigated the social and personality correlates of video game play (Dominick, 1984; Gibb, Bailey, Lambirth, & Wilson, 1983; Morlock, Yando, & Nigolean, 1985). There has also been a lot of speculation about whether computer and video technology requires and develops various cognitive skills. Ball (1978) speculated that video games could teach eye-hand coordination, decision making, the following of directions, numerical concepts, and word recognition skills. Lowery and Knirk (1982–1983) proposed that video game playing might play a role in enhancing eye–hand coordination.

Greenfield (1983, 1984, 1990, 1993) suggested that there might be a set of literacy skills associated with computers and the video screen that are distinct from the traditional literacy skills required for print media (Greenfield, 1972). This idea has stimulated research as to whether video games might have beneficial effects on various cognitive processes (Greenfield, Brannon, & Lohr, 1994; Greenfield, Camaioni, et al., 1994; Greenfield, deWinstanley, Kilpatrick, & Kaye, 1994; Okagaki & Frensch, 1994). Possibly, video games are also a means of informal education that develop computer and video literacy skills that are distinct from the traditional print literacy skills taught at school (Greenfield, 1972, 1990, 1993).

These speculations about the effect of video game training fit Vygotsky's (1978) view that cultural tools and artifacts are related to cognitive developmental processes. Given the growing importance of computers and video games as modern tools, their effect on cognitive skills is of interest from both a theoretical and practical perspective.

Skill in spatial representation is one example of everyday cognitive skills utilized and developed by video games and other computer applications (Greenfield, 1993). These skills build on the foundation laid down by television (Greenfield, 1984; Salomon, 1979). Spatial representation is better thought of as a domain of skills rather than as a single ability or skill (Pellegrino & Kail, 1982). Multivariate studies (Lohman, 1979) have identified three important factors in the domain of spatial abilities: (1) spatial relations ability, which refers to the capacity to rapidly transform objects in the mind, as is required when one "mentally rotates" an object about its center; (2) spatial visualization, which is the ability to deal with complex visual problems that require imagining the relative movements of internal parts of a visual image, as in the folding and unfolding of flat patterns; and (3) perceptual speed, a visual-spatial factor, which involves rapid encoding and comparison of visual forms.

Although this is not commonly acknowledged in the literature on spatial skills, it is important to recognize that spatial tests assess skill in dealing with two-dimensional images of hypothetical two- or three-dimensional space, and not skill in navigating, comprehending, or representing real world, three-dimensional spaces. In this respect, spatial tests contrast with the spatial skill development studied by researchers such as Acredolo, Pick, and Olsen (1975), Hart and Berzok (1982), and DeLoache (1993).

Skills in utilizing two-dimensional representations of hypothetical space are important in a variety of computer applications, including word processing (Gomez, Egan, & Bowers, 1986; Gomez, Egan, Wheeler, Sharma, & Gruchacz, 1983) and programming (Roberts, 1984), as well as the recreational medium of action video games. These skills may be one component of the ability to "read" and utilize the information on computer screens.

Task analyses of video games led to early speculation that they could be a tool for the development of spatial skills (Ball, 1978; Greenfield, 1983, 1984; Lowery & Knirk, 1982–1983). This was of particular interest because of repeated findings revealing male superiority in this area. After a review of over 1,000 research reports on gender differences, Maccoby and Jacklin (1974) concluded that gender differences were "fairly well established" in the cognitive area of spatial skills. More recent work has confirmed that gender differences in spatial skills may indeed exist (Halpern, 1986; Hyde, 1981; Kerns & Berenbaum, 1991; Linn & Petersen, 1985; McGee, 1979; Peterson & Crockett, 1985). Even when male and female performance is equal on a spatial task, there is sometimes a gender difference in strategy: Males generally show preference for a more visual solution strategy whereas most females show preference for a more verbal strategy (Pezaris & Casey, 1991).

Lowery and Knirk (1982–1983) reasoned that if spatial skills are indeed built up over a period of time and repeated interactions, as suggested by research, then microcomputer video games should be an excellent mechanism for training these skills. In one of the first experimental studies utilizing video game training, Gagnon (1985) studied the effect of 5 hr video game practice on undergraduate and graduate students. Subjects in the experimental group played two games (Targ and Battlezone) for 2½ hr each whereas subjects in the control group received no video game practice. The pattern of correlations indicated that the two different video games utilized different although overlapping skills.

Gagnon (1985) reported that at the start of the study, men scored higher than women on spatial orientation, spatial visualization, and the game Targ, whereas women scored higher on eye-hand coordination. Following 5 hr of video game practice, there were no significant differences between men and women on the final scores on Targ and spatial visualization. However, the gender differences found at the start continued to be present on spatial orientation (in favor of men) and eye-hand coordination (in favor of women). In addition, subjects with less video game experience at the outset improved in spatial skills as a result of video game practice, whereas more experienced players did not. There was also a large overlap between the less experienced and women. Finally, it was found that subjects who reported they had played more video games in the past tended to score higher on both the video games and the spatial tests. Thus, both gender and amount of past video game practice were related to subjects' scores on video games and spatial skills. Although we cannot say with certainty that gender differences cause differences in exposure to video games, it does seem to be the case that females, on average, seek out video games less than males do (Lockheed, 1985).

In another set of practice studies, Pepin and Dorval (1986) and Dorval and Pepin (1986) provided eight sessions of training on the video game Zaxxon (each session included five games of Zaxxon) to 70 undergraduate students in Quebec city. Training was also provided to 101 seventh-grade students in Quebec city, although the children received fewer practice sessions because of time constraints. A control group was given only the pretest and posttest and received no training. Scores on the Space Relations Test of the Differential Aptitude Test (DAT), Forms A and B, were used as measures of spatial ability.

In the adult experiment, there were no significant gender-related differences in visual-spatial skills, although there was a tendency toward a difference in favor of men. Furthermore, both men and women gained significantly and equally on the spatial measures from playing Zaxxon. In the experiment with adolescents, there was no initial gender difference in visual-spatial skills and no significant improvement in spatial skills following training on Zaxxon. One possible reason that adults but not adolescents improved is that the adult sample had no prior experience with video games, whereas the adolescent sample had some experience (although very limited).

McClurg and Chaillé (1987) also reported that playing computer games enhanced the development of the spatial skill of three-dimensional mental rotation in fifth-, seventh-, and ninth-grade students, with the treatment benefiting both boys and girls at all three grade levels equally. It is interesting to note that in their study there was an initial gender difference in spatial skill, with boys performing better than the girls; it is not clear from their article whether this difference continued to be present at the end of the study. Miller and Kapel (1985) found a positive effect of similar computer games on two-dimensional mental rotation in seventh and eighth graders.

A thesis by Chatters (1984) found a significant positive effect of $3\frac{3}{4}$ hr of practice with Space Invaders on the Wechsler Intelligence Scale for Children (WISC) Block Design subtest for sixth-grade children. No gender differences were observed.

Thus, there is evidence that in some age groups, with some games, video games are a tool of cognitive socialization for some skills of spatial representation. There is also evidence that these games can reduce some gender differences in the spatial skills of adults. Our question was whether this effect could be obtained in a stronger form if we gave video game practice to children at the point in development when gender differences in spatial skills are first consistently detectable (Johnson & Meade, 1987).

According to Halpern (1986), there is "still some confusion about the youngest age at which gender differences in spatial abilities are found" (p. 51). Petersen and Crockett (1985) obtained gender differences in mental rotation tests for children in elementary school. In a large study of over 1,800 public school students, Johnson and Meade (1987) used a battery of seven spatial tests tailored to the developmental levels of the children and concluded that a reliable male advantage in spatial performance appeared by age 10. This means that gender differences in spatial skills are consistently detectable by the time children are about 10 years old. Although Johnson and Meade did not speculate about the theoretical rationale for these differences, there is evidence to indicate that they are the cumulative effect of the nature and nurture interaction (Pezaris & Casey, 1991).

The issue of gender differences in video game playing is also of relevance here. In a survey of video game use among fourth through sixth graders in the San Francisco Bay area, it was found that boys played video games more often both in arcades and at home (Linn & Lepper, 1987). In another survey of 10th and 11th graders in three high schools in northeast Georgia, Dominick (1984) reported that the average playing time per week was about $1\frac{1}{2}$ hr for boys compared to less than 1 hr for girls. Among college students, the relationship between gender and frequency of video game playing was similar (Morlock et al., 1985). Finally, video arcades were found to be basically male preserves (Kiesler, Sproull, & Eccles, 1985). The greater popularity of video games with males is not surprising, given the fact that in most games the player controls a male character (Provenzo, 1991; Rushbrook, 1986) who is carrying out activities that are perceived as being male oriented (Hess & Miura, 1985). In view of the male bias in video game design and video game play, Lepper (1982), Loftus and Loftus (1983), Greenfield (1984), and Kiesler et al. (1985) all expressed the concern that females might be at a disadvantage where computer usage is concerned, because computer and video games might provide an easy lead-in to computer literacy.

If we consider the research that shows a relationship between video game playing and spatial skill, it is reasonable to suppose that gender differences in spatial skills may be related to differences in video game play. Other research has implicated both training and practice in related activities as being relevant to the development of spatial skills (Baenninger & Newcombe, 1989; Brinkmann, 1966; Embretson, 1987; Gilger & Ho, 1989; Kyllonen, Lohman, & Snow, 1984; Newcombe, Bandura, & Taylor, 1983). Indeed, one study showed that brief training could eliminate gender differences favoring males on standard tests of visual-spatial skills (Stericker & LeVesconte, 1982), although another study found that initial gender differences remained after training (Embretson, 1987).

The purpose of the study presented here was to examine the relationship among gender, video game experience, and spatial skills. Based on earlier re-search, it was hypothesized that there would be gender differences favoring boys in both spatial skills and past video game experience. Also, we expected to find that gender and past experience would contribute to spatial scores prior to the experimental practice. We did not know whether video game practice would improve spatial skills equally in boys and girls (as in McClurg & Chaillé, 1987), improve them more in boys because of a possible biological component (Hier & Crowley, 1982), or improve them more in girls because of their lack of relevant previous experience (as in Gagnon, 1985). Because we wanted to maximize the possibility of reducing gender differences in spatial skills, we selected the age— 10 years old—at which gender differences in spatial skills first become reliably evident (Johnson & Meade, 1987).

Our decision to work with 10-year-olds was driven more by empirical facts than theory. We wanted to be able to detect effects of video game training; thus we selected 10-year-olds because past research shows that gender differences in spatial skill are reliably detected by this age. We also thought that gender differ-ences in spatial skills might be more easily eradicated when they first appeared, rather than at a later point in development.

Our study used a computerized spatial battery developed by Pellegrino, Hunt, Abate, and Farr (1987). This battery was chosen because it uses the same medi-um (the computer) as the video game. Also, it has been suggested that the ability to deal with objects in motion is separate from the ability to deal with the stationary displays used in conventional tests (Hunt et al., 1987). The dynamic-skill subtests of the computerized battery involve movement and are interactive in nature; because these features are present in video games, it was felt that the computerized battery would be most effective in measuring changes in spatial skill following training on video games. In other words, it was considered prudent to establish near transfer before testing for far transfer effects. In addi-tion, these dynamic tests assess spatial skills in the context of spatial activity, an important influence on real-world spatial knowledge (Gauvain, 1993).

METHOD

Subjects
The sample included 61 subjects (28 boys, 33 girls) divided randomly into an experimental and a control group. The experimental group was made up of 15 boys and 15 girls, whereas the control group consisted of 13 boys and 18 girls. The subjects were in the fifth grade and were between $10^{1}/_2$ and $11^{1}/_2$ years of age ($M = 11$ years, 1 month; $SD = 3.5$ months).

All participants attended a private school in West Hollywood, Los Angeles. Five subjects did not complete the study: Two girls and two boys were not present on the final day of testing and one boy did not wish to take the posttest. These subjects were eliminated in all analyses of pre- and posttest change.

Materials

A questionnaire was used to record the subjects' past experiences with video games and was adapted from Rushbrook (1986). Items in the questionnaire concerned information about the number of days a subject played a video game (home or arcade) and the average time played at each sitting. Questions were also asked about a subject's favorite games, the setting in which the games were played, and who accompanied the subject while he or she played the games.

The video game Marble Madness (Harvey, 1986) was used as the experimental treatment in our study. This game, available in video arcades and on Nintendo game sets, was run on Apple II computers. The game involves guiding a marble along a three-dimensional grid using a joystick. Players have to be careful to keep the marble on the path and try and prevent it from falling off the grid. They also have to fight a black ball that tries to push the marble off and avoid small wormlike creatures that cause the marble to disappear temporarily on contact.

The game has increasing levels of difficulty. At lower levels, players have to simply trace a given path, taking care to prevent the marble from falling off and to avoid the black ball and the wormlike creatures. At higher levels, the grid becomes more complex and even involves a maze in the final level. At all levels, the players have to reach the end point of one level within the time allotted before they can move on to the next higher level. If players are unsuccessful at a given level, they have to start again at the first level and work their way up.

The video game Marble Madness was selected because it involves the use of: the spatial skills of guiding objects, judging speeds and distances of moving objects, and intercepting objects. In addition, preliminary use indicated that it is a challenging and motivating game that children enjoy playing. The game has very little violence and aggression. The purpose of the study being the examination of gender differences, this feature was a major factor in the selection of Marble Madness because it has been found that boys are especially likely to play games requiring aggressive competition (Heller, 1982, cited in Morlock et al., 1985; Kiesler et al., 1985; Linn & Lepper, 1987), whereas girls are turned off by violent themes (Malone, 1981). The paths in the different levels were charted out on graph paper to keep track of the point where a player failed on a particular trial.

Another computer game, Conjecture (1986), was used as a control condition in the study. This is a word game and does not involve any spatial skills. It involves solving puzzles in which, using some initial cues, the player has to fill in blanks in words that stand for phrases, capitals, and things. It is similar in structure and content to the television show "Wheel of Fortune."

Spatial abilities were measured using a computer-based test battery (Pellegrino et al., 1987). The test was run on Apple II+ and IIe computers using monochrome monitors. The test had 10 subtests: 5 of which measured static and 5 measured dynamic spatial skills. Three of the subtests measuring dynamic spatial skills were used; it should be recalled that dynamic spatial skills

are the skills involved in dealing with objects in motion. The test developers reported no information about any gender differences in performance on the subtests.

The three subtests used were Memory Lane, Extrapolation, and Intercept;
they were chosen because they appeared to measure the dynamic spatial skills
that were relevant to performance on Marble Madness. In Memory Lane, each
subject was presented with three sequential displays consisting of three small
squares moving across the screen. Of these three paths, either the first or the third
was different from the second. The subject had to judge which of the paths (either
the first or the third) was different from the second one. In Extrapolation, the
subject had to extrapolate mentally the location of a trajectory (straight, sine, or
parabola) and then use a joystick to move an arrow to the point where he or she
estimated the line would end. In Intercept, the subject had to press the space bar
of the keyboard to trigger a missile in order to intercept a UFO that was released.
The UFO would trace a path that was either a straight line, a sine curve, or a
parabola. The reliability coefficients of the three tests ranged from .50 to .74,
and the intercorrelations between them ranged from .12 to .22.

The subtests involved random presentation of stimuli, and the subjects had to
respond by pressing the appropriate keys on the keyboard for Memory Lane and
Intercept; however, for Extrapolation the subject had to use a joystick. The
computer recorded the responses for each subject on a separate disk. The test also
had software that analyzed and printed the results.

Design and Procedure
The study used a 2 × 2 × 2 design where gender and experimental condition
were between-subject independent variables, time of testing (pre- and posttest)
was a within-subject independent variable, and spatial skill was the dependent
variable. The study involved a pretest, a training period, and a posttest. Testing
and practice required five sessions for each subject.

At the start of the experiment, all the subjects were given the questionnaire to
fill out; subjects took an average of 5 min to answer all the questions. At this
point subjects were asked whether they had played Marble Madness before.
Following Rushbrook (1986), the questionnaires were given at the start of the
study to get an index of video game experience prior to the playing of Marble
Madness.

Next, all subjects were administered the spatial skill pretest on the computer;
instructions were provided on the screen and subjects had to proceed only after
indicating that they had been understood. Also, three practice trials were given
before the test stimuli were presented. For the pretest, three subtests—Memory
Lane, Extrapolation, and Intercept—were used; the total time taken was 45 min.
The order of presentation of the subtests was counterbalanced to remove order
effects; within each subtest, the computer presented the stimuli in a random order
that varied from subject to subject. Testing took place individually at computers
in a computer lab or in the library.

After the pretest, boys and girls were randomly divided into the experimental and control groups. Subjects in the experimental group were asked to play the game Marble Madness for a total of 2 hr and 15 min. This period was broken down into three sessions of 45 min each, which took place on different days; the sessions were from 1 day to 1 week apart.

Subjects in the control group were asked to play the game Conjecture, also on the computer, for the same time period. This period was again broken down into three sessions of 45 min each. Subjects in the control group were told that they would be given an opportunity to play Marble Madness at the end of the study, and vice versa for the experimental group.

Following the training sessions, all the subjects were given the posttest. The posttest took about 30 min to administer and was similar to the pretest except that only two of the subtests, Extrapolation and Intercept, were used. This was done because many of the children found Memory Lane boring; it was observed that children were often not attending to the stimuli and were simply guessing their responses. We therefore felt that it would not be advisable to run it a second time. The order of administration of the subtests was again counterbalanced.

Analysis
The software for the computerized test performed the analysis for the pre- and posttests. Scores on the subtests Extrapolation and Intercept were in terms of absolute error (in pixels) whereas scores on the subtest Memory Lane stood for average difficulty level of correct responses. Pearson product-moment correlations revealed a significant positive relation between each subject's pretest scores on the Extrapolation and Intercept subtests, r (48) $= .55$, $p < .01$. It was therefore decided to form a composite spatial ability score by combining them. The scores on the Extrapolation and Intercept subtests were transformed into z scores to make them comparable with each other. These scores were then averaged for each subject to obtain the composite score for spatial ability. This score was computed for both the pre- and posttest. In cases where data from one of the two tests were lost because of random software failures, the single available score was used. (Four subjects were missing two pretest scores and one different subject was missing two posttest scores because of random software failure; these subjects were eliminated from the relevant analyses.[1]) Due to the fact that Memory Lane could not be administered on the posttest and because the children's behavior while taking the pretest cast doubts on its accuracy, it was decided not to use Memory Lane scores in reporting results.

The information obtained from the questionnaire was used to calculate an index of the subjects' past experiences with video games in terms of the number

---

[1]For a given subject, software failure on the pretest was theoretically independent of software failure on the posttest.

of hours played per week. The children were also asked whether they had ever played Marble Madness. For the experimental group, initial and final levels of performance on Marble Madness on each trial were also noted.[2]

RESULTS

To analyze whether there were gender differences in spatial ability and past experience with video games at the start of the study, mean scores on these variables were analyzed using t tests. As predicted, there were gender differences in baseline spatial performance scores, with boys having significantly lower error scores ($M = -0.27$) than the girls ($M = 0.29$), t (56) $= -2.50$; $p = .01$). It was also found that, as predicted, there was a significant difference between boys ($M = 4.16$) and girls ($M = 1.80$) in the estimated number of hours spent weekly playing video games, t (58) $= 2.06$, $p < .05$ (see Footnote 2 and Table 1).

To determine whether variables other than gender, specifically those related to past experience, would help to predict spatial ability at the start of the study, a stepwise multiple regression was performed. The dependent variable was the composite spatial ability score obtained from the pretest; the independent variables were gender of the subject, past video game experience, and past experience with the video game Marble Madness. Gender and past experience with Marble Madness were coded as dichotomous variables whereas past video game experience was coded as a continuous variable.

Only gender contributed significantly to the overall adjusted R^2 of .073, F (1, 54) $= 5.36$, $p < .05$, accounting for about 7% of the total variance in spatial ability at the start of the study.

To determine the effect of video game practice on error scores, a $2 \times 2 \times 2$ (Time of Test $\times$ Training $\times$ Gender) repeated-measures analysis of variance (ANOVA) was performed, with the composite spatial ability score as a repeated measure and gender and experimental conditions as the between-subjects variables. This analysis would also provide information about any differential effect of video game practice for boys versus girls.

Analysis indicated a significant two-way interaction of experimental condition and time of test, F (1, 47) $= 5.00$, $p = .03$. The two-way interaction, shown in Figure 1, indicates that video game practice (video game group) resulted in improved relative performance on the spatial tests whereas the computerized word game (control group) did not. No main effect or interaction effect involving gender was obtained.

---

[2]Because of experimenter error, two subjects lacked information on past video game experience, one subject lacked an initial score on Marble Madness, and two subjects lacked a final score on Marble Madness. These subjects were dropped from the relevant analyses. No subject was missing data on more than one variable, including pretest and posttest scores.

TABLE 1
Means and Standard Deviations of Spatial Error Z Scores and Video Game
Experience as a Function of Gender

Variable	Boys			Girls		
	n	*M*	*SD*	*n*	*M*	*SD*
Spatial Score						
Pretest**	28	−0.27	0.67	29	0.29	0.99
Posttest	26	−0.12	0.70	29	0.16	0.89
Video Game						
Experience*	28	4.16	4.98	31	1.86	3.89

*p < .05. **p < .01.

T tests indicated that there was no significant difference between the video
game and control group on pretest scores; however, the video game group
showed significantly smaller spatial error on the posttest *t* (54) = −2.26, *p* =
.02. (Note that in this and all other *t* tests, each datum point entered into only one
test and so a normal unprotected *t* test was considered appropriate.)

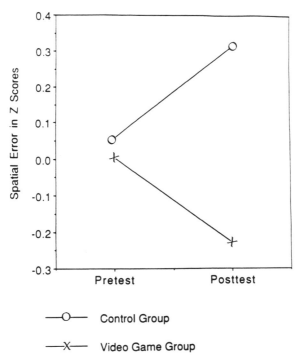

Figure 1. Effect of video game practice on error reduction in spatial task performance. The
video game group played Marble Madness. The control group played a computer word game,
Conjecture.

In the absence of an interaction involving gender, it was thought that the critical variable determining effectiveness of training might be pretest spatial skill. Although girls had significantly poorer spatial scores on the pretest than did boys, there was considerable overlap between the two groups. (The range of absolute error scores for boys was 13.82–34.02; for girls, it was 15.48–55.78.)

A Pearson product-moment correlation was computed between initial spatial ability and change scores (difference between the pre- and posttest scores) for the experimental group. It was found that there was a significant negative correlation between initial spatial scores and change scores, r (24) $=$ $-.69$, $p <$ .001, indicating that subjects who initially did poorly on the pretest showed the greatest improvement in spatial skills after training.

A new repeated-measures ANOVA was therefore run with pretest spatial skill replacing gender. The group with relatively strong preexisting spatial skills had error scores in which z equaled zero or less. The group considered to have relatively weak spatial skills had z scores above zero. The other two variables (experimental treatment as the between-subjects variable and pre- vs. posttest as the repeated-measures variable) remained the same as in the first ANOVA. In addition to replicating the experimental effect demonstrated from the first analysis, this analysis revealed significant interactions involving pretest spatial skill. Pretest spatial skill entered into a significant two-way interaction with time of test, F (1, 47) $=$ 5.38, $p =$ .025), and a significant three-way interaction with experimental condition and time of tests, (F (1, 47) $=$ 6.13, $p = 0.17$. Because the latter effect is stronger, explains the former, and is of theoretical interest, the three-way interaction will be the focus of our description; it is graphed in Figure 2.

As predicted, subjects who were initially low in spatial skills (high spatial error) benefited significantly from video game practice, $t(11) = 3.65, p = .004$. Neither subjects who started out with strong spatial skills (low spatial error) nor control group subjects were significantly affected by their experimental treatments. As expected, most but not all the members of the low spatial skills pretest group (21 out of 30) were girls; most but not all members of the high spatial skills pretest group (17 out of 26) were boys. Although subjects who initially scored poorly on the spatial tests improved significantly as a result of video game play, they did not catch up with the groups who started out with high spatial skills on the pretest. At the posttest, their spatial performance was still significantly poorer than that of both the experimental, t (24) $=$ 2.07, $p <$ .05, and control subjects t (27) $=$ 3.81, $p <$ .001, who began the experiment with strong spatial skills. This is precisely the pattern of effect one would expect from a short-term training experience. The failure of the experimental subjects, who started out with good spatial performance, to improve was not attributable to a ceiling effect. In absolute terms, the experimental subjects with strong pretest spatial skills committed an average error of 18 pixels on the pretest. Their absolute error scores stayed constant at the posttest, whereas the group of subjects who started out with poorer spatial performance reduced the mean error from 26 to 22 pixels as a result of video game practice.

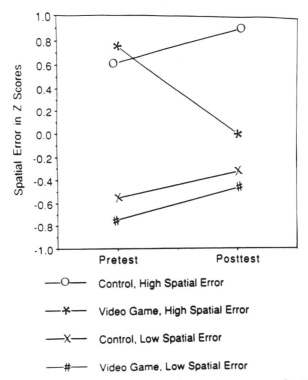

Figure 2. Effect of video game practice on spatial test performance as a function of experimental condition and pretest spatial skill.

Having demonstrated that video game practice can improve spatial skills, we wondered whether the reverse would also hold: Would better spatial skills enhance the acquisition of video game skill? Pearson product-moment correlations indicated that there was no significant relation between initial spatial scores and initial performance on the video game Marble Madness; however, initial spatial scores were significantly correlated with the final levels of video game performance, $r (26) = -.33, p < .056$. The results indicate that spatial skill enhances video game learning, just as video game practice enhances the acquisition of spatial skills.

To check whether practice helped boys and girls gain equally on video game performance, t tests were carried out to compare their mean performance scores at the beginning and end of the study. It was found that there were no significant gender differences in video game performance at the beginning; however, a significant gender difference favoring boys was found after repeated game practice, $t (27) = 6.18, p < .001$ (see Table 2).

TABLE 2
Means and Standard Deviations of Performance Scores for Boys and Girls in the Experimental Group

	Boys			Girls		
Variable	n	M	SD	n	M	SD
Marble Madness						
Initial Score	15	1.40	0.51	14	1.28	0.47
Final Score*	15	3.53	0.64	13	2.23	0.44

*$p < .001$.

DISCUSSION

The data are in agreement with earlier research (Johnson & Meade, 1987; Petersen & Crockett, 1985) that found a gender difference in spatial ability; boys made smaller errors than girls while judging speeds and distances. Also, the results confirm that gender differences may appear as early as 10 years of age, during the prepubertal period. However, there was also considerable overlap in initial spatial skills between boys and girls, with the best boy performing just slightly better than the best girl, but the worst girl performing much worse than the worst boy.

Video game practice, but not practice on a computerized word game, led to significant improvement in dynamic spatial skills, an improvement that was concentrated in those subjects who started out with relatively poor spatial performance. The results showed strongly that, irrespective of gender, video game practice could serve as compensatory education for relatively weak spatial skills. The results confirm the thesis that video games are cultural artifacts that provide informal education for spatial skills. As the meta-analysis of Baenninger and Newcombe (1989) shows, the effects of training on spatial skills do not differ for males and females. Therefore, video games can provide a cultural push that sends both boys and girls down the developmental path of spatial skill development.

However, girls take this path less frequently. In line with earlier findings (e.g., Dominick, 1984), boys estimated that they spent significantly more time per week playing video games. Although estimates of past video game experience did not predict initial spatial performance, video game practice in our experiment did produce improved spatial performance on the posttest. Nevertheless, this study did not address the issue of the stability of transfer following short training on a video game.

The connection between spatial skills and video game expertise was further strengthened by the finding that initial spatial skills predicted ultimate video game performance in the experiment. This pattern of results indicates that strong dynamic spatial skills enhance the mastery of a video game, whereas video game practice improves relatively weak dynamic spatial skills.

The lack of relation between estimates of past video game experience and error scores on the spatial tests may be because of various factors. First, there could have been a bias in the subjects' self-reports as to how often they played video games. Second, the questionnaire dealt with video games in general and did not distinguish between games on the basis of whether or not they utilized particular spatial skills. It is possible then that our index of past experience may have included exposure to games that both involved and did not involve the spatial skills tested in our study and, therefore, did not contribute to measured spatial performance. Indeed, after our data were collected and analyzed, Kuhlman and Beitel (1991) found that more reported video game experience was significantly associated with better performance on anticipation of coincidence (a dynamic spatial task related to our test of Extrapolation) in 7- to 9-year-old children.

The ability to learn a video game (as represented in personal best performance) was strongly related to spatial skill: Initial spatial skill significantly predicted ultimate attainment on Marble Madness. However, it did not predict initial levels of performance. One possible reason for there being no relation between spatial skill and initial performance on Marble Madness could be that the index of game performance was not very sensitive to differences at the beginning, when almost all subjects failed on the first level, leading to a nonsignificant result. This interpretation is supported by the findings of Bliss, Kennedy, Turnage, and Dunlap (1991), who found that correlations between spatial tracking tests and video game performance steadily increased with increasing practice on both the tests and the video games.

Video game practice tended to equalize spatial performance among groups, but it had the opposite effect on video game performance. In the experimental group, there were no gender differences in initial scores on Marble Madness; but after several hours of practice, boys showed significantly better performance than girls did. Thus, the same amount of video game practice led to lesser improvement in game skill for girls. One factor may be that because of boys' greater previous video game experience, they "learned how to learn" a new video game better than girls.

A second factor may be revealed in our informal observation that boys were much more enthusiastic about participating in our experiment than girls were. Indeed, in a coeducational sports camp where we tried to recruit additional volunteer subjects, not one girl returned a permission slip. (Because we needed to have both boys and girls in our sample, we therefore were unable to use this setting to recruit volunteer subjects.) Clearly, girls lacked motivation to do the computer-related activities that were part of our experiment.

This research leaves questions regarding breadth of transfer unanswered. In this study, care was taken to choose a video game that involved skills similar to those measured in the spatial ability subtests. It is possible that practice on

Marble Madness was effective because of this similarity in skills. However, McClurg and Chaillé (1987) found a transfer effect from practice on a dynamic video game to a static paper-and-pencil spatial test. Nonetheless, in general we do not expect very broad transfer as a result of training on video games.

It is clear that this study involved low-road transfer through extensive practice, not high-road transfer through intentional mindful abstraction of a concept, followed by its application in a new context (Salomon & Perkins, 1989). Low-road transfer is generally narrower than high-road transfer in which an abstract schema is formulated. However, the more automatic nature of the spatial skills developed through extensive and varied practice (part of the nature of a video game) in low-road transfer may be particularly useful as foundational visual literacy skills upon which more conceptual applications of computer technology may depend.

Other studies of video game training that obtained mild, mixed, or no effects of training (Dorval & Pepin, 1986; Gagnon, 1985; Greenfield, Brannon, et al., 1994; Greenfield, Camaioni, et al., 1994) used older subjects: junior high, high school, undergraduate, and graduate students. In contrast, this study focused on fifth graders or 10-year-olds and found strong effects. It seemed possible that this was the age when spatial abilities were emerging and developing and were therefore more susceptible to the effects of training—a kind of sensitive period. However, a study by McClurg and Chaillé (1987) obtained a training effect for seventh- and ninth-grade children, as well as for fifth graders. Our sensitive period hypothesis was subsequently tested and refuted by Okagaki and Frensch (1994), who showed training effects of video game practice on the spatial skills of late adolescents.

As mentioned earlier, there is evidence that individual and gender differences in spatial skills are a product of both nature and nurture (Pezaris & Casey, 1991). The study reported in this article exemplified the effect of nurture (in our case, repeated practice with a video game) on spatial skill development. Yet research has also shown that participation in spatial activities, of which video games could be considered an example, is affected by age of pubertal maturation (nature; Newcombe & Bandura, 1983). The influences of nature and nurture on spatial skill development are thus complementary and inseparable.

In conclusion, we can say that if the right game is selected and practice is given, video games may serve as important tools in programs designed to improve spatial abilities. Such programs are especially useful for training personnel on jobs that require a high level of spatial skills, such as mechanical tasks, machinery operation tasks, and jobs using radars for tracking purposes (Hunt et al., 1987). Performance on video games can also be used in place of traditional paper-and-pencil tests to identify personnel best suited for jobs requiring high levels of spatial skill, specifically dynamic skills.

Finally, nonviolent video games may be very useful to narrow the gender gap in both spatial skills and computer usage. With computers fast becoming the dominant technology of the day, video games may serve as an informal technique for equipping girls and women with the skills and motivation they need to ensure that they are not left behind in the future.

REFERENCES

Acredolo, L.P., Pick, H.L., Olsen, M.G. (1975). Environmental differentiation and familiarity as determinants of children's memory for spatial location. *Developmental Psychology, 11*, 495–501.

Alperowicz, C. (1983). Videogames, what's the score? *React, 12*, 10–11.

Baenninger, M., & Newcombe, N. (1989). The role of experience in spatial test performance: A meta-analysis. *Sex Roles, 20*, 327–344.

Ball, H.G. (1978). Telegrams teach more than you think. *Audiovisual Interaction, May*, 24–26.

Bliss, J., Kennedy, R.S., Turnage, J.J., & Dunlap, W.P. (1991). Communality of videogame performances with tracking tasks. *Perceptual and Motor Skills, 73*, 23–30.

Brinkmann, E.H. (1966). Programed instruction as a technique for improving spatial visualization. *Journal of Applied Psychology, 50*, 179–184.

Chatters, L.B. (1984). *An assessment of the effects of video game practice on the visual motor perceptual skills of sixth grade children.* Unpublished doctoral dissertation, University of Toledo, Toledo, OH.

Conjecture. (1986). [Computer program]. Auburn, WA: Robert Scott Enterprises.

DeLoache, J.S. (1993). Distancing and dual representation. In R.R. Cocking & K.A. Renninger (Eds.), *The development and meaning of psychological distance* (pp. 91–108). Hillsdale, NJ: Erlbaum.

Dominick, J.R. (1984, Spring). Videogames, television violence and aggression in teenagers. *Journal of Communication, 34*, 136–147.

Dorval, M., & Pepin, M. (1986). Effect of playing a video game on a measure of spatial visualization. *Perceptual and Motor Skills, 62*, 159–162.

Embretson, S.E. (1987). Improving the measurement of spatial aptitude by dynamic testing. *Intelligence, 11*, 333–358.

Gagnon, D. (1985). Videogames and spatial skills: An exploratory study. *Educational Communication and Technology Journal, 33*, 263–275.

Gauvain, M. (1993). The development of spatial thinking in everyday activity. *Developmental Review, 13*, 92–121.

Gibb, G.D., Bailey, J.R., Lambirth, T.T., & Wilson, W.P. (1983). Personality differences between high and low electronic video game users. *The Journal of Psychology, 114*, 159–165.

Gilger, J.W., & Ho, H. (1989). Gender differences in adult spatial information processing: Their relationship to pubertal timing, adolescent activities, and sex-typing of personality. *Cognitive Development, 4*, 197–214.

Gomez, L.M., Egan, D.E., & Bowers, C. (1986). Learning to use a text editor: Some learner characteristics that predict success. *Human–Computer Interaction, 2*, 1–23.

Gomez, L.M., Egan, D.E., Wheeler, E.A., Sharma, D.K., & Gruchacz, A.M. (1983, December). How interface design determines who has difficulty learning to use a text editor. In *Proceedings of CHI '83 Conference on Human Factors in Computer Systems* (pp. 176–181). New York Association for Computing Machinery.

Greenfield, P.M. (1972). Oral vs. written language: The consequences for cognitive development in Africa, the United States, and England. *Language and Speech, 15*, 169–178.

Greenfield, P.M. (1983). Video games and cognitive skill. In *Video games and human development: Research agenda for the '80s* (pp. 19–24). Cambridge, MA: Monroe C. Gutman Library, Graduate School of Education.

Greenfield, P.M. (1984). *Mind and media: The effects of television, video games, and computers.* Cambridge, MA: Harvard University Press.

Greenfield, P.M. (1990). Video screens: Are they changing how children learn? *Harvard Education Letter, 6*(2), 1–4.

Greenfield, P.M. (1993). Representation competence in shared symbol systems: Electronic media from radio to video games. In R.R. Cocking & K.A. Renninger (Eds.), *The development and meaning of psychological distance* (pp. 161–183). Hillsdale, NJ: Erlbaum.

Greenfield, P.M., Brannon, C., & Lohr, D. (1994). Two-dimensional representation of movement through three-dimensional space: The role of video game experience. *Journal of Applied Developmental Psychology, 15*, 87–103.

Greenfield, P.M., Camaioni, L., Ercolani, P., Weiss, L., Lauber, B.A., & Perrucchini, P. (1994). Cognitive socialization by computer games in two cultures: Inductive discovery or mastery of an iconic code? *Journal of Applied Developmental Psychology, 15*, 59–85.

Greenfield, P.M., & Childs, C.P. (1991). Developmental continuity in biocultural context. In R. Cohen & A.W. Siegel (Eds.), *Context and development* (pp. 135–159). Hillsdale, NJ: Erlbaum.

Greenfield, P.M., deWinstanley, P., Kilpatrick, H., & Kaye, D. (1994). Action video games and informal education: Effects on strategies for dividing visual attention. *Journal of Applied Developmental Psychology, 15*, 105–123.

Greenfield, P.M., & Lave, J. (1982). Cognitive aspects of informal education. In D. Wagner & H. Stevenson (Eds.), *Cultural perspectives on child development* (pp. 181–207). San Francisco: Freeman.

Guberman, S.R., & Greenfield, P.M. (1991). Learning and transfer in everyday cognition. *Cognitive Development, 6*, 233–260.

Halpern, D.F. (1986). *Sex differences in cognitive abilities.* Hillsdale, NJ: Erlbaum.

Hart, R., & Berzok, M. (1982). Children's strategies for mapping the geographic-scale environment. In M. Potegal (Ed.), *Spatial abilities: Development and physiological foundations* (pp. 147–172). New York: Academic.

Harvey, W. (1986). *Apple marble madness* [Computer program]. Atari Games Corporation. San Maleo, CA: Electronic Arts.

Hess, R.D., & Miura, I.T. (1985). Gender differences in enrollment in computer camps and classes. *Sex Roles, 13*, 193–204.

Hier, D.B., & Crowley, W.F., Jr. (1982). Spatial ability in androgen-deficient men. *The New England Journal of Medicine, 20*, 1202–1204.

Hunt, E., Pellegrino, J.W., Abate, R., Alderton, D., Farr, S., Frick, R., & McDonald, T. (1987). *Computer controlled testing of spatial-visual ability* (Tech. Rep.). San Diego: Naval Personal Research and Development Center.

Hyde, J.S. (1981). How large are cognitive gender differences? *American Psychologist, 36*, 892–901.

Johnson, E.S., & Meade, A.C. (1987). Developmental patterns of spatial ability: An early sex difference. *Child Development, 58*, 725–740.

Kerns, K.A., & Berenbaum, S.A. (1991). Sex differences in spatial ability in children. *Behavior Genetics, 21.* 383–396.

Kiesler, S., Sproull, L., & Eccles, J.S. (1985). Pool halls, chips, and war games: Women in the culture of computing. *Psychology of Women Quarterly, 9*, 451–462.

Kuhlman, J.S., & Beitel, P.A. (1991). Videogame experience: A possible explanation for differences in anticipation of coincidence. *Perceptual and Motor Skills, 72*, 483–488.

Kyllonen, P.C., Lohman, D.F., & Snow, R.E. (1984). Effects of aptitudes, strategy training, and task facets on spatial task performance. *Journal of Educational Psychology, 76*, 130–145.

Lepper, M.R. (1982, August). *Microcomputers in education: Motivational and social issues.* Paper presented at the American Psychological Association, Washington, DC.

Linn, M.C., & Petersen, A.C. (1985). Emergence and characterization of sex differences in spatial ability: A meta-analysis. *Child Development, 56,* 1479–1498.

Linn, S., & Lepper, M. (1987). Correlates of children's usage of video games and computers. *Journal of Applied Social Psychology, 17,* 72–93.

Lockheed, M.E. (1985). Women, girls, and computers: A first look at the evidence. *Sex Roles, 13,* 115–122.

Loftus, G.R., & Loftus, E.F. (1983). *Mind at play.* New York: Basic Books.

Lohman, D.F. (1979). *Spatial ability: A review and reanalysis of the correlational literature* (Tech. Rep. No. 8). Palo Alto, CA: Stanford University Aptitude Research Project.

Lowery, B.R., & Knirk, F.G. (1982–1983). Micro-computer video games and spatial visualization acquisition. *Journal of Educational Technology Systems, 11,* 155–166.

Maccoby, E.E., & Jacklin, C.N. (1974). *The psychology of sex differences.* Stanford, CA: Stanford University Press.

Malone, T.W. (1981). Toward a theory of intrinsically motivating instruction. *Cognitive Science, 5,* 333–370.

Mayfield, M. (1982, November 10). Video games only fit for old. *USA Today,* p. 1.

McClurg, P.A., & Chaillé, C. (1987). Computer games: Environments for developing spatial cognition? *Journal of Educational Computing Research, 3,* 95–111.

McGee, M.G. (1979). Human spatial abilities: Psychometric studies and environmental, genetic, hormonal, and neurological influences. *Psychological Bulletin, 86,* 889–918.

Miller, G.G., & Kapel, D.E. (1985). Can non-verbal, puzzle type microcomputer software affect spatial discrimination and sequential thinking skills of 7th and 8th graders? *Education, 106,* 160–167.

Morlock, H., Yando, T., & Nigolean, K. (1985). Motivation of video game players. *Psychological Reports, 57,* 247–250.

Newcombe, N., & Bandura, M.M. (1983). Effect of age of puberty on spatial ability in girls: A question of mechanism. *Developmental Psychology, 19,* 215–224.

Newcombe, N., Bandura, M.M., & Taylor, D.G. (1983). Sex differences in spatial ability and spatial activities. *Sex Roles, 9,* 377–386.

Okagaki, L., & Frensch, P.A. (1994). Effects of video game playing on measures of spatial performance: Gender effects in late adolescents. *Journal of Applied Developmental Psychology, 15,* 33–58.

Pea, R.D. (1985). Beyond amplification: Using the computer to reorganize mental functioning. *Educational Psychologist, 20,* 167–182.

Pellegrino, J.W., Hunt, E.B., Abate, R., & Farr, S. (1987). A computer-based test battery for the assessment of static and dynamic spatial reasoning abilities. *Behavior Research Methods, 19,* 231–236.

Pellegrino, J.W., & Kail, R. (1982). Process analyses of spatial aptitude. In R.J. Sternberg (Ed.), *Advances in the psychology of human intelligence* (Vol. 1, pp. 311–365). Hillsdale, NJ: Erlbaum.

Pepin, M., & Dorval, M. (1986, April). *Effect of playing a video game on adults' and adolescents' spatial visualization.* Paper presented at the annual meeting of the American Educational Research Association, San Francisco, CA.

Petersen, A.C., & Crockett, L. (1985, August). Factors influencing sex differences in spatial abilities during adolescence. In S.L. Willis (Chair), *Sex differences in spatial ability across the life-span.* Symposium conducted at the 93rd Annual Convention of the American Psychological Association, Los Angeles, CA.

Pezaris, E., & Casey, M.B. (1991). Girls who use "masculine" problem-solving strategies on a spatial task: Proposed genetic and environmental factors. *Brain and Cognition, 17,* 1–22.

Provenzo, E.F., Jr. (1991). *Video kids: Making sense of Nintendo*. Cambridge, MA: Harvard University Press.

Roberts, R.J., Jr. (1984, April). *The role of prior knowledge in learning computer programming*. Paper presented at the Western Psychological Association, Los Angeles, CA.

Rogers, E.M., Vale, M.E., & Sood, R. (1984, May). *Diffusion of video games among teenagers in Silicon Valley*. Paper presented at the 34th Annual Conference of the International Communication Association, San Francisco, CA.

Rogoff, B., & Lave, J. (Eds.). (1984). *Everyday cognition: Its development in social context*. Cambridge, MA: Harvard University Press.

Rushbrook, S. (1986). *"Messages" of video games: Socialization implications*. Unpublished doctoral dissertation, University of California, Los Angeles.

Salomon, G. (1979). *Interaction of media, cognition, and learning*. San Francisco: Jossey-Bass.

Salomon, G., & Perkins, D.N. (1989). Rocky roads to transfer: Rethinking mechanisms of a neglected phenomenon. *Educational Psychologist, 24*, 113–142.

Salomon, G., Perkins, D., & Globerson, T. (1988, August). *Partners in cognition: Extending human intelligence with intelligent technologies*. Paper presented at the XXIV International Congress of Psychology, Sydney, Australia.

Saxe, G.B. (1991). *Culture and cognitive development: Studies in mathematical understanding*. Hillsdale, NJ: Erlbaum.

Scribner, S. (1986). Thinking in action: Some characteristics of practical thought. In R.J. Sternberg & R.K. Wagner (Eds.), *Practical intelligence: Nature and origin of competence in the everyday world* (pp. 13–30). Cambridge, England: Cambridge University Press.

Scribner, S., & Cole, M. (1981). *The psychology of literacy*. Cambridge, MA: Harvard University Press.

Stericker, A., & LeVesconte, S. (1982). Effect of brief training on sex-related differences in visual-spatial skill. *Journal of Personality and Social Psychology, 43*, 1018–1029.

Vygotsky, L.S. (1978). *Mind in society*. Cambridge, MA: Harvard University Press.

Chapter 8

Effects of Video Game Playing on Measures of Spatial Performance: Gender Effects in Late Adolescence

Lynn Okagaki

Purdue University

Peter A. Frensch

University of Missouri at Columbia

Educators and behavioral scientists have long recognized the value of play in children's development (e.g., Almy, 1967; Athey, 1984). In particular, games have been identified as an important facilitator of children's cognitive, social, and moral development (e.g., Kamii & DeVries, 1980; Piaget, 1965; Selman, 1980). Currently, one of the most popular varieties of games for both children and adolescents is the video game. The meteoric rise of video games over the last decade has led to a corresponding rise in the emotional debate regarding the consequences of video game playing. Do video games, like other games, provide a context that encourages positive development?

The research presented here is guided by the belief that, partly because of their enormously and intrinsically motivating qualities (Malone, 1981), video

This research was supported, in part, by a summer research fellowship and a Research Council Grant from the graduate division of the University of Missouri at Columbia to Peter A. Frensch. We thank Jody Crow, Brian Donaldson, Staci Enger, David Foreman, Sharmie Guha, Joellyn Hotes, Maggie Loewe, Randy Mitchell, Roger Pharr, Janet Remedios, Tiffany Schuster, Tony Turk, and Debbie Zukerman for their assistance with data collection. We also thank the Nintendo Corporation of America, Inc., for providing us with the Nintendo setups and game cartridges used in the research presented here.

Correspondence and requests for reprints should be sent to Lynn Okagaki, Department of Child Development and Family Studies, Purdue University, West Lafayette, IN 47907–1267.

games do indeed have great potential as educational tools. Empirical research on the impact of video game playing is scarce, however. Most of the existing research has dealt with social and emotional factors. For those interested in cognitive domains, researchers have proposed that spatial skills are the cognitive skills that are most likely to benefit from video game practice (e.g., Greenfield, 1984; Loftus & Loftus, 1983; Lowery & Knirk, 1982–1983). Indeed, spatial skills are the focus of two of the empirical articles in this special issue (Greenfield, Brannon, & Lohr, 1994; Subrahmanyam & Greenfield, 1994). Improvement of spatial skills could be particularly beneficial for females, who reportedly do not do as well as males on some spatial performance tasks (for reviews, see Halpern, 1986; Maccoby & Jacklin, 1974; McGee, 1979).

EFFECTS OF VIDEO GAME PRACTICE ON MEASURES OF COGNITIVE AND PERCEPTUAL PERFORMANCE

The few existing studies examining the impact of video game practice on cognitive and perceptual variables have obtained mixed results. Some studies have obtained limited effects of video game practice on performance of spatial tasks (e.g., Gagnon, 1985; Pepin & Dorval, 1986 [cited by Subrahmanyam & Greenfield, 1994]; Strein, 1987). In contrast, however, some studies have found that positive benefits can be obtained from video game playing (e.g., Dorval & Pepin, 1986; Forsyth & Lancy, 1987; Subrahmanyam & Greenfield, 1994). Reasons for the discrepancies in the findings may lie in the variety of spatial skills that were tapped by the video games and by the spatial performance tests, the degree of transfer required between the video game and spatial performance test, and differences in the ages of the participants.

With respect to variation in spatial skills, Linn and Petersen (1985) suggested that spatial tasks may in fact require three different types of spatial skills: (1) spatial perception, (2) mental rotation, and (3) spatial visualization. Spatial perception is the ability to infer the orientation of an object with respect to one's own orientation. Mental rotation is the ability to imagine the rotation of a visual stimulus. Spatial visualization is the most difficult ability to describe precisely. According to Linn and Petersen, spatial visualization tasks "involve complicated, multistep manipulations of spatially presented information. These tasks may involve the processes required for spatial perception and mental rotations but are distinguished by the possibility of multiple solution strategies" (p. 1,484). That is, spatial visualization requires multiple mental manipulations of spatially represented objects. In addition, spatial visualization tasks can be accomplished using analytic strategies. It is also important to note that the spatial tasks that are referred to are tasks that require the individual to manipulate mental representations of objects and not to manipulate actual physical objects in real space. Whether or not studies obtain differences on spatial tasks after video game practice may depend on the type of spatial skills that are utilized and on the match between the spatial skills involved in the video game and the skills that are tested on the transfer task.

In a study with an undergraduate and graduate student sample, Gagnon (1985) had the experimental group play two video games for a total of 5 hr over a 1-week period. The two video games were: (1) Targ, in which a spaceship is manipulated through a two-dimensional grid while shooting enemy spaceships; and (2) Battlezone, in which the participant drives a tank through a battleground while shooting enemy tanks. In Battlezone, the participant views a three-dimensional representation of the battlefield (as if looking out of the tank's window) and has a two-dimensional aerial view (the view generated by a radar screen) of the field. Both games require spatial visualization and spatial perception skills. Three paper-and-pencil measures were used as pre- and posttests of spatial performance. In the Guilford-Zimmerman Spatial Orientation Test, the participant compares pairs of pictures to determine how a figure (the prow of a boat) must have moved to get from its position in Picture 1 to its position in Picture 2. In the Guilford-Zimmerman Spatial Visualization Test, an alarm clock is shown in an initial orientation, with arrows showing how it will be rotated, and the subject must determine which picture depicts the clock after it has been rotated. The third test was the Visual Pursuit Test (not part of Linn & Petersen's, 1985, taxonomy), in which the subject traces a line from beginning to end on a circuit board as it crosses several other lines on the circuit board.

Initial scores on Targ were correlated with pretest scores on the Visual Pursuit Test, but not with pretest scores on the other two spatial performance tests. It appeared that players were relying on visual tracking skills during their initial playing of the video game. In contrast, it seemed that playing Targ did not utilize spatial orientation and spatial visualization skills to the same degree. Initial scores on Battlezone were not significantly correlated with any of the paper-and-pencil tests. However, final scores on Battlezone were correlated with the Visual Pursuit and Spatial Visualization pretests. Gagnon (1985) suggested that because Battlezone was more complex than Targ, it might simply have taken longer for subjects to figure out how to play the game. In addition, final scores on Battlezone were correlated with posttest Visual Pursuit scores, which suggests that playing Battlezone may have influenced participants' Visual Pursuit performance.

Although Gagnon (1985) did not obtain overall differences between experimental subjects and control subjects on paper-and-pencil Spatial Visualization, Spatial Orientation, and Visual Pursuit tests, post hoc analyses indicated that women in the experimental group showed more improvement on the Spatial Visualization posttest than women in the control group. There were no differences among the men on any test. Gagnon suggested that because the women did not perform as well as the men initially on all of the pretests, they might have been able to benefit from playing the video games whereas men did not do so.

Because the 5 hr of video game practice all occurred within a 1-week period and 5 hr were equally split between two different games, it is possible that subjects did not have enough time to gain much expertise in these video games. Alternatively, Gagnon may have found limited gains in spatial skill performance after playing Targ and Battlezone because the measures of spatial skill were static, paper-and-pencil measures of the skills and consequently different from the utilization of those skills during video game play.

Dorval and Pepin (1986; Pepin & Dorval, 1986 [cited by Subrahmanyam & Greenfield, 1994]) also had limited success in obtaining improvement in spatial skill performance after video game practice. In a study of 70 French Canadian undergraduates who had no prior experience playing video games, Dorval and Pepin (1986) found that after eight sessions of practice, pretest-to-posttest improvement on a paper-and-pencil spatial visualization test was greater for experimental subjects than for control subjects. In this experiment, each practice session included five games of Zaxxon, and the subjects could play no more than two sessions within each week. In Zaxxon, the player manipulates a spaceship through three-dimensional space while shooting down enemy ships. However, using the same materials, Pepin and Dorval (1986 [cited by Subrahmanyam & Greenfield, 1994]) did not obtain similar improvement of experimental subjects over control subjects with a sample of 101 seventh-grade students.

Others have found stronger support for the hypothesis that video game playing can improve spatial skill performance (e.g., Forsyth & Lancy, 1987; McClurg & Chaillé, 1987; Subrahmanyam & Greenfield, 1994). For example, McClurg and Chaillé (1987) found that fifth, seventh, and ninth graders' mental rotation performance as measured by a paper-and-pencil test improved after video game practice. In their experiment, participants in the experimental conditions played either the video game Factory or the video game Stellar 7 for 45 min twice a week for 6 weeks. In Factory, participants must visualize what will happen to a sheet of metal as it goes through an assembly line of punch, stripe, and rotate machines in order to create a particular product. Because players initially see an overhead view of the metal sheet and then see side views of the machines, they must be able to mentally rotate the image and imagine the effect of the punch, stripe, and rotate machines on the metal sheet. In Stellar, a spaceship is manipulated through three-dimensional space while avoiding objects and shooting enemy targets. The players see objects at different distances and in different orientations and must learn to recognize the enemy targets in their various orientations. Both games rely on mental rotation and spatial visualization skills. The transfer task was a paper-and-pencil mental rotation test in which subjects saw a three-dimensional target shape in one orientation and had to determine whether another shape was the same as the target shape but in a different orientation, or whether it was a different shape.

Also using tests that closely matched the skills used in the practice sessions, Subrahmanyam and Greenfield (1994) found that after only three 45-min sessions, children 10 years, 5 months–11 years, 5 months who had played the video game Marble Madness showed more improvement on the spatial skill tests than did control subjects who had played a computerized word game. They suggested that their success in obtaining training effects might have been due to the age of the subjects. That is, late childhood to early adolescence may be a time when spatial abilities are developing and are more easily affected by training. They also observed that both the spatial skill tests and the video game utilized dynamic spatial skills involving judging speeds and distances of moving objects and intercepting moving targets. Hence, transfer from the video game to the spatial skills was a close transfer of skills between relatively similar contexts.

GENDER DIFFERENCES IN THE EFFECTS OF VIDEO GAME PLAYING ON MEASURES OF COGNITIVE AND PERCEPTUAL PERFORMANCE

In video game research, gender differences on spatial performance tests have not been consistently obtained. For example, in the previously cited studies by Dorval and Pepin (1986; Pepin & Dorval, 1986 [cited by Subrahmanyam & Greenfield, 1994]), there were no gender differences on pre- and posttest scores for either the undergraduates or the seventh graders. In contrast, Gagnon (1985) found that men outperformed women on spatial orientation pre- and posttests, and on the spatial visualization pretest. However, there was no difference between the men and women on the spatial visualization posttest. As mentioned earlier, Gagnon found that women improved their spatial visualization scores after practice on the video games, but there was no improvement for the men. She argued that the lack of difference between men and women on the spatial visualization posttest was most likely due to the practice on the video games.

Although there appears to be some evidence for a gender difference on tests of spatial skills (e.g., Halpern, 1986; Maccoby & Jacklin, 1974; McGee, 1979), the magnitude of the gender difference, the specificity of the difference with respect to type of spatial skills, and the ages when gender differences emerge have been questioned (e.g., Caplan, MacPherson, & Tobin, 1985; Hyde, 1981). For example, Hyde (1981) argued, on the basis of a meta-analysis of visual-spatial ability studies, that the magnitude of the difference between males and females is very small. Others (e.g., Caplan, et al., 1985) have argued that the data are very inconsistent and reflect the lack of consensus about the specific skills that comprise visual-spatial abilities and their operationalization.

Basing their observations on the results of their meta-analysis of spatial ability studies, Linn and Petersen (1985) suggested that: (a) on spatial orientation tasks, reliable effect sizes indicating gender differences different from zero occurred only for subjects over 18 years old, (b) on mental rotation tasks, gender differences were found at all ages, with the largest effect sizes occurring on more complex mental rotation tasks (e.g., those using three-dimensional figures); and

(c) on spatial visualization tasks, the average effect size for gender differences did not differ from zero. Hence, whether gender differences on spatial ability tasks are obtained appears to be a function of both the type of spatial ability task used and the ages of the participants.

In their frequently cited review, Maccoby and Jacklin (1974) concluded that from early adolescence on, males typically outperform females on visual spatial tasks (e.g., spatial orientation, spatial relationships, spatial visualization tasks). Subrahmanyam and Greenfield (1994) suggested that one reason Maccoby and Jacklin might have obtained gender differences in both performance and training effects, was that late childhood and early adolescence might be a particularly sensitive period in the development of spatial abilities.

The main goal of the research presented here was to examine three specific aspects of the relation between video game play and spatial skills among older adolescents. First, we examined whether gender differences can be obtained in initial visual spatial performance and in video game play in a sample of older adolescents. Second, we examined the impact of video game play on spatial performance in the same sample. In essence, a replication of Subrahmanyam and Greenfield's (1994) findings with an older sample is provided. Third, we studied the effect of video game play on the specific component of spatial skills utilized in the game. That is, if a video game relies heavily on two spatial skills, is the impact on those skills predictable? We present two experiments in which measures of spatial performance were obtained from subjects both before and after they practiced the video game Tetris. In Experiment 1, paper-and-pencil measures of spatial performance were used, and in Experiment 2, computerized measures of spatial performance were used.

EXPERIMENT 1

Tetris is a game that requires the rapid rotation and placement of two-dimensional stimuli. In Experiment 1, subjects were given four paper-and-pencil tests assessing mental rotation, spatial visualization, and perceptual speed. We examined whether performance on spatial performance tests, game playing performance, and the impact of playing Tetris on spatial performance differed for males and females. In general, we anticipated that scores on measures that assess rotation and spatial visualization should have increased as a result of playing Tetris because playing this game requires the participant to practice mental rotation and spatial visualization. Conversely, scores on the measure of perceptual speed should have been affected to a much lesser degree, if at all. The perceptual speed test consisted of encoding and differentiating letters, functions that are highly overlearned and likely to be at ceiling for most subjects. Hence, practicing Tetris for 6 hr was not likely to affect performance on the perceptual speed task.

METHOD

Subjects

Fifty-seven undergraduate students (28 males, 29 females, M age $= 19.93$ years, $SD = 4.33$) were recruited from introductory psychology classes at the University of Missouri-Columbia and either participated in the study for course credit or for payment ($10). At their first session, all subjects completed the questionnaire about their previous video game experience. None of the subjects reported any prior experience with Tetris.

Materials

Participants in the experimental group played the video game Tetris on a Nintendo game set. In Tetris, seven different two-dimensional shapes, each consisting of four squares, must be placed into openings in a wall so that there are no holes in the wall. The target shapes appear at the top of the screen and fall at a set rate toward the wall at the bottom of the screen (see Figure 1). The wall is 10 squares wide and the target shapes initially appear over the center of the wall. The shapes may be placed in the wall in their original orientation or they may be rotated to obtain a better fit. In addition, the shapes may be moved left or right to fall into more suitable openings. The object of the game is to prevent the wall from

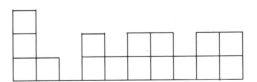

Figure 1. Example of Tetris shape and wall.

building up to the top of the screen and thereby ending the game. Whenever a row is completely filled (i.e., there are no holes or gaps in it), the row disappears, the height of the wall drops down, and players score one "line." The speed at which the target shapes fall increases as the level of difficulty increases. Successful play requires players to compare the presented shapes in their original and rotated orientations with the various openings (or spaces) in the wall to determine their best possible fit. That is, players must not only mentally represent the shapes in different orientations (mental rotation skill), but must also mentally visualize what would happen if the shapes were dropped into a particular opening in the wall (spatial visualization skill).

Subjects in both the experimental and control groups completed four paper-and-pencil tests taken from the French Kit (French, Ekstrom, & Price, 1963): (1) Finding A's, a perceptual speed measure; (2) the card rotations test, a two-dimensional mental rotation task; (3) the cube comparisons test, a three-dimensional mental rotation task; and (4) the form board test, a spatial visualization measure. For the perceptual speed task, subjects are presented with several lists of words and must cross out words that contain the letter A. For the card rotations test, subjects must determine whether a two-dimensional figure is the same as the target figure (i.e., the figure can be rotated to match the target) or whether it is different from the target (see Figure 2A). In the cube comparisons

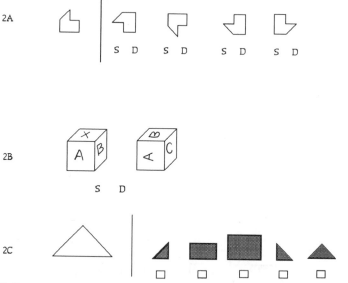

Figure 2. Figure 2A is an example of a card rotation item. Figure 2B is an example of a cube comparisons item. Figure 2C is an example of a form board item. Used by permission of the Educational Testing Service, the copyright owner.

task, subjects see two cubes lying side by side (see Figure 2B). Three sides of each cube are visible and on each side there is a letter. Subjects must decide whether the cubes are the same (i.e., one cube can be rotated so that the three visible sides will match those of the other cube) or different. For the form board test, Subjects see a target shape and must determine which of the shapes from a set of five could be combined to form the target shape (see Figure 2C). All four tests are timed tests. There were two versions of each test, one for the pretest (Time 1) and one for the posttest (Time 2). Half of all subjects received Version 1 at Time 1 and Version 2 at Time 2; the other half received Version 2 at Time 1 and Version 1 at Time 2.

Procedure

Participants were randomly assigned either to the experimental or the control group. During the first and last sessions, both experimental and control participants completed the four paper-and-pencil tasks as the Time 1 and Time 2 measures of their spatial and perceptual speed performance. Tests were administered to groups of 3 to 8 subjects at a time. The time between testing was 14 days, on average, for the experimental and control groups. In addition to the paper-and-pencil tests, both groups completed a brief questionnaire about their prior video game playing experience during the first session.

At the end of the Time 1 assessment session, practice sessions for playing Tetris were scheduled for the experimental group participants. Individual practice sessions for each subject were scheduled 1 day apart, except for weekends. At the first practice session, subjects were given instructions in booklet form for playing Tetris. Each of the 30 experimental subjects (15 males, 15 females) played Tetris for twelve 30-min sessions for a total of 6 hr of playing time. The subjects' first and last practice sessions were videotaped, and they usually took the posttests the day after the last practice session.

The 27 control group participants (13 males, 14 females) completed the Time 1 measures and returned 2 weeks later to do the Time 2 assessment. During that time, they reportedly refrained from playing any video games.

Design

The dependent variables of interest were subjects' scores on the paper-and-pencil spatial performance measures as well as measures representing the quality of game-playing performance for subjects in the experimental condition. The independent variables were *group* (between-subjects; experimental vs. control), *gender* (between-subjects; male vs. female), and *time of testing* (within-subjects; Time 1 vs. Time 2).

RESULTS AND DISCUSSION

For clarity of presentation, the results have been organized into two main sections. In the first section, we present analyses testing for gender differences on paper-and-pencil spatial and perceptual speed tests and game performance at the beginning of the experiment. The second section contains the results pertaining to the effects of video game playing on improving performance on spatial performance tests.

Initial Effects of Gender

Spatial Performance Tests. Table 1 contains the mean pretest scores on the four spatial performance tests as a function of gender. To test whether males and females differed on their initial performances on the spatial performance tests, we performed a one-way multivariate analysis of variance (MANOVA) with gender as a between-subjects variable on the scores from the four spatial skill and perceptual speed tests. In this analysis, the gender effect was reliable, Wilks' $\Lambda = 0.81$, $F(4, 52) = 2.98$, $p < .05$. Separate follow-up analyses of variance (ANOVAs) on the scores from the four spatial skill and perceptual speed tests yielded reliable effects of gender for the card rotations test, $F(1, 55) = 5.61$, $p < .05$, the cube comparisons test, $F(1, 55) = 3.98$, $p < .05$, and the form board test, $F(1, 55) = 5.04$, $p < .05$, but no reliable effect of gender for the perceptual speed test, $F(1, 55) = 1.03$, $p > .31$. As can be seen in Table 1, the Time 1 spatial performance test scores favored males.

Game-Playing Performance. For subjects in the experimental group, we tested whether males and females differed on their initial game-playing performances. The videotapes of the first and last video game playing sessions were coded for two variables that captured the quality of performance: (1) the mean number of points achieved per game and (2) the mean number of lines created per game. (In Tetris, each line represents a row of blocks in which there are no holes or gaps in it.) Table 2 contains the average scores for the number of lines and points at Time 1 (first video game playing session) separately for males and females. A one-way MANOVA with gender as between-subjects variable on the two dependent variables number of lines and number of points at Time 1 yielded

TABLE 1
Initial (Time 1) Scores on Spatial Performance Measures
for Men and Women (Experiment 1)

	Males		Females	
Perceptual Speed	32.32	(7.97)	34.28	(6.02)
Card Rotation	68.33	(7.97)	62.26	(11.40)
Cube Comparison	14.53	(2.71)	13.14	(2.47)
Form Board	74.44	(21.46)	62.33	(18.03)

Note. Standard deviations are given in parentheses. Scores on each test represent number of correct responses.

TABLE 2
Time 1 and Time 2 Scores on Spatial Performance Measures and Game Playing Indices for Men and Women (Experiment 1)

Experimental Condition

	Males		Females	
	Pretest	Posttest	Pretest	Posttest
Perceptual Speed	32.00 (9.19)	36.01 (6.59)	31.17 (4.37)	37.01 (4.75)
Card Rotation	67.99 (8.73)	72.22 (6.30)	65.45 (12.66)	67.53 (13.13)
Cube Comparison	14.21 (2.99)	17.88 (1.53)	13.66 (2.17)	13.73 (3.64)
Form Board	66.43 (25.71)	83.30 (20.51)	61.86 (21.33)	65.82 (18.74)
No. of Lines	18.6 (6.7)	58.4 (24.8)	7.7 (5.8)	52.9 (17.0)
No. of Points	2,716.9 (1,759.9)	16,964.0 (9,915.0)	808.3 (667.0)	13,271.00 (6,230.0)

Control Condition

	Males		Females	
	Pretest	Posttest	Pretest	Posttest
Perceptual Speed	32.63 (6.89)	37.06 (11.33)	38.64 (5.39)	38.60 (8.57)
Card Rotation	68.66 (7.43)	71.56 (5.14)	57.80 (7.94)	62.61 (13.00)
Cube Comparison	14.83 (2.47)	15.38 (3.20)	12.40 (2.80)	13.00 (2.91)
Form Board	71.99 (13.29)	71.09 (9.75)	63.00 (13.16)	68.60 (22.34)

Note. Standard deviations are given in parentheses. Scores on each test represent number of correct responses. Number of lines and points are explained in the text.

125

a reliable gender effect, Wilks' $\Lambda = 0.55$, $F(2, 27) = 11.18$, $p < .001$. Separate ANOVAs yielded reliable effects of gender, with males outperforming females on both variables, $F(1, 28) = 22.53$, $p < .001$, and $F(1, 28) = 14.58$, $p < .001$, for the number of lines and the number of points, respectively. To determine whether the effects of gender on initial game-playing performance were due to initial gender differences in spatial performance, we repeated the analyses as analyses of covariance (ANCOVA), partialing gender differences on the Time 1 spatial performance scores. Even after partialing the gender differences in spatial performance, the gender differences on initial game-playing performance remained reliable, suggesting that these differences were not solely due to differences in spatial performance, but might have been due to the effects of other variables as well (e.g., overall experience with video games).

Effects of Game Playing on Spatial Performance Scores
Table 2 also contains the mean scores of the four spatial performance measures for both the experimental and the control conditions at Times 1 and 2, again separately for males and females. To determine whether subjects' game-playing performance did, in fact, improve as a result of practice, we performed a two-factorial MANOVA with gender (between-subjects) and time (within-subjects) as independent variables on the dependent variables number of lines and number of points. (Note that Time 2 scores for numbers of lines and points represent the quality of subjects' performance during the last video game session.) In this analysis, only the main effect of time was reliable, Wilks' $\Lambda = 0.18$, $F(2, 26) = 57.85$, $p < .001$. Separate ANOVAs on the two dependent variables with gender as between-subjects variable and time as within-subjects variable yielded a reliable main effect for time for both the number of lines and the number of points, $F(1, 27) = 118.13$, $p < .001$, and $F(1, 27) = 69.37$, $p < .001$, respectively. Thus, the quality of game playing improved reliably over the 12 practice sessions. Because the interaction between time and gender was not reliable in any of the analyses, we concluded that males and females did not differ in how much their game-playing performance improved over the 6 hr of practice.

To test whether game playing improved subjects' scores on the spatial performance measures, we ran four separate ANOVAs with group (experimental vs. control) and gender as between-subjects variables. The dependent variables were subjects' change scores (Time 2 minus Time 1) on the four spatial performance measures. The only reliable effects obtained with these analyses were a main effect of gender, $F(1, 53) = 5.28$, $p < .05$, with males improving more than females did and an interaction between gender and group, $F(1, 53) = 5.62$, $p < .05$, on the cube comparisons test. Because the general pattern of scores shown in Table 2 appears to indicate that males tend to show greater improvements in spatial performance than females as a result of game playing, we performed one-way ANOVAs, with group as the between-subjects variable on card rotations, cube comparisons, and form board tests, separately for males and females. For males, the main effect of group was reliable for both the cube comparisons and form boards tests, $F(1, 31) = 14.07, p < .001$, and $F(1, 31) = 4.56, p < .05$, respectively. In contrast, none of the effects were reliable for females (all p's $> .70$). These results indicate reliable improvements for males as a result of video game practice on the cube comparisons and form board tests, but no reliable change for females.

To test whether the amount of improvement on the spatial performance scores could be reliably predicted by amount of improvement in game-playing skill, we computed the correlations between the changes, from Time 1 to Time 2, in the four spatial performance measures and the change in the number of lines and points. None of the resulting eight correlations was reliable (all p's $> .05$), indicating that the amount of improvement in spatial performance was not predicted by amount of improvement in game-playing performance.

Furthermore, final game-playing performance did not reliably predict final spatial performance on any of the four measures, nor did initial spatial performance reliably predict either initial or final game-playing performance (all p's $> .40$).

In sum, Experiment 1 demonstrated that video game playing has the potential to improve performance on spatial performance measures. However, it appeared that improvements were generally greater for males than they were for females. In fact, none of the spatial performance measures we employed demonstrated reliable change after practice for females. In contrast, scores on two of the three measures that we had predicted would improve as a result of game playing did indeed improve for males.

Theoretically, the lack of an effect for females could be explained by assuming that more practice on video game playing was needed for such an effect to appear (notice that our results demonstrated a male superiority in initial game-playing performance that was not entirely due to the male subjects' advantage in spatial performance), and/or that females' spatial performance did, in fact, improve but our dependent measures were not sensitive enough to pick up the improvement. Experiment 2 dealt with the second possibility. In lieu of the paper-and-pencil measures of spatial performance employed in Experiment 1, Experiment 2 utilized computerized tests that were specifically constructed to measure mental rotation and spatial visualization performance as they are practiced in the video game Tetris. We hoped that the use of the reaction time measure instead of number correct, as in paper-and-pencil measures, would increase the sensitivity of the dependent measures. In addition, because the computerized tasks were much more similar to the Tetris game than the paper-and-pencil measures were, they constituted a closer transfer task from the video game; for this reason, greater effects from the video game practice might be observed.

As reported in Experiment 1, males and females already differed in their game-playing performances at the first time of testing. Although gender differences no longer existed at the end of the 6 hr of practice, Wilks' $\Lambda = 0.94$, $F(2,$

26) < 1, it is possible that the initial gender differences may have affected our results. Therefore, we included in Experiment 2 only subjects who had not played *any* video game during the past year, thus hoping to eliminate the initial gender difference in game-playing performance.

EXPERIMENT 2

Experiment 2 was essentially a replication of the first experiment. The main goals of Experiment 2 were to examine whether spatial performance scores, game-playing performances, and the impact of playing Tetris on spatial performance scores differed for males and females; and whether playing the video game Tetris would improve spatial performance scores.

METHOD

Subjects

A total of 53 undergraduate students (27 males, 26 females), M age = 19.85, SD = 3.52) recruited from an introductory psychology class participated in the experiment either for credit or for a small payment ($10). At their first session, all subjects completed the questionnaire about their previous video game experience. None of the subjects reported any prior experience with Tetris. In addition, none of the subjects reportedly had played any video game during the past year.

Materials

Visualization Task. For this experiment, two computerized spatial performance tests were designed. Both tasks were presented on Macintosh SE computers. The first task was a spatial visualization task in which the subjects saw a shape at the top of the screen and had to decide whether the shape would fit into the hole or gap in the wall at the bottom of the screen by imagining what would happen if the shape was moved into the hole. To qualify as fitting into the hole, the shape had to completely "disappear" into the wall, such that no part of the shape was left above the wall and there were no enclosed or completely surrounded empty spaces or gaps in the wall. In addition, the shape had to fit the hole in its presented orientation—that is, subjects could not mentally rotate the shape to make it fit into the wall (see Figure 3).

A total of 10 shapes were used, each consisting of four basic squares. Five shapes were the same as the shapes used in the Tetris game (Tetris shapes). For these five shapes, the four squares were arranged such that at least one side of each square was connected to the side of another square (see Figure 1). The remaining five shapes were different from the Tetris game shapes (non-Tetris shapes). For these non-Tetris shapes, the four squares were arranged such that each square was connected either to the side of another square or to the corner of

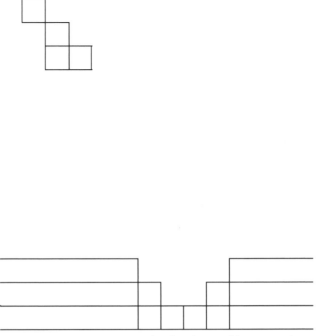

Figure 3. Example of a non-Tetris shape and wall as they would appear in the computerized spatial visualization task.

another square (see Figure 3). Notice that because all possible shapes consisting of four squares with connected sides were utilized in Tetris, our non-Tetris shapes necessarily differed from the Tetris shapes in terms of complexity. In 50% of the trials, the correct response was that the shape fit into the hole (fit); for 50% of the instances, the correct response was that the shape did not fit the hole (no-fit).

Instructions for the task were presented on the computer screen at a subject-controlled pace. After reading the instructions, subjects pressed the space bar to begin 10 practice trials. After each practice trial, subjects received feedback as to whether the response was correct or not. At the end of the practice trials, subjects could either stop and ask the experimenter for clarification of the task, reread the instructions, or begin the actual test.

Mental Rotation Task. The second computerized task was a mental rotation task in which a reference shape was presented to subjects along with a second shape. Subjects had to decide whether the second shape was the same as the reference shape—that is, whether or not it could be mentally rotated within the plane to look exactly like the reference shape, or whether the second shape was different from the reference shape, in which case it was the mirror image of the reference shape. The exact same shapes used in the visualization task were used again in the mental rotation task. In exactly 60% of the trials, the correct response was that the shapes were the same; in the remaining 40% of the trials, the correct response was that the shapes were different.

As in the spatial visualization task, instructions for the task were presented on the computer screen at a subject-controlled pace. After reading the instructions, subjects completed 10 practice trials and received feedback after each response. At the end of the practice trials, subjects could either stop and ask the experimenter for clarification of the task, reread the instructions, or begin the actual test.

At the first time of testing, half of the subjects in the experimental and control conditions received the visualization task first and the mental rotation task second; for the remaining subjects the order was the reverse. At the second time of testing, subjects received the two tasks in the reverse order that they received them at Time 1.

Subjects in the experimental group practiced the video game Tetris according to the exact specifications provided for Experiment 1. As in the first experiment, the first and last game-playing sessions were videotaped.

Procedure

Subjects were randomly assigned either to the experimental or the control group. At their first session, all subjects were individually tested on the two computerized measures of spatial performance, and they completed the questionnaire about their previous video game experience.

At the end of the initial testing session, individual practice sessions for each experimental subject were scheduled one day apart, except for weekends. At the first practice session, subjects were given instructions in booklet form for playing Tetris. Each of the 25 experimental subjects (13 males, 12 females) played Tetris for twelve 30-min sessions. The control group was comprised of 28 undergraduate students (14 males, 14 females) who reportedly refrained from playing any video games during the pre- to posttest periods. The time between testing was 14 days, on average, for each of the two groups.

Design

The dependent variables of interest were subjects' reaction times on the mental rotation task and the visualization task as well as measures representing the quality of game-playing performances for subjects in the experimental condition. The independent variables were group (between-subjects; experimental vs. control), gender (between-subjects; males vs. females), and time of testing (within-subjects; Time 1 vs. Time 2).

RESULTS AND DISCUSSION

For clarity of presentation, the results have again been organized into two main sections. In the first section, we present analyses testing whether males and females differed on our new measures of spatial performance and on game performance at the beginning of Experiment 2. The second section contains the results pertaining to the effects of video game play on the improvement of spatial performance. Because there were no systematic differences in error rates, we will present the results for reaction times only.

Initial Effects of Gender

Mental Rotation Task. For each subject, the median reaction time (RT) of correct "yes" responses in the mental rotation task was determined separately for Tetris and non-Tetris shapes at each of the seven different angles used in the experiment (i.e., 45°, 90°, 135°, 180°, 225°, 270°, 315°). Initial analyses indicated a nonlinear, inverted U-shaped relation between degree of angle and RT. That is, shapes that were presented at angles between 180° and 315° were mentally rotated in the opposite direction to that of shapes that were presented at angles between 45° and 180°. Therefore, the average time needed to rotate a shape by 1° of angle was determined separately using RTs from angles varying from 45° to 180°, and angles varying from 180° to 315°. The estimates for the time taken to rotate a shape by 1° of angle were computed separately for each subject and each type of shape (Tetris vs. non-Tetris) by performing a series of multiple regressions using degree of angle as predictor of RT. The numerical estimates for rotation time correspond to the B values in the best-fitting multiple regression equations. Because the results obtained with the two ranges of angles (i.e., 45°–180° vs. 180°–315°) were qualitatively identical, we averaged the two estimates obtained for each subject and each type of shape. All results described in the following are therefore based on the average of the two estimates of mental rotation time.

Table 3 contains the mean Time 1 (pretest) scores on the measure of mental

TABLE 3
Initial (Time 1) Scores on Spatial Performance Measures
for Males and Females (Experiment 2)

	Males		Females	
Mental Rotation Time				
Tetris Shapes	4.04	(1.30)	3.90	(1.03)
Non-Tetris Shapes	4.11	(0.84)	5.36	(0.93)
Visualization Time				
Tetris-Fit	1,914	(725)	1,987	(742)
Tetris-No-Fit	2,183	(645)	2,078	(717)
Non-Tetris-Fit	2,589	(953)	2,566	(913)
Non-Tetris-No-Fit	2,637	(893)	2,610	(749)

Note. Means and standard deviations (in parentheses) for mental rotation time are in milliseconds per degree of rotation; for visualization time, means and standard deviations are in milliseconds.

rotation time for both Tetris and non-Tetris shapes as a function of gender. The means represent mental rotation time as the number of milliseconds needed to rotate a Tetris or non-Tetris shape by 1° of angle. To test whether males and females differed on their initial mental rotation times, we performed a one-way ANOVA with gender as a between-subjects variable and type of shape (Tetris vs. non-Tetris) as a within-subjects variable. In this analysis, reliable main effects of gender and type of shape were obtained, $F(1, 51) = 7.71, p < .01, F(1, 51) = 13.47, p < .001$, respectively. In addition, there was a reliable interaction between gender and type of shape, $F(1, 51) = 11.24, p < .001$. Follow-up ANOVAs indicated that the gender effect was reliable for non-Tetris shapes, $F(1, 51) = 24.93, p < .001$, but was not reliable for Tetris shapes, $F(1, 51) < 1$. This finding suggests that gender differences in mental rotation time vary with the degree of complexity and is consistent with Linn and Petersen's (1985) observations that effect sizes for gender differences on mental rotation tasks vary with task complexity and that large effect sizes are obtained on more complex mental rotation tasks. Notice that our interpretation emphasizes complexity rather than familiarity because for the initial spatial tests, neither the simpler Tetris shapes nor the more complex non-Tetris shapes had been previously seen by the subjects. The familiarity dimension only entered into the situation after the subjects had practiced Tetris.

Visualization Task. For each subject, the median RT of correct responses was determined separately for Tetris and non-Tetris shapes that either fit or did not fit into the wall pattern displayed on the screen. Table 3 contains the means in milliseconds for Tetris-fit, non-Tetris-fit, Tetris-no-fit, and non-Tetris-no-fit shapes computed for Time 1, separately for males and females. A three-way ANOVA with gender as a between-subjects variable, and type of shape (Tetris vs. non-Tetris) and fit (fit vs. no-fit) as within-subjects variables on subjects' RTs for Time 1, yielded a reliable main effect of type of shape, $F(1, 51) = 199.83, p < .001$, a marginally reliable main effect of fit, $F(1, 51) = 3.12, p < .08$, and a reliable interaction between type of shape and fit, $F(1, 51) = 5.38, p < .05$. Non-Tetris shapes were processed more slowly, on average, than the less complex Tetris shapes. In addition, subjects were faster when a given shape fit the wall pattern than when it did not fit the wall pattern. The interaction between type of shape and fit indicated that the difference between shapes that fit and did not fit the wall pattern was larger for Tetris than for non-Tetris shapes. Most important, neither the main effect of gender nor any of the interactions involving gender were reliable, all $ps > .05$. Thus, males and females did not differ initially in terms of visualization time.

Game-Playing Performance. To test whether males and females differed on their initial game-playing performances, we coded, for subjects in the experimental group only, the videotapes of the first video game playing session for two variables that captured the quality of performance: (1) the mean number of points per game achieved and (2) the mean number of lines created per game. Table 4 contains the average scores on the number of lines and points for the experimental condition at Time 1 and Time 2, again separately for males and females. On the Time 1 scores for number of lines and points, we performed a one-way MANOVA with gender as between-subjects variable. In this analysis, the main effect of gender was not reliable, $p > .39$. However, as can be seen in Table 4, the average scores for males were again slightly higher than the average scores for females as was found in Experiment 1.

Effects of Game Playing on Spatial Performance Measures

To test whether subjects' game-playing performance did in fact improve as a result of video game practice, we performed a MANOVA with gender as between-subjects variable and time (Time 1 vs. Time 2) as within-subjects variable on the number of lines and points on the dependent variables. In this analysis, only the main effect of time was reliable, Wilks' $\Lambda = 0.31$, $F(2, 20) = 22.92$, $p < .001$. Separate ANOVAs on the two dependent variables indicated that the main effect of time was reliable with both the number of lines, $F(1, 21) = 32.97$, $p < .001$, and number of points, $F(1, 21) = 36.73$, $p < .001$, indicating that subjects' quality of game playing improved reliably over the course of the practice sessions. Neither the main effect of gender nor the interaction between time and gender was reliable in any of the analyses, all $Fs < 1$. Thus, males and females did not differ in the amount of improvement, with practice, that they demonstrated in game-playing performance.

Mental Rotation Time. Table 4 also contains the mean scores on the measure of mental rotation time for both the Tetris and non-Tetris shapes and the experimental and control conditions at Times 1 and 2, again separately for males and females. To test whether game practice improved subjects' scores on the mental rotation time measure, we performed an ANOVA with group (experimental vs. control) and gender as between-subjects variables and type of shape (Tetris vs. non-Tetris) as within-subjects variable. Subjects' change scores (Time 1 minus Time 2) on the time-of-rotation measures were the dependent variables. In this analysis, only the main effect of group was reliable, $F(1, 49) = 19.20$, $p < .001$; for all other effects, $p > .30$. The average change score was 1.19 ms per degree of rotation, $SD = 1.01$, for the experimental group, and 0.01 ms per degree of rotation, $SD = 0.95$, for the control group.

Neither the main effect of gender nor any of the interactions involving gender were reliable in this analysis, indicating that males and females did not differ in the amount of improvement in mental rotation time resulting from video game practice.

Separate follow-up analyses indicated that the decrease in mental rotation time was reliable for the experimental group, $F(1, 24) = 34.49$, $p < .001$.

TABLE 4
Time 1 and Time 2 Scores on Mental Rotation Task and Game-Playing Indices for Men and Women (Experiment 2)

	Males		Females	
	Pretest	Posttest	Pretest	Posttest
Experimental Condition				
Tetris Shapes	4.01 (1.35)	2.80 (1.65)	3.80 (0.86)	2.83 (1.01)
Non-Tetris Shapes	4.16 (0.62)	2.63 (1.19)	5.39 (0.91)	4.24 (1.21)
No. of Lines	14.4 (20.5)	60.0 (27.8)	9.8 (14.6)	57.6 (19.7)
No. of Points	1,603.4 (1,789.9)	17,746.6 (12,769.5)	1,391.5 (1020.3)	16,615.3 (12,022.0)
Control Condition				
Tetris Shapes	4.06 (1.32)	4.02 (0.71)	3.99 (1.19)	4.10 (0.98)
Non-Tetris Shapes	4.06 (1.02)	4.26 (1.25)	5.32 (0.98)	5.05 (1.17)

Note. Means and standard deviations (in parentheses) for Tetris and non-Tetris shapes are in milliseconds per degree of rotation. Number of lines and points are explained in the text.

The change in mental rotation time was not reliable for the control group, $F(1, 27) < 1$.

Visualization Time. Table 5 contains the mean scores on various measures of visualization time for the experimental and control conditions at Times 1 and 2, again separately for males and females. To test whether game practice improved subjects' scores on the visualization time measure, we performed an ANOVA with group (experimental vs. control) and gender as between-subjects variables, and type of shape (Tetris vs. non-Tetris) and fit (fit vs. no-fit) as within-subjects variables. Subjects' change scores (Time 1 minus Time 2) on the visualization time measures were the dependent variables. In this analysis, only the main effect of group was reliable, $F(1, 49) = 9.12, p < .01$; however, the main effect of type of shape approached significance, $F(1, 49) = 3.49, p < .07$. The average improvement for the experimental group was larger than the average improvement for the control group, and the improvement for non-Tetris shapes was larger than the improvement for Tetris shapes.

Again, neither the main effect of gender nor any of the interactions involving gender were reliable in this analysis, indicating that males and females did not differ in the amount of improvement in visualization time resulting from video game practice.

Separate follow-up analyses indicated that the decrease in visualization time from Time 1 to Time 2 was reliable for all four measures in the experimental group, all $ps < .05$, but was not reliable in the control group, all $ps > .05$. In addition, the advantage of the experimental group over the control group was reliable for all four measures, all $ps < .05$.

TABLE 5
Time 1 and Time 2 Scores on Spatial Visualization Task for Men and Women (Experiment 2)

	Males				Females			
	Pretest		Posttest		Pretest		Posttest	
Experimental Condition								
Tetris-Fit	1,983	(670)	1,448	(542)	2,072	(789)	1,294	(395)
Tetris-No-Fit	2,176	(674)	1,612	(726)	2,211	(573)	1,570	(791)
Non-Tetris-Fit	2,684	(820)	2,121	(804)	2,759	(976)	1,879	(608)
Non-Tetris-No-Fit	2,743	(1,039)	1,940	(823)	2,688	(778)	1,910	(622)
Control Condition								
Tetris-Fit	1,857	(790)	1,899	(867)	1,906	(711)	2,088	(844)
Tetris-No-Fit	2,189	(650)	2,164	(1,087)	1,953	(829)	1,992	(787)
Non-Tetris-Fit	2,510	(1,081)	2,361	(899)	2,386	(839)	2,453	(832)
Non-Tetris-No-Fit	2,549	(786)	2,583	(1,325)	2,537	(738)	2,520	(1,143)

Note. Means and standard deviations (in parentheses) are in milliseconds.

Game Playing and Spatial Performance Measures. To test whether the amount of improvement on the spatial performance measures could be directly predicted by amount of improvement in game-playing skill, we computed the correlations between changes in all six spatial performance measures and changes in the number of lines and points. Of the resulting 12 correlations, 4 were reliable—namely, the correlations between the change in number of lines and two measures of visualization performance, Tetris-fit, $r(23) = -.43$, and non-Tetris-fit, $r(23) = -.46$, and the correlations between the change in points and the same two measures of visualization performance, Tetris-fit, $r(23) = -.41$, and non-Tetris-fit, $r(23) = -.44$. The negative sign indicates that the amount of improvement in game playing was related to the amount of decrease in RT on the two measures of visualization performance. In contrast, the changes in the two measures of mental rotation performance were not related to amount of improvement in game playing.

To summarize the main results of Experiment 2, practicing Tetris for a total of 6 hr did reliably improve both mental rotation time and spatial visualization skill for both Tetris and non-Tetris shapes. The improvement in spatial skill did not differ for men and women.

GENERAL DISCUSSION

The playing of video games and their counterparts, arcade and computer games, is a ubiquitous feature of the culture of today's children and youth. Yet very little is known about the impact of playing video games on cognitive skills. Taken together, our two experiments, like earlier research, obtained mixed results in finding a relation between video game playing and improvements in spatial skills, and in finding gender differences in performances on spatial performance tasks. We begin our discussion by focusing on the effects of gender on spatial skills performance and then examine the impact playing Tetris had on spatial skills.

Effects of Gender on Spatial Skills Performance

Consistent with Linn and Petersen's (1985) meta-analysis of spatial-ability research, we found reliable and consistent differences favoring males on complex mental rotation tasks (i.e., the cube comparison and the mental rotation of non-Tetris shapes) and obtained mixed results for simple rotation tasks. On the paper-and-pencil card rotation task, males did better than females. However, for the RT measure of mental rotation on the relatively simple Tetris shapes, there was no difference between males and females. If large effect sizes for gender differences are only obtained on complex mental rotation tasks, then on simple tasks one would not expect to consistently obtain reliable gender differences.

On the spatial visualization tasks, males did better than females on the form board test, but not on the computerized visualization task. In both Linn and Petersen's review (1985) and in Maccoby and Jacklin's (1974) review, the authors concluded that for spatial visualization tasks there are no consistent gender differences.

Effects of Playing Tetris on Mental Rotation and Spatial Visualization Performance

In the first experiment, we found that males' scores on the cube rotation and the form board tests did improve, but females' scores did not improve on any measures. In light of Baenninger and Newcombe's (1989) meta-analysis of spatial-skill training studies, in which they found that the impact of training on males and females did *not* differ, we replicated our experiment using more sensitive (i.e., RT) measures of spatial skills. It was possible that the females might have improved, but the measures were not sensitive enough to detect that improvement. Experiment 2 also used tests presented in the same (computer) medium as that of the video game training. In contrast to Experiment 1, therefore, Experiment 2 required relatively near transfer.

In the second experiment, we found that mental rotation time and visualization time decreased reliably for both males and females and that the amount of improvement on these two measures of spatial performance did not differ for males and females. Thus, the findings presented here replicate Subrahmanyam and Greenfield's (1994) finding that practice on a spatially oriented video game positively affects closely related spatial skills. Because our replication used an older sample than did Subrahmanyam and Greenfield's the data suggest that the effectiveness of video game practice for improvement of spatial skills may have more to do with the similarity between the video game and the transfer task than with a particularly sensitive period for the development of spatial skills. The video game and the transfer tasks shared a common medium (i.e., the computer), at least some common shapes for manipulations (i.e., the Tetris shapes), and common skills (e.g., mental rotation of shapes, visualizing whether a shape would fit into a hole in a wall). This explanation is also consistent with Baenninger and Newcombe's (1989) observation that the effectiveness of spatial training is a function of the similarity between the training task and the testing task. The greater sensitivity of the reaction time measures in Experiment 2 may also have contributed to the demonstration of transfer for females in Experiment 2, but not in Experiment 1.

Numerous training studies (e.g., Connor, Schackman, & Serbin, 1978; Embretson, 1987; McGee, 1978; see also Baenninger & Newcombe, 1989, for meta-analysis of training studies) have found that spatial performance can be improved through practice. The importance of this study is that the gains in spatial performance occurred as a by-product of playing a popular video game for only 6 hr. The implication is that adolescent video game players can accrue some specific cognitive benefits from the time they spend playing video games.

Transfer of Skills Gained in Video Game Context to Other Tasks

The second study demonstrated that skills acquired through playing Tetris can be generalized to different shapes. On the visualization task, improvement of Tetris scores was correlated with both placement of the Tetris shapes and with placement of the non-Tetris, complex shapes. Thus, visualization skill developed in Tetris could be transferred to the visualization and mental manipulation of different (non-Tetris) stimuli. It is also important to note that even though the visualization task was designed to be similar to the placement of shapes within the Tetris game context, the requirements for shapes "fitting" in the wall in the visualization task were somewhat different than the requirements for placing shapes in the Tetris game. Effective strategies for placing shapes in the Tetris game do no necessarily require players to make sure there are no empty spaces enclosed by the shape and the wall. There are times in the Tetris game in which the best placement of a shape will leave some empty spaces, and knowing which kinds of spaces are easier to fix than others is important for successful game playing. Consequently, there were some differences in the rules that governed effective Tetris placement and correct placement decisions in the placement task. Although the transfer of spatial visualization skill from Tetris to the visualization task may on the surface appear trivial, studies have shown that transfer of skill when stimuli are changed is not always obtained (e.g., Lantz, 1979; Scribner, 1984).

In summary, spatially oriented video games do have potential to improve late adolescents' mental rotation and spatial visualization skills. However, without a formal test of the variety of contexts to which spatial skills developed within a particular video game can be successfully transferred, it is difficult to say how generalizable these skills might be. Although there were differences between the Tetris game and the transfer task, the tasks shared many similar features. Thus, along with other research our studies suggest that spatial skills developed through video game practice or practice on other spatial skills training tasks may be contextualized or tied to contexts closely linked to the practice setting. Development of spatial skills within the video game context may be another example of what Brown, Collins, and Duguid (1989) called "situated cognition." If this is the case, those wishing to capitalize on the motivational aspect of video games for spatial skills training will need to find or develop games that are similar to the actual contexts in which the spatial skills will eventually be used.

REFERENCES

Almy, M. (1967). Spontaneous play: An avenue for intellectual development. *Young Children, 22,* 265–277.

Athey, I. (1984). Contributions of play to development. In T. Yawkey & A. Pellegrini (Eds.), *Children's play: Developmental and applied* (pp. 9–27). Hillsdale, NJ: Erlbaum.

Baenninger, M., & Newcombe, N. (1989). The role of experience in spatial test performance: A meta-analysis. *Sex Roles, 20,.* 327–344.

Brown, J.S., Collins, A., & Duguid, P. (1989). Situated cognition and the culture of learning. *Educational Researcher, 33,* 32–42.

Caplan, P.J., MacPherson, G.M., & Tobin, P. (1985). Do sex-related differences in spatial abilities exist? A multilevel critique with new data. *American Psychologist, 40,* 786–799.

Connor, J.M., Schackman, M., & Serbin, L.A. (1978). Sex related differences in response to practice on a visual spatial test and generalization to a related test. *Child Development, 49,* 24–29.

Dorval, M., & Pepin, M. (1986). Effect of playing a video game on a measure of spatial visualization. *Perceptual and Motor Skills, 62,* 159–162.

Embretson, S.E. (1987). Improving the measurement of spatial aptitude by dynamic testing. *Intelligence, 11,* 333–358.

Forsyth, A.S., & Lancy, D.F. (1987). Simulated travel and place location learning in a computer adventure game. *Journal of Educational Computing Research, 3,* 377–394.

French, J.W., Ekstrom, R.B., & Price, L.A. (1963). *Kit of reference tests for cognitive factors.* Princeton, NJ: Educational Testing Service.

Gagnon, D. (1985). Videogames and spatial skills: An exploratory study. *Educational Communication and Technology Journal, 33* 263–275.

Greenfield, P.M. (1984). *Mind and media: The effects of television, video games, and computers.* Cambridge, MA: Harvard University Press.

Greenfield, P.M., Brannon, C., & Lohr, D. (1994). Two dimensional representation of movement through three-dimensional space: The role of video game expertise. *Journal of Applied Developmental Psychology, 15,* 87–103.

Halpern, D.F. (1986). *Sex differences in cognitive abilities.* Hillsdale, NJ: Erlbaum.

Hyde, J.S. (1981). How large are cognitive gender differences? A meta-analysis using ω^2 and *d.* *American Psychologist, 36,* 892–901.

Kamii, C., & DeVries, R. (1980). *Group games in early education: Piaget's theory.* Washington, DC: National Association for the Education of Young Children.

Lantz, D. (1979). A cross-cultural comparison of communication abilities: Some effects of age, schooling and culture. *International Journal of Psychology, 14,* 171–183.

Linn, M.C., & Petersen, A.C. (1985). Emergence and characterization of sex differences in spatial ability: A meta-analysis. *Child Development,* 1479–1498.

Loftus, G.R., & Loftus, E.F. (1983). *Mind at play: The psychology of video games.* New York: Basic Books.

Lowery, B.R., & Knirk, F.G. (1982–1983). Micro-computer video games and spatial visualization acquisition. *Journal of Educational Technology Systems, 11,* 1155–1166.

Maccoby, E.E., & Jacklin, C.N. (1974). *The psychology of sex differences* (Vol. 1). Stanford, CA: Stanford University Press.

Malone, T.W. (1981). Toward a theory of intrinsically motivating instruction. *Cognitive Science, 4,* 333–369.

McClurg, P.A., & Chaillé, C. (1987). Computer games: Environments for developing spatial cognition? *Journal of Educational Computing Research, 3,* 95–111.

McGee, M.G. (1978). Effects of training and practice on sex differences in mental rotation test score. *Journal of Psychology, 100,* 87–90.

McGee, M.G. (1979). Human spatial abilities: Psychometric studies and environmental, genetic, hormonal, and neurological influences. *Psychological Bulletin, 86,* 889–918.

Pepin, M., & Dorval, M. (1986, April). *Effect of playing a video game on adults' and adolescents' spatial visualization.* Paper presented at the American Educational Research Association annual meeting, San Francisco, CA.

Piaget, P. (1965). *The moral judgment of the child.* New York: Free Press.

Scribner, S. (1984). Studying working intelligence. In B. Rogoff & J. Lave (Eds.), *Everyday cognition* (pp. 9–40). Cambridge, MA: Harvard University Press.

Selman, R. (1980). *The growth of interpersonal understanding: Developmental and clinical analyses.* New York: Academic.

Strein, W. (1987). Effects of age and visual-motor skills on preschool children's computer-game performance. *Journal of Research and Development in Education, 20,* 70–72.

Subrahmanyam, K., & Greenfield, P.M. (1994). Effect of video game practice on spatial skills in girls and boys. *Journal of Applied Developmental Psychology, 15,* 13–32.

Chapter 9

Cognitive Socialization by Computer Games in Two Cultures: Inductive Discovery or Mastery of an Iconic Code?

PATRICIA M. GREENFIELD
University of California, Los Angeles

LUIGIA CAMAIONI
PAOLA ERCOLANI
University of Rome

LAURA WEISS
BENNETT A. LAUBER
University of California, Los Angeles

PAOLA PERUCCHINI
University of Rome

We would like to thank Marisa Fragassa, Patti Rosenwald Frasen, Claire Lipsom, Kaveri Subrahmanyam, Daniel Kaye, and Lisa Kendig for their contributions to the research and manuscript preparation. Special thanks to Laurel Smith for the statistical analyses and to Ben Loh for the graphs. This research was supported by NATO Collaborative Research Grant 283/89 awarded to Patricia M. Greenfield and Luigia Camaioni by the Gold Shield Faculty Prize, a UCLA University Research Grant, a Visiting Professorship at the University of Rome awarded to Patricia M. Greenfield, and by a grant from the Italian National Research Council awarded to Luigia Camaioni.

An earlier version of this article was presented as a poster at the 1991 biennial meeting of the Society for Research in Child Development in Seattle under the title *Video Game as a Tool of Cognitive Socialization: A Cross-Cultural Examination in the United States and Italy.*

Laura Weiss is now at the University of Connecticut.

Correspondence and requests for reprints should be sent to Patricia M. Greenfield, Department of Psychology, University of California, Los Angeles, 405 Hilgard Avenue, Los Angeles, CA. 90024–1563.

Games generally socialize children for the adult roles valued and needed by a particular society (Roberts & Sutton-Smith, 1962). One aspect of such socialization is the provision of cognitive skills required by adult work. Video games have become a mass medium, particularly for children. It is therefore of great interest to know whether these games are providing cognitive socialization for the adult skills required by contemporary society.

One of the most interesting points about video games is that no one tells you the rules in advance. The rules must be figured out by observation, trial and error, and a process of hypothesis testing (Greenfield, 1983, 1984, 1993). Several other researchers have also noted the problem-solving/discovery aspect of video games (Strover, 1984; Turkle, 1984).

In essence, players create a part of a complex, dynamic representational system using a joystick; they must figure out how their representation interacts with screen objects controlled by the computer. The rules go beyond the decoding of meaning for individual icons on the screen. In addition to figuring out what the symbols mean, players must discover how they act.

This process of making observations, formulating hypotheses, and figuring out the rules governing the behavior of a dynamic representation through a trial-and-error process is basically the cognitive process of inductive discovery. It is the process by which individuals learn much about the world, and, at a more formal level, it is the thought process behind scientific thinking and discovery. If video games functioned to train this process, they would have great educational and social importance. They would indeed provide cognitive socialization for the much needed scientific work of contemporary society.

To test this idea, the process of inductive discovery in the course of video game mastery was documented. The ultimate goal was to determine whether video games could function as a method of informal education for the inductive discovery processes so fundamental to the scientific method. Our goal was to investigate whether discovery skills could transfer from an entertaining action video game to a scientific–technical representation. The scientific–technical representation selected for study was an animated computer simulation of the logic of computer circuitry. The study had a cross-cultural aspect as well, involving a comparison between students in Los Angeles and students in Rome, where computer technology is less widespread (Camaioni, Ercolani, Perucchini, & Greenfield, 1990; Sensales & Greenfield, 1991, in press).

COMPUTER GAMES

From the simplicity of Pong, an early video game in which a spot of light moves across an electronic tennis court, action or "arcade-style" video games have evolved to a creative and complex form of entertainment used frequently by today's youth. When video games first became popular and highly visible, many people, including former Surgeon General C. Everett Koop, believed that the time spent playing video games was, from society's point of view, wasted time (Rebellion Against Video, 1983). Malone (1981), Strover (1984), Turkle (1984), Greenfield (1983, 1984), and Loftus and Loftus (1983) disagreed.

Malone (1981), on the basis of the first experimental research on video games, concluded that the informational features of video games that make them intrinsically motivating should be applied to instructional environments in general. Turkle (1984) stated, "There is nothing mindless about mastering a video game. The games demand skills that are complex and differentiated. Some of them begin to constitute a socialization into the computer culture" (p. 67). Strover (1984) also emphasized this latter point.

Greenfield (1983, 1984), in trying to promote more research on effects of video game play, hypothesized that playing arcade-style action games could develop skills in inductive discovery, iconic object constancy across visual transformations (required to recognize Pac-Man as both a whole yellow circle and minus a wedge-shaped piece), parallel processing (exemplified by the necessity to take in information from more than one screen location simultaneously during a video game), and skills in spatial representation (e.g., interpreting a two-dimensional display in the third dimension and coordinating visual information coming from multiple perspectives). Loftus and Loftus (1983), in an attempt to explain the psychology of video games, proposed video games as potential training aids for cognitive and perceptual disorders, for treating eye dysfunctions, and for developing memory skills.

Indeed, the U.S. Army and Air Force experimented with arcade-style games as training devices for skills such as rapid information processing and "multiplex" thinking (i.e., parallel processing; Trachtman, 1981). That video games do indeed involve complex cognitive skills was demonstrated by Rabbit, Banerji, and Szymanski (1989), who found that IQ, as measured by a standardized test, was highly predictive both of rate of learning and practiced performance on an action video game.

Low-cost microcomputers brought action video games into many American households; a 1982 report showed that 1 in every 10 households in the U.S. owned a home video game system (Perry, Truxal, & Wallach, 1982). A 1985–1986 survey in southern California found that 94% of all 10-year-old children had played some video games (Rushbrook, 1986). As of December 1988, the Nintendo phenomenon brought video game sets into 14 million homes in the U.S. The numbers have continued to increase: In 1992, Nintendo figures indicated that approximately 44% of all U.S. households had video game systems. Despite such wide acceptance of video games by the population, little empirical research has been conducted either on the cognitive effects of video games or the cognitive processes that the games engage.

It is important to distinguish noneducational action games, the focus of our study, from games with educational content. Games with varying graphic and action elements have been designed to teach a variety of educational subjects, including logic (e.g., Bank Street College Project in Science and Mathematics, 1984; Burton & Brown, 1979; Char, 1983; Dugdale & Kibbey, 1982; Levin, 1981; Piestrup, 1982; Robinett, 1982; Wood, 1980), and some have also been the subject of empirical research on cognitive processes and educational effects (Burbules & Reese, 1984; Burton & Brown, 1979; Char, 1983; Levin, 1981; Piestrup, 1982; Stein & Linn, 1985; Wood, 1980). Research and development have also focused on the use of arcade-style, action game formats to teach academic subjects such as mathematics (e.g., Chaffin, 1983; Chaffin, Maxwell, & Thompson, 1982; Mick, Konneman, O'Farrell, & Isaacs, 1983). However, the focus has been on the learning of particular academic skills specific to the *content* of a given game.

In contrast, the focus of our research is the acquisition of a general cognitive strategy inherent in the *format* of the whole class of noneducational action video games. To use McLuhan's (1964) terminology, we were interested in the unintentional cognitive "message" of a new medium: the recreational video game as a means of informal cognitive education (Greenfield & Lave, 1982). Our focus is on the popular action games, rather than on the adventure games that allow time for reflective decision making.

At the outset, the only study on the subject (and the inspiration for our research) was conducted by Gagnon (1985), who found positive effects of arcade-style video games on standardized paper-and-pencil tests of spatial ability after 5 hr of play on two games. Although men were initially better players than women, women improved during the 5 hr game play to achieve game scores equal to those of their male counterparts, and they simultaneously improved their performance in spatial skill. Gagnon's results also showed that experienced video game players were better than inexperienced video game players on a number of spatial skills at the outset of the experiment.

In contrast to the cognitive effects orientation of Gagnon's (1985) research, Craig (1987) and Roberts and his colleagues (Roberts, Aman, & Canfield, 1989; Roberts, Brown, Wiebke, & Haith, 1991) ; Roberts, Wiebke, Valaer, Matthias, & Ondrejko, in press) recently explored the cognitive processes involved in the mastery of action video games. Craig found that the progression from novice to expert in the course of mastering Passport to Paris, an action game requiring logical problem solving, involved developing systematic organization, sensitivity to efficient use of constrained resources (time, money), and evaluation and revision. Roberts (1989; described in Roberts et al., 1991) found developmental differences in the efficiency of learning strategies: 12- and 20-year-olds showed improvement with practice in a version of the video game Asteroids, whereas 4- and 7-year-olds did not. Roberts and Ondrejko and Roberts, Brown, et al. found that expert video game players used anticipatory eye movements that helped calibrate future action.

Lancy and his colleagues experimented with the cognitive aspects of two nonaction genres of computer games—fantasy adventure games and interactive fiction—as well as with the cognitive effects of action video games (Forsyth & Lancy, 1987; Hayes, Lancy, & Evans, 1985; Lancy, 1987; Lancy, Cohen, Evans, Levine, & Nevin, 1985; Lancy & Hayes, 1988). An adventure game, Winnie the Pooh, led to the acquisition of game-related spatial knowledge (Forsyth, 1986; Forsyth & Lancy, 1987), whereas interactive fiction, requiring a great deal of reading, was enjoyed by reluctant readers (Lancy, 1987; Lancy & Hayes, 1988).

In terms of transfer to nongame cognitive tasks, the effects of two action games, Star Raiders and Missile Commanders, on a Piagetian-flavored battery of tests (Lancy et al., 1985) were ambiguous because of the nature of the design. The effects of the two games did not differ. However, without a no-treatment control group, it is impossible to know whether both or neither of the games produced a transfer effect. Issues of video game transfer with adults were explored by Frederiksen and White (1989). Their study was part of a large research program that focused on the learning processes and training conditions by which mastery of a complex action video game is achieved (Donchin, Fabiani, & Sanders, 1989).

INDUCTIVE DISCOVERY PROCESSES

Action video games have the interesting property that no one tells the player the rules in advance. The player must figure these rules out by observation, trial and error, and hypothesis testing. Essentially, this describes a process of inductive discovery: The player receives input of specific data on the video screen and must formulate (not necessarily on a verbal level) general rules, patterns, and strategies in order to become a skilled player. This process must include perceptual observation as well as learning action contingencies.

Mastery of other more traditional games, such as chess, involve inducing high-level strategies, but in these games the player is told the basic rules (e.g., the permitted moves for each piece) in advance. This is not the case for video games. Home games for the computer often have no printed instructions, and arcade machines have very minimal ones. In addition to the fact that most players never read whatever instructions exist (according to an informal survey of a few hundred UCLA students and Lancy, 1987), each video game has a huge number of rule-bound patterns programmed into it that are not to be found in the printed instructions on the machine. Talking about Pac-Man, which marked the beginning of the arcade game craze in the U.S., a young player stated, "At first it was thought to be incredibly hard. Then people realized it wasn't random and figured out the patterns" (M. Greenfield, personal communication, 1983).

Strover (1984) concluded that "in contrast to other games . . . video games involve discovering the rules rather than playing by those that are established *a prior*" (p. 17). For this reason, Turkle (1984) felt that the development of game strategy therefore involved "achieving a meeting of the mind with the program" (p. 68). Yet how are the rules discovered? How does this meeting of the minds come about? David Sudnow presented us with a first-person account in *Pilgrim in the Microworld* (1983) and Myers (1984) offered ethnographic evidence, but no experimental research on these questions currently exists. Our study was designed to fill the gap.

Two interrelated goals of our study were to establish the existence and explore the nature of this inductive process of rule discovery. Our major technique for establishing the existence of inductive processing was to document the gradual acquisition of rule knowledge through the repeated administration of questionnaires at various stages of video game play in one of our experimental conditions (the questions group, to be described later).

The process of inductive discovery as studied in information processing experiments (the earliest example being Bruner, Goodnow, & Austin, 1956) and modeled in artificial intelligence (e.g., Holland, Holyoak, Nisbett, & Thagard, 1986; Salzberg, 1985) has two major components: (1) a purely inductive component, in which the person goes from the specific to the general; and (2) a more deductive component, in which the generalizations from the first component become hypotheses to be tested with specific data (cf. Peirce, 1931, cited in Deacon, 1976). The results of such tests then confirm the hypotheses or generate new ones, and there is another cycle of the process. As Holland et al. (1986) pointed out, the initial observations never occur in a vacuum but are always guided by prior knowledge. From this perspective, the cycle in a given situation actually begins with a deductive component based on the application of general knowledge acquired in previously encountered situations.

We thought that this cycle of deductive and inductive thought processes would apply to video games where prior experience would guide initial hypotheses, which then would be tested by actual play. Because play is rapid and feedback instantaneous, many cycles of hypothesis–trial–feedback–new hypothesis could occur in a relatively short period of time. For inexperienced players or novel aspects of the game, the cycle would start with an inductive rather than deductive component.

In terms of induction tasks used in classic experimental studies (Pellegrino, 1985), action video games are most similar to series completion tasks, where one must induce repetitive patterns from one or a few examples. However, a major difference between any experimental test of induction and a video game is that the former uses static stimuli extended in space whereas a video game involves dynamic stimuli extended in both space and time. Although the nature of the rules in a video game could be precisely specified by analyzing the computer program behind the game, from the player's point of view there are a number of alternative formulations of the rules and so the rules may appear more imprecise than in an experimental test of induction. The rules of a video game are generally more complex as well.

As part of our exploration of the nature of inductive discovery processes in video game mastery, we wanted to separate the role of the inductive and deductive components of the discovery process. For this purpose, we created two specific experimental groups. In one, the subjects were free to use any and all cognitive processes as they moved toward game mastery in $2\frac{1}{2}$ hr of play. (This was the play group, to be described in more detail later.) In the other, we provided a detailed and specific basis for initial deduction by demonstrating the game, via slides and videotape, along with verbal commentary describing all rules, patterns, and some game-playing strategies. It was thought that this group (originally labeled the rule-instructed group) would learn how to use these rules in a fairly deductive way, moving from the generalizations provided in our instructions (plus any prior knowledge) to specific applications in the game situation. We therefore thought that the balance between induction and deduction would lie more toward deduction for the rule-instructed group.

The rule-instructed group was also relevant to the question of how much video game expertise is acquired independently and how much can be acquired through watching and talking to other people. In essence, subjects in the rule-instructed group were given the opportunity to watch an expert play and receive verbal instruction.

Another aspect of the experimental design specifically assessed the role of prior knowledge and experience in the inductive process occurring during the mastery of a particular game. By comparing novice and experienced players, we were able to investigate the deductive component by which previous experience is applied to the acquisition of knowledge in a new situation.

A third major goal of our study was to demonstrate that arcade-style video games train inductive discovery skills that transfer to other domains of clear social importance. Because inductive discovery is the heart of scientific thinking and technical problem solving, as classically described, we chose this domain to examine transfer. Hence, we developed a test of inductive discovery in which the subject had to make generalizations concerning the logic of electronic circuitry from viewing schematic, animated demonstrations of circuits on a computer screen. Experimental groups received this test before and after playing an arcade-style video game for $2\frac{1}{2}$ hr. Improvement from pre- to posttest (in comparison with the performance of control subjects) was our measure of transfer of inductive discovery processes.

The nature of inductive discovery processes required in the game and in the pre- and posttests was thought to be similar in several respects: In both cases the subject had to figure out rules governing the operation of computer-generated moving visual stimuli, and the context provided complete information with no extraneous events to confuse the learner. In this respect, the cognitive requirements of the tasks were probably closer to technical problem solving than to science, where the relevant information is usually open-ended and noise in the system is the rule.

One must also note that the test of scientific–technical discovery involved a representation of computer circuitry rather than the circuits themselves. However, scientists and technicians (e.g., medical doctors) increasingly deal with representations of physical data rather than with the data themselves. Ochs, Jacoby, & Gonzales (1994), for example, studied the communication processes that go on in a physics laboratory in which all data are read from a screen or dial and the primary phenomena remain invisible to the scientists. Consequently, the application of inductive discovery processes to computer representations of scientific or technical data will become increasingly important in the conduct of science.

The inclusion of more and less experienced players in the study served to test the ecological validity of our conclusions regarding video games as training devices for more general inductive discovery skills. Our hypothesis was that the video game experience in the real world possessed by experienced players would give them generalizable skill in inductive discovery processes—skill that would then transfer to scientific–technical discovery processes as measured by our screen-based test. This skill was hypothesized to result in higher scores on our pretest of scientific–technical discovery in experienced, as opposed to novice, video game players.

THE CROSS-CULTURAL COMPONENT

A problem of experimental design arose in the U.S. It was impossible to design a pure experiment to study the impact of video games because the population had already been universally exposed to the games, at least to some degree. The opportunity to extend our experiment to Italy meant an opportunity to expose subjects experimentally to video games for the very first time and, more generally, to have a population of more novices available. Indeed, Italy provided a setting in which computer technology was less diffused among the general population and where attitudes toward computers differed from those in the U.S. (Sensales & Greenfield, 1991, in press). Perhaps most important for present purposes, Italian university students have significantly more negative attitudes toward video games than do students in the U.S. (Sensales & Greenfield, 1991, in press). The addition of the Italian component therefore meant that we could assess the impact of being socialized in cultures with different levels of experience and comfort with computer technology.

Because the Italian component of the study was run after the American component, it also provided an opportunity to extend the study by adding conditions to the experiment. Two more control conditions were added: (1) a computer memory game condition, which provided *noninductive* computer game experience; and (2) a mechanical memory game condition, which provided exactly the same game experience without the computer medium.

METHOD

Subjects

Our sample was composed of 206 psychology students in Los Angeles and Rome. Table 1 shows the breakdown of the sample according to the background variables that were thought to relate to computer and video game exposure: culture, gender, and video game experience.

Subjects were considered experienced video game players if they scored 5,500 or better on a screening test of Pac-Man or reported having played more than 100 video games up to that time. These two criteria were used because we considered both practice and skill to be components of video game experience. The use of alternative criteria was especially important in Rome where Pac-Man was not nearly as widespread as it was in the U.S. In Rome, the skills of a relatively experienced player could have been underestimated from the Pac-Man test alone.

It is clear from Table 1 that most experienced players were men and most novices were women in both cultures. Chi-square tests indicated that the association between gender and video game experience was highly significant in both Rome and Los Angeles, ($\chi^2 = 13.895, p < .01; \chi^2 = 6.800, p < .01$, respectively. Whereas gender was not an original interest in carrying out the research, it was not possible to ignore its influence in analyzing the results.

Of the 206 subjects, 200 completed the experiment through the posttest. This subset of 200 therefore constituted the sample for assessing the experimental effects.

Design, Materials, and Procedure

The research basically used a pretest–posttest design, with one of six conditions inserted in between.

TABLE 1
Description of Sample

	Experienced Video Game Players	Novice Video Game Players
Rome[a]		
Male	20	26
Female	10	65
Los Angeles[b]		
Male	17	31
Female	4	33

Note. N = psychology students.
[a]M age = 21 years. [b]M age = 19 years.

Conditions. Four conditions were initially run in Los Angeles. When the study was subsequently extended to Rome, two more control conditions were added (Camaioni et al., 1990).

Three of the original four conditions involved playing a relatively nonviolent video game, Evolution, for $2\frac{1}{2}$ hr on an Apple II computer. Game play was spread over three sessions with two 5-min breaks in each session. Evolution consisted of six diverse levels of game play. Each level comprised a new set of rules and patterns to discover.

In one condition (play only), subjects simply practiced the game. In a second condition (game demonstration and instructions followed by play), subjects were shown the game via a lecture illustrated with slides of the game screens and a video recording of the computer screen during expert play before the game practice period began; the purpose of this condition was to see whether a more deductive approach to learning a video game would produce the same result. In the third condition (play plus questions), subjects filled out a questionnaire during each of the two 5-min breaks and at the end of each session. Subjects were allowed to finish the current game before each break. The questionnaire was designed to assess the development of inductively based game knowledge. The fourth condition was a no-treatment control group.

In Rome, two additional control conditions were added. The first was a computer memory game designed to provide computer experience without the discovery component. The game, resembling the traditional game of Concentration, was much simpler than Evolution and was explained in advance.

The second control condition, the mechanical memory game, held the content of activity constant while varying its medium; it presented the same game in a mechanical medium.

Within a given level of video game experience, subjects were randomly assigned to conditions in each city. There were two exceptions to random assignment: In the U.S., the group of subjects who were presented with game rules before playing the game for $2\frac{1}{2}$ hr were added after the other groups were run as an additional control for inductive experience and consisted entirely of novices. This additional group was drawn from the same source (introductory psychology students) as the other Los Angeles groups; the students enrolled in the course the previous quarter. In Rome, because of a shortage of experienced players, the memory groups consisted entirely of novice players.

Pretest–Posttest of Simulated Scientific–Technical Discovery. We wanted to design a test that would involve forming generalized rules about dynamic processes in the domain of science, just as video games involve generalized patterns of dynamic processes in the domain of fantasy. For this test several dynamic video displays from Rocky's Boots (Robinett, 1982), an educational video game designed to teach the logic of computer circuitry, were used as stimulus material. Although it is hard to get across the nature of a dynamic color demonstration with

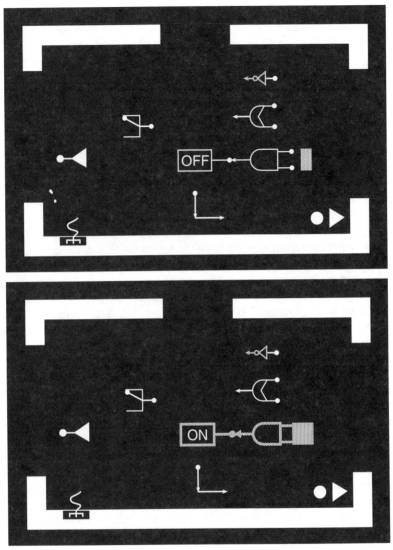

Figure 1. Two screens from the pretest–posttest of scientific–technical discovery. Shaded areas, which were orange in the actual displays, represent the flow of power.

static black-and-white visuals, Figure 1 gives an example of what the subjects saw.

The pair of pictures in the illustration show a sequence in the demonstration of a circuit. It represents the activation of an on/off indicator (middle element in both screens). The shaded quadrilateral in each screen represents a power source.

The lollipop-shaped protuberances are input locations. The pair of screens in Figure 1 shows the power source near a working *and-gate* attached to the on/off indicator. Electricity flows through an *and-gate* when the power source touches both its inputs, as in the bottom screen (shading indicates the flow of power). In the bottom screen, the *and-gate* has been activated in this way, turning the on/off indicator from "off" (top screen) to "on."

In addition to the concepts illustrated in Figure 1, displays exemplified concepts such as *not-gates* and *or-gates*. A *not-gate* (shown at the top right of both screens in Figure 1) is activated when there is not a power source touching the input; the power source deactivates a *not-gate*. An *or-gate* (shown under the not-gate in both screens of Figure 1) activates when the power source touches either one or the other (or both) of its two inputs. Other elements can be made to function if electricity flows through their input end; for example, the bell shown to the left of the *or* element in Figure 1 "rings" when a power source touches its input end. The bell was used in a number of circuit demonstrations. Although many elements were simultaneously on the screen, as Figure 1 shows, the relevant ones for a particular demonstration could be discerned because they were in motion or were involved in some sort of change of state.

The experimenter presented these schematic circuit diagrams on a color video monitor. Subjects were not told that the diagrams they were seeing represented circuits, nor anything else about what they were seeing. They merely were asked to watch carefully and try to figure out what was going on, so that they could answer questions about it afterward.

It is important to note that from the subjects' point of view, the pretest and posttest were in no way games. Although the materials were originally developed for a learning game, they were presented simply as screen displays in our experiment. That is, subjects did not "play": They were not given a joystick or keyboard and they therefore had no control over the displays. They merely watched about 5 min of demonstrations of circuits in operation on the video screen. Thus, at the very least, any transfer involved generalizing discovery strategies acquired in a game situation to a nongame context.

Subjects were shown at least three examples of every element tested so that they could observe the rules that governed their use. Immediately following each group of demonstrations, subjects answered questions about the displays on a paper-and-pencil test. No displays were visible while they were answering the questions. A sample page of questions is presented in Figure 2.

The pre- and posttest were developed to examine skill in inducing generalizations from a few specific examples of each circuit element. All but one of the test questions required the generalization of principles abstracted from the displays to new combinations of elements not shown in the demonstrations. In this way, the possibility that the questions could be answered by simply remembering the displays was eliminated. Instead, some level of inductive generalization was required. Some degree of generalization was also required because subjects had to go from dynamic color displays as shown on a video screen to interpreting

NAME:

DATE: FORM B

What does this represent?

What is its function?

How would you get the orange
color to flow through the
following game elements?

Figure 2. Sample questions from Form B of the pretest–posttest of scientific–technical discovery. The rectangle represents the power source. Both the power source and the flow of power were represented by orange in the screen displays of the pre- and posttest.

primitive black-and-white drawings in a different medium, print, on the test. In addition, the very use of words to answer some of the questions involved forming generalizations from specific visual examples, for as Vygotsky (1962) pointed out, every word is ipso facto a generalization that transcends particular instances. Or, to use different terminology, subjects had to move from the procedural level of the game to the conceptual level of the test.

Two alternate forms of this paper-and-pencil test were developed so that subjects would receive different questions on pre- and posttests. One of the two forms of the test was assigned randomly to each subject, and the alternate form of the test was used during the subsequent testing session, thus counterbalancing for any effect of form of test. Although the questions on each form of the test were different, the video demonstrations were the same. Because the Italian data revealed that the forms were not of equal difficulty (Camaioni et al., 1990), order of forms was used as an independent variable in the relevant analyses of variance (ANOVAs) to reduce variance accruing from this error factor.

Subjects in the experimental conditions were pretested about a week before their experimental treatment. They were posttested between 1 and 3 days after completing the treatment conditions. No-treatment control subjects were pre- and posttested at the same time as the experimental subjects, so that they had the same amount of time between pre- and posttest.

The test was administered to subjects in groups of two to four. There were four blocks of demonstrations, each followed by a block of questions on a printed questionnaire.

The test had a total of 17 questions. Subjects were free to answer the questions either with a short answer and/or by drawing a small diagram.

Coding and Recording of Data

Two points were awarded for each correct answer on the pre- and posttests, making 34 the total possible score. One point was awarded for answers that showed some understanding of the concept being tested but were not totally correct. Zero points were awarded, of course, for answers that indicated no understanding of the concept being tested and for questions left blank or marked, "Don't know."

Only certain questions had partially correct answers. For example, in answer to the question "How would you get the orange color to flow through an *or-gate?*", the subject could get one point by noting that the power source had to touch one or the other of the inputs, and a second point by noting that the power source could also touch both inputs.

In the U.S., interrater reliability was .94, based on a Pearson correlation coefficient calculated from a subset of 22 subjects (both pretest and posttest).

Each answer was also scored for the mode of representation used to present the answer: 1 = verbal representation, 2 = answers that mixed verbal and iconic representation, and 3 = iconic representation. A percentage score of iconic representation was then calculated based on the first eight items, which were considered most diagnostic for mode of representation. Examples of the different modes of representation used to answer one question are shown in Figure 3.

In the U.S., interrater reliability was .95, based on a Pearson correlation coefficient calculated from the same subset of subjects. Coding was calibrated in Rome and Los Angeles through communication of scoring rules and discussion of scoring decisions. In addition, calibrated scoring was facilitated by a visit of the senior author to Rome to collaborate on data analysis.

DIFFERENT MODES OF REPRESENTATION

Verbal

I would touch both spurs with the energizer
one is not enough.

Iconic

Mixed

     Touch both simultaneously.

Figure 3. Different modes of representation used to answer pretest–posttest questions. The question being answered is shown in Figure 2.

In Los Angeles, subjects kept track of their Evolution game scores on a log sheet. Although inaccuracies were possible, there were no reward contingencies within the experiment that would provide a motivation to lie about scores; any inaccuracies should therefore have been random. In Rome, the experimenters corroborated subjects' Evolution game scores. The average of the first three Evolution game scores was calculated as a baseline measure, and the average of the best three Evolution scores was calculated as a measure of optimal performance.

RESULTS

A 2 (Experienced vs. Novice) $\times$ 2 (United States vs. Italy) $\times$ 2 (Male vs. Female) ANOVA explored the relationship of indices of past video game experience to pretest scores on the test of scientific–technical discovery skills. The analysis yielded main effects of video game experience, $F(1, 198) = 6.395$, $p < .025$; culture, $F(1, 198) = 10.477$, $p < .005$; and gender, $F(1, 198) = 12.034$, $p < .005$. There were no significant interactions. In line with their relative exposure to video games, experienced players, Americans, and males performed significantly better on the screen-based test of scientific–technical

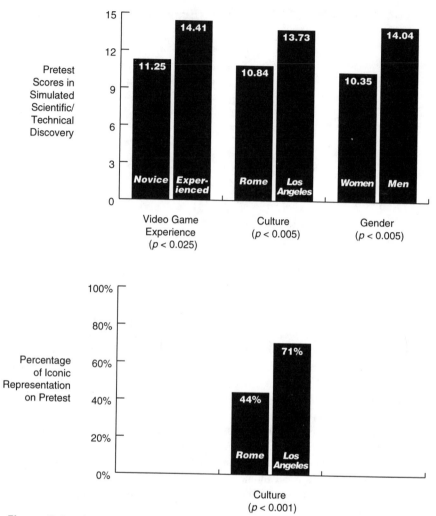

Figure 4. Significant long-term influences on simulated scientific–technical discovery and mode of representation.

discovery than did novices, Italians, and females, respectively (see Figure 4). In addition, a parallel ANOVA was done, using iconic versus verbal representation of pretest answers as the dependent variable. The analysis yielded a main effect of culture, $F(1, 198) = 176.463$, $p < .001$, showing that Americans preferred to use diagrams whereas Italians preferred to use words in formulating answers to the test. These results are shown in Figure 4. Again, there were no significant interaction effects.

The influence of culture was not surprising; as hoped, there was a significant subgroup ($n = 17$) of Italian novices who never played a video game before the experiment. In the U.S., as anticipated, this phenomenon was rare ($n = 2$). Probably because of this significant difference in group composition, $\chi^2 = 8.158$, $p < .005$, Italian novices attained significantly lower maximum video game scores during the experimental treatments than did novices in the U.S., $t = 8.11$, $p < .001$, although there was no difference in the practiced performance of experienced players in the two countries.

Consistent with the results presented up to now, previous game experience, culture, and gender were highly related to video game performance in the course of the experiment. A $2 \times 2 \times 2$ ANOVA showed that the best video game scores were significantly affected by previous video game experience, $F(1, 169) = 97.829$, $p < .001$; culture, $F(1, 169) = 25.944$, $p < .001$; and gender, $F(1, 169) = 17.146$, $p < .001$. Significantly higher Evolution scores were attained by more experienced players, by Americans, and by males. There was also an interaction between experience and culture, $F(1, 169) = 18.948$, $p < .001$; its nature was elucidated by the t test described in the preceeding paragraph.

These factors affected initial scores as well as ultimate levels of game play. A second $2 \times 2 \times 2$ ANOVA using the same variables showed that players' first three video game scores were also affected by video game experience, $F(1, 168) = 78.257$, $p < .001$; culture, $F(1, 168) = 124.245$, $p < .001$; and gender, $F(1, 168) = 11.622$, $p < .001$, just as their best three scores were. Significantly higher initial game scores were attained by more experienced players, by Americans, and by males. Again, there was a significant interaction between experience and culture, $F(1, 168) = 15.366$, $p < .001$. Novices in Italy initially scored lower on Evolution than did novices in the U.S., $t = 9.81$, $p < .001$, although there was no difference between initial scores for experienced players in the two countries. Thus experienced players, Americans, and males seemed to start playing Evolution with some combination of better initial hypotheses and better manual skills.

The effectiveness of actual discovery processes during $2\frac{1}{2}$ hr of game play did not seem to differ very much; for example, men and women each came close to quintupling their video game scores from their first games to their best games, as did both novices and more experienced players. Gender, experience, and culture seemed to affect initial game knowledge and skills more than they affected the cognitive processes of discovery.

The results indicating long-term developmental influences of video game and related central experiences on discovery skills were confirmed by the experimental results. An ANOVA using pretest and posttest as a repeated measure, with treatment group, video game experience, and order of test forms as between-subject variables revealed a significant two-way interaction between treatment group and pretest–posttest change, $F(5, 180) = 2.46$, $p < .05$, as well as a significant three-way interaction between treatment group, video game experi-

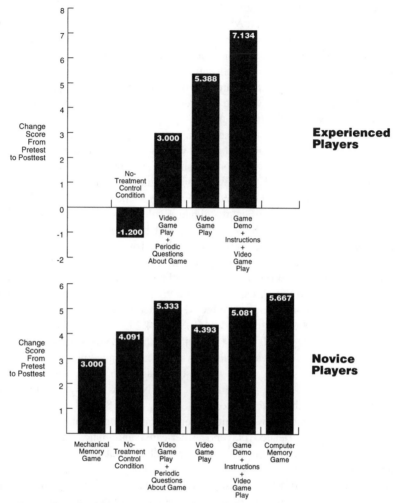

Figure 5. Pretest–posttest change in understanding a scientific–technical simulation: experienced and novice players under different experimental conditions.

ence, and pretest–posttest change, $F(3, 180) = 3.10, p < .05$. This interaction is graphed in Figure 5.

One import of the three-way interaction is to show that the transfer performance of experienced players benefits significantly more than that of novice players from game demonstrations and instructions before starting to play the game (Tukey test, $p < .05$). Apparently, off-line video game instructions have more effect if the recipient has more on-line experience with the games. In contrast, periodic questions during game play benefit novice transfer performance significantly more than they benefit that of experienced players (Tukey test, $p < .05$).

Further analysis of the three-way interaction showed that experimental effects were more pronounced for the experienced than the novice video game players. The Tukey test revealed that posttest improvement in comprehending scientific–technical material on the screen differed significantly for experienced players under every experimental condition to which they were exposed, $p < .05$. This was not the case for novice players. (This difference is manifest descriptively in the difference between the slopes of the bars in the two graphs in Figure 5.)

Taken together, the graphs indicate that the video game and computer memory groups improved the most from pretest to posttest, whereas two control groups (no-treatment, mechanical memory) improved the least. This major feature of the three-way interaction is preserved in the significant two-way interaction between treatment group and pretest–posttest change: According to a post-hoc Tukey test, each of the computer and video game conditions produced significantly greater pretest–posttest improvement than did either the mechanical memory or no-play groups, $p < .05$.

The pattern of results indicates that there is meaningful transfer from video and computer game experience to informal scientific–technical discovery in a screen-based task, but that, contrary to prediction, the degree of induction required makes no difference to the amount of transfer. Of all the conditions, the video and slide demonstration with verbal instructions before video game play produced the most improvement among experienced players (Tukey test, $p < .05$); yet it is the least inductive condition to which this group was exposed. For the novices, the computer memory game, the least inductive condition of all, stimulated pretest–posttest change that was significantly greater (Tukey test, $p < .05$) than the change produced by simply practicing a video game, the most inductive condition. These results went contrary to the original prediction.

Most interesting was the fact that the computer memory group improved in their understanding of the scientific–technical simulation significantly more than did the mechanical memory group (Tukey test, $p < .05$). The computer medium made a difference, even though game content was identical in the two conditions. Practice with a particular medium of presentation and representation contributed more to discovering the meaning of the animated scientific–technical simulation than did the opportunity to exercise inductive discovery processes.

Although inductive processes per se did not appear responsible for the transfer effect, periodic questioning about game knowledge in the game play plus questions group provided evidence that game experience nonetheless led to discovery of game knowledge. Figure 6 shows the gradual and significant increase in game knowledge from after 15 min of play to after about $2\frac{1}{4}$ hr of play that took place in the questions group in Rome, $F(5, 70) = 14.52$, $p < .001$. A Tukey test for multiple comparisons indicated significant, $p < .05$, improvement in the pre-

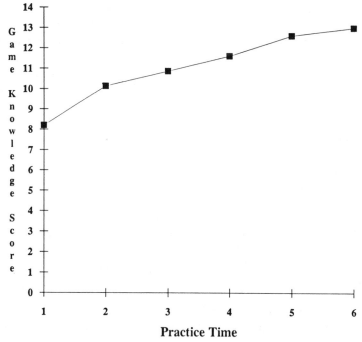

Figure 6. Induction of game knowledge through video game practice.

dicted direction between Times 1 and 2 and between Times 2 and 5. Of course, all improvements between more distant times (e.g., Time 1, Time 6) were also statistically significant at the .05 level.

We have seen that the provision of knowledge that could be used deductively to master a video game maximized transfer for experienced players; however, such knowledge was of little or no use in mastering the video game itself. A comparison of the ultimate skill level (the best three Evolution scores) of subjects who merely played the game (a more inductive condition) with that of subjects who, before playing, were given demonstrations and audiovisual descriptions of rules and patterns (a condition that involves more deductive elements), showed that there was no difference in maximum performance for either experienced or novice players (using initial scores as a covariate in an ANOVA).

Computer game experience made mode of representation more iconic. An ANOVA using pretest and posttest modes of representation as repeated measures, with treatment group and test order as independent variables, revealed a significant interaction between repeated measure and treatment group, $F(5, 142) = 3.09, p < .025$. This shift was mainly due to the computer memory game, which produced a significant shift toward iconic representation, $t = 3.84, p < .01$, two-tailed test. It was most interesting to note that despite the fact that mode of representation was independent of correctness from a measurement point of view, the two measures were positively correlated on the pretest, $r = .2308$, $p < .005$. More iconic representation was associated with better scores on the screen-based test of scientific–technical discovery.

The role of video games in producing the experimental effect was further strengthened by the fact that there was a significant positive correlation between the best video game scores and amount of pretest–posttest improvement on the test of simulated scientific–technical discovery, $r = .1883$, $p < .025$. The number of science courses taken significantly predicted pretest scores on the test of simulated scientific–technical discovery, $r = .2682$, $p < .001$. However, science background significantly predicted neither posttest nor improvement scores. Video game scores did: The correlation between best three video game scores and posttest was .3894 ($p < .001$). As might be expected from this pattern of results, all correlations remained significant with science background partialed out.

DISCUSSION

Our study succeeded in establishing that knowledge of a video game is acquired as a result of the inductive experience of playing the game as Greenfield (1983, 1984) theorized. We documented a significant and steady increase in knowledge of rules, regularities, and strategies as a function of time spent playing the video game Evolution. At the same time, we also established that the provision of initial information through slides, verbal instructions, and modeling did not make a difference in the ultimate game skill attained by subjects. Thus, it was necessary for players to form hypotheses from their own experience and test them inductively in the course of the game. A model and explanations that could aid deductive processes at the outset of the learning process were of no advantage for either novices or more experienced players.

In other words, we established that inductive discovery is crucial to mastery of an arcade-style action video game. On the other hand, Harris (1992) observed that "in video game play, young children as novices are introduced to game play by more experienced players, and once the basics are mastered, the novice further develops his skills on his own through interaction with the games. . . . more experienced players share secrets with less experienced players, often modeling game strategies or providing verbal guidance through difficult moves" (p. 6). At the same time, other research has indicated that explicit instructions beginning after some inductive practice can be of use in mastering a video game (Newell, Carlton, Fisher, & Rutter, 1989).

Given these observations concerning the role of expert instruction in the learning process, why did visual demonstrations accompanied by verbal instructions not make a positive difference in mastering the video game Evolution? One important factor may be the interactive and scaffolded nature of the novice–

master relationship described by Harris (1992). In other words, the experienced player can observe the learner's level and specific needs for information as the learner plays the game, and the learner can communicate his or her specific informational needs to the master. The master–novice interaction described by Harris (1992) occurs while the learner is on-line with the game, receiving inductively relevant input. The learner creates a representational model of the game by interacting both with the game and with other players simultaneously. A second, related factor may be the timing; Newell et al.'s (1989) findings indicate the possibility that video game instructions would be more useful after, rather than before, game play has begun.

We also established that experience with "noneducational" video and computer games can produce transfer to skill in acquiring knowledge from a scientific–technical computer application. For both novice and experienced players, practice on an activity utilizing the computer medium led to greater transfer; the absence of the computer medium (mechanical memory condition, no-treatment control condition) greatly reduced pretest–posttest improvement in the acquisition of knowledge from an animated computer simulation of the logic of electronic circuitry.

Most telling in relation to the impact of action video games was the following finding: The level of subjects' best performance on the arcade-style video game Evolution was significantly correlated both with pretest–posttest improvement and with posttest scores on the screen-based test of scientific–technical discovery. That this test actually tapped scientific skills is attested to by the fact that science background was a significant predictor of pretest performance. Yet science background did not significantly predict either posttest scores or improvement in the course of the experiment. Video game performance, in contrast, did.

Despite these experimental and correlational results, inductive discovery did not seem to be at the heart of the transfer that took place. First of all, recall that for experienced players, the most effective conditions in promoting transfer involved receiving explicit communication concerning the rules, regularities, and strategies of the video game before actually playing the game. This condition was less effective for the novices, whose most effective condition was one that minimized the necessity for inductive activity even more: the computer memory game, in which the very simple rules were all explained in advance to the subjects. Contrary to the original hypothesis, game play alone (the most inductive condition) was not the most effective in improving test performance for either novices or experienced players.

Another result that militates against the idea that video games provide training in inductive discovery skills was the fact that novice players improved their Evolution scores at about the same rate as more experienced players, indicating equivalent skill in discovering new rules, patterns, and strategies through game play.

If inductive discovery was not the cognitive key to transfer, what process was? Or, to put the question another way, what skill was being transferred and what skill was being tested? Several results led to the conclusion that the transferable skill was not induction but rather skill in decoding and encoding the iconic representational code of the computer medium. First, in the scale of transfer shown for novices in Figure 5, all computer conditions were at the top whereas the mechanical memory condition, the only condition involving a different medium of representation, was at the bottom.

Second, the fact that periodic questioning was more effective at generating transfer for the novices than for the experienced players might also constitute evidence that mastery of an iconic code was at play. As the sample questions in Figure 2 show, these questions called attention to the code units, perhaps helping novice players to identify the basic nature of symbolic elements on a computer screen. Because the experienced players started off with greater knowledge of this code (as shown by their significantly higher pretest scores), the basic level of screen symbolism addressed by the questions condition may have been of less use to them.

More direct evidence that the basis of transfer was mastery of an iconic code lay in two other results: (1) $2\frac{1}{2}$ hr of playing the computer memory game produced a significant increase in iconic (as opposed to verbal) representation of the posttest, and (2) relatively greater use of iconic representation on the pretest was significantly associated with more correct answers on that test. In summary, whereas we had originally conceptualized the pretests–posttests as tests of scientific–technical discovery, the results made us emphasize that scientific content was being conveyed in a particular medium and code of representation, that of animated computer graphics. Not surprisingly, skill with the code facilitated comprehension of the content.

That computer games activate visual–spatial rather than verbal–symbolic processes was confirmed in a study by Logie, Baddeley, Mane, Donchin, and Sheptak (1988). These researchers found that after 3 hr of practice on an action video game, Space Fortress, performance was more disrupted by concurrent visual–spatial tasks than by concurrent verbal tasks.

Overall, the pattern of results led to the conclusion that it was not inductive discovery experience per se, but rather experience with a particular medium and code of symbolic representation that was at the heart of the transfer. What was being tested was not merely the process of scientific–technical discovery, but also the ability to decode scientific–technical information from schematic animated computer graphics. Results indicated that the construction of meaning was the important process underlying transfer; contrary to the hypothesis, it did not matter whether such meaning was constructed more inductively or more deductively.

Why was the computer memory condition the most effective in promoting a preference for iconic rather than verbal representation? One reason may have been that its schematic graphics were more similar to those of the transfer tests than were the graphics of Evolution; the graphics used in the computer memory game were also more prototypical of the computer medium than were those of Evolution. Another reason may have been that the action in the computer memory game was slower and, unlike that of arcade-style games, totally under the control of the player; the faster, uncontrollable action of Evolution may have been relatively distracting. And, finally, the computer memory game was simpler, perhaps allowing greater concentration on the code itself.

Our results indicate that mastery of an iconic code is a crucial element in computer literacy. This finding is very much in tune with Salomon's (1979) theoretical view that each medium has its own symbol system. Applying this view to computers, Salomon (1988) suggested that symbolic forms used by computer tools can be internalized as cognitive modes of representation through the process of human–computer interaction. Given the importance of mastering the symbolic codes of the computer screen, a possible pedagogical implication of our findings is that children should be exposed to prototypical computer graphics representing simple or familiar content before they are expected to use this medium to decode complex new information. As in print literacy, knowledge of the basic code must precede use of that code to attain new information. In terms of the relation of noneducational computer games to scientific and technical education, mastery of the symbolic codes used in computer graphics becomes increasingly important as more and more science and technology comes to be done on computer screens rather than in the material world.

As a corroboration of our results concerning short-term experimental influences, we found that long-term influences that subjects brought with them into the study also had an impact on the ability to decode scientific–technical information from a computer screen. The groups who had been more exposed to computer screens over the long term—males, Americans, and more experienced video game players—had at the outset of the experiment more skill than females, Italians, and less experienced video game players in decoding graphically presented information about the logic of computer circuitry. Finally, Americans were more iconic than Italians in their way of representing and communicating this information, possibly because of their greater exposure to computer screens and other sources of iconic visual imagery.

An important side effect of the computer revolution may turn out to be a shift from more verbal and symbolic representation to more iconic modes. Our study also showed that the representational skills developed by computer games transfer to scientific computer applications. In other words, entertaining computer games provide informal education for the scientific or technical use of computers. Contrary to early popular views of video games (summarized in Greenfield, 1984), they are not simply a waste of time. Lastly, computer games are cultural tools that, like other cultural tools, exist in a societal context. Our results indicate that the availability of computer tools in a particular society affects the representational competence of its members in communicating with computers across a range of specific applications. By influencing representational competence in a medium of symbolic communication, computer games serve as a cultural tool of cognitive socialization.

REFERENCES

Bank Street College Project in Science and Mathematics (1984). *Voyage of the Mimi.* New York: Author.

Bruner, J.S., Goodnow, J., & Austin, G. (1956). *A study of thinking.* New York: Wiley.

Burbules, N.C., & Reese, P. (1984). *Teaching logic to children: An exploratory study of "Rocky's Boots."* Berkeley: University of California, Lawrence Hall of Science.

Burton, R.R., & Brown, J.S. (1979). An investigation of computer coaching for informal learning activities. *International Journal of Man–Machine Studies, 11,* 5–24.

Camaioni, L., Ercolani, A.P., Perucchini, P., & Greenfield, P.M. (1990). Video-giochi e abilita cognitive: L'ipotesi del transfer [Video-games and cognitive ability: The hypothesis of transfer]. *Giornale Italiano di Psicologia, 17,* 331–348.

Chaffin, J. (1983, May). *Motivational features of video arcade games.* Paper presented at the Harvard Graduate School of Education Symposium on Video Games and Human Development, Cambridge, MA.

Chaffin, J.D., Maxwell, B., & Thompson, B. (1982). ARC-ED curriculum: The application of video game formats to educational software. *Exceptional Children, 49,* 173–178.

Char, C. (1983). Research and design issues concerning the development of educational software for children. In *Chameleon in the classroom: Developing roles for computers.* Symposium presented at the annual meeting of the American Educational Research Association, Montreal.

Craig, E.M. (1987). *Expert and novice problem solving in a complex computer game.* Unpublished doctoral dissertation, University of California, Los Angeles.

Deacon, T.W., (1976). *Semiotics and cybernetics: The relevance of C.S. Peirce.* Unpublished manuscript, Western Washington University, Bellingham, WA.

Donchin, E., Fabiani, M., & Sanders, A. (Eds.). (1989). The learning strategies program: An examination of the strategies in skill acquisition. *Acta Psychologica, 71,* 1–310.

Dugdale, S., & Kibbey, D. (1982). *Green globs and graphing equations* [Computer program]. Pleasantville, NY: Sunburst Communications.

Forsyth, A.S., Jr. (1986). A computer adventure game and place location learning: Effects of map type and player gender. Unpublished doctoral dissertation, Utah State University, Logan.

Forsyth, A.S., Jr., & Lancy, D.F. (1987). Simulated travel and place location learning in a computer adventure game. *Journal of Educational Computing Research, 3,* 377–394.

Frederiksen, J.R., & White, B.Y. (1989). An approach to training based on principled task decomposition. *Acta Psychologica, 71,* 89–146.

Gagnon, D. (1985). Videogames and spatial skills: An exploratory study. *Educational Communication and Technology Journal, 33,* 263–275.

Greenfield, P.M. (1983). Video games and cognitive skills. In *Video games and human development: Research agenda for the '80s* (pp. 19–24). Cambridge, MA: Monroe C. Gutman Library, Graduate School of Education.

Greenfield, P.M. (1984). *Mind and media: The effects of television, video games and computers.* Cambridge, MA: Harvard University Press.

Greenfield, P.M. (1993). Representational competence in shared symbol systems: Electronic media from radio to video games. In R.R. Cocking & K.A. Renninger (Eds.), *The development and meaning of psychological distance* (pp. 161–183). Hillsdale, NJ: Erlbaum.

Greenfield, P., & Lave, J. (1982). Cognitive aspects of information education. In D. Wagner &

H. Stevenson (Eds.), *Cultural perspectives on child development* (pp. 181–207). San Francisco: Freeman.

Harris, S. (1992). *Media influences on cognitive development.* Unpublished manuscript.

Hayes, B., Lancy, D.F., & Evans, B. (1985). Computer adventure games and the development of information-processing skills. In G.H. McNick (Ed.), *Comprehension, computers, and communication* (pp. 60–66). Athens, GA: University of Georgia Press.

Holland, J.H., Holyoak, K.J., Nisbett, R.E., & Thagard, P.R. (1986). *Induction: Processes of inference, learning, and discovery.* Cambridge, MA: MIT Press.

Lancy, D.F. (1987). Will video games alter the relationship between play and development? In G.A. Fine (Ed.), *Meaningful play, playful meanings* (pp. 219–230). Champaign, IL: Human Kinetics.

Lancy, D.F., Cohen, H., Evans, B., Levine, N., & Nevin, M.L. (1985). Using the joystick as a tool to promote intellectual growth and social interaction. *Laboratory for the Comparative Study of Human Cognition Newsletter, 7,* 119–125.

Lancy, D.F., & Hayes, B.L. (1988). Interactive fiction and the reluctant reader. *The English Journal, 77,* 42–46.

Levin, J.A. (1981). Estimation techniques for arithmetic: Everyday math and mathematics instruction. *Educational Studies in Mathematics, 12,* 421–434.

Loftus, G.R., & Loftus, E.F. (1983). *Mind at play: The psychology of video games.* New York: Basic Books.

Logie, R.H., Baddeley, A.D., Mane, A., Donchin, E., & Sheptak, R. (1988). Visual working memory in the acquisition of complex cognitive skills. In M. Denis, J. Engelkamp, & J.T.E. Richardson (Eds.), *Cognitive and neuropsychological approaches to mental imagery* (pp. 191–201). Dordrecht, Netherlands: Martinus Nijhoff Publishers.

Malone, T.W. (1981). Towards a theory of intrinsically motivating instruction. *Cognitive Science, 4,* 333–369.

McLuhan, M. (1964). *Understanding media: The extensions of man.* New York: McGraw-Hill.

Mick, D., Konneman, M., O'Farrell, R., & Isaacs, J. (1983). *Algebra arcade* [Computer program]. Fairfield, CT: Queue.

Myers, D. (1984). The patterns of player–game relationships: A study of computer game players. *Simulation & Games, 15,* 159–185.

Newell, K.M., Carlton, M.J., Fisher, A.T., & Rutter, B.G. (1989). Whole-part training strategies for learning the response dynamics of microprocessor driven simulators. *Acta Psychologica, 71,* 197–216.

Ochs, E., Jacoby, S., & Gonzales, P. (1994). Interpretive journeys: How physicists talk and travel through graphic space. *Configurations, 2,* 151–172.

Pellegrino. J.W. (1985). Inductive reasoning ability. In R.J. Sternberg (Ed.), *Human abilities: An information-processing approach* (pp. 195–225). New York: W.H. Freeman.

Perry, T., Truxal, C., & Wallach, D. (1982). Videogames: The electronic big bang. *IEEE Spectrum, 19,* 20–33.

Piestrup, A.M. (1982). *Young children use computer graphics.* Portola Valley, CA: Learning Company.

Rabbit, P., Banerji, N., & Szymanski, A. (1989). Space fortress as an IQ test? Predictions of learning of practised performance in a complex interactive video-game. *Acta Psychologica, 71,* 243–257.

Rebellion against video games spreads. (April 24, 1983). *Los Angeles Times,* Part III, p. 3.

Roberts, J.M., & Sutton-Smith, B. (1962). Child training and game involvement. *Ethnology, 1,* 166–185.

Roberts, R.J., Jr., Aman, C., & Canfield, R. (1989, April). *Developmental differences in learning a new skill: The role of self-imposed constraints.* Paper presented at the biennial meeting of the Society of Research in Child Development, Kansas City, MO.

Roberts, R.J., Jr., Brown, D., Wiebke, S., & Haith, M.M. (1991). A computer-automated laboratory for studying complex perception-action skills. *Behavior Research Methods, Instruments and Computers, 23,* 493–504

Roberts, R.J., Jr., & Ondrejko, M. (in press). Perception, action, and skill: Looking ahead to meet the present. In M.M. Haith, J.B. Benson, R.J. Roberts, Jr., & B.F. Pennington (Eds.), *The development of future-oriented processes.* Chicago: University of Chicago Press.

Robinett, W. (1982). *Rocky's Boots.* Portola Valley, CA: Learning Company.

Rushbrook, S. (1986). *"Messages" of video games: Socialization implications.* Unpublished doctoral dissertation, University of California, Los Angeles.

Salomon, G. (1979). *Interaction of media, cognition, and learning.* San Francisco: Jossey-Bass.

Salzberg, S. (1985). Heuristics for inductive learning. *Proceedings of the Ninth International Joint Conference on Artificial Intelligence:* Vol. 1 (pp. 603–609). Los Altos, CA: Morgan Kaufman.

Sensales, G., & Greenfield, P.M. (1991). *Computer, scienza e tecnologia: Un confronto transculturale fra gli atteggiamenti di studenti italiani e statunitensi* [Computers, science, and technology: A cross-cultural comparison between the attitudes of Italian and U.S. students]. *Giornale Italiano di Psicologia, 18,* 45–57.

Sensales, G., & Greenfield, P.M. (in press). Attitudes toward computers, science, and technology: A cross-cultural comparison between students in Rome and Los Angeles. *Journal of Cross-Cultural Psychology.*

Stein, J.S., & Linn, M. (1985). Capitalizing on computer-based interactive feedback: An investigation of Rocky's Boots. In M. Chen & W. Paisley (Eds.), *Children and microcomputers: Research on the newest medium* (pp. 213–227). Beverly Hills, CA: Sage.

Strover, S. (1984, May). *Games in the information age.* Paper presented at the meeting of the International Communication Association, San Francisco, CA.

Sudnow, D. (1983). *Pilgrim in the microworld.* New York: Warner Books.

Trachtman, P. (1981). A generation meets computers—and they are friendly. *Smithsonian, 12,* 50–61.

Turkle, S. (1984). *The second self: Computers and the human spirit.* New York: Simon & Schuster.

Vygotsky, L.S. (1962). *Thought and language.* Cambridge, MA: MIT Press.

Wood, L.E. (1980). An "intelligent" program to teach logical thinking skills. *Behavior Research Methods & Instrumentation, 12,* 256–258.

Chapter 10

Two-Dimensional Representation of Movement Through Three-Dimensional Space: The Role of Video Game Expertise

Patricia M. Greenfield
Craig Brannon
University of California, Los Angeles

David Lohr
North Los Angeles Regional Center

Cognitive processes—the basic processes by which we take in, transform, remember, create, and communicate information—are universal. A culture has the power to selectively encourage some cognitive processes and let others stay in a relatively undeveloped state. As shared symbol systems, media are potent cultural tools for the selective sculpting of profiles of cognitive processes. A medium is not simply an information channel; as a particular mode of representation, it is also a potential influence on information processing.

The notion of symbol systems as cultural tools for cognitive development can be traced to Vygotsky (1962, 1978) and Bruner (1965, 1966). For Vygotsky, it

This article was prepared with the aid of a UCLA College Institute Award, a Science Fellowship from the Bunting Institute, Radcliffe College and the Office of Naval Research, the UCLA Gold Shield Faculty Prize, and a grant from the Spencer Foundation. The authors gratefully acknowledge the assistance of Peter Bentler for statistical analysis and Lisa Kendig for manuscript preparation.

Correspondence and requests for reprints should be sent to Patricia M. Greenfield, Department of Psychology, University of California, Los Angeles, 405 Hilgard Avenue, Los Angeles, CA 90024–1563.

was the internalization of a cultural tool or symbol system that constituted and produced cognitive development. For Bruner, it was the need for a match between external symbol systems and internal modes of representation that stimulated cognitive development. As applied to media, this notion was significantly expanded by Bruner and Olson (1973) and Salomon (1979). These researchers were the first to recognize communication media as distinct symbol systems.

Media of communication and representation tend to be embodied in various cultural artifacts. The role of cultural artifacts in developing representational and problem-solving skills has been extensively studied by Saxe (e.g., 1991) and reviewed by Guberman and Greenfield (1991). People engage with cultural artifacts not merely in the rarefied atmosphere of the psychology laboratory, but in their everyday lives. Hence, much of the cognitive activity that these artifacts engage falls under the rubric of "everyday cognition" (Rogoff & Lave, 1984).

A central aspect of human cognitive processes is representational competence. Sigel and Cocking (1977) saw the development of an understanding of various media of representation, such as pictures, verbalizations, and gestures, as part of representational competence. Nonetheless, each medium has its particular design features such that it presents certain kinds of information easily and well and other kinds poorly and with difficulty. Each medium, therefore, presents certain opportunities to construct particular kinds of representations. As a consequence, each medium stimulates different kinds of representational processes; it provides a particular kind of cognitive socialization.

The interactive television set we call a video game has entered our society on a mass scale. From the point of view of development and socialization, video games are particularly important because they affect children during the formative years of childhood, when socialization is taking place. For most children, the video game is one of the first opportunities they have to interact with computer technology.

Video games have risen from relative obscurity in the early 1970s to their assimilation in U.S. culture. In 1982, the video arcade business grossed about $8 billion; sales of home video games were worth less than half that amount (Condry & Keith, 1983). That same year, according to Condry and Keith (1983), the home video market reached 12 million homes, in contrast to the 75 million reached by television. Rushbrook (1986) showed that 94% of 10-year-old children in Southern California (Orange County) played video games. Still, the penetration of the home market continued; by the end of 1991, Nintendo game sets alone had entered 45 million homes. Such mass penetration led Provenzo (1991) to carry out a social and cultural analysis of the "Nintendo phenomenon." Although the overwhelming mass of research on children and computers has involved studies of children either programming or using "educational" software, video games are, in fact, much more pervasive elements in children's *everyday* cognition (Greenfield, 1983, 1984, 1993).

If the video game is indeed an interactive television, then it is not surprising that as a means of representation, it shares design features with television itself. Compared with pictorial representation, the video screen, possessed by both television and video games, adds two new interrelated dimensions—time and motion—to the iconic imagery of pictorial representation. These two new dimensions have implications for the representation of three-dimensional space. One would expect television and video games to require common representational skills.

The central thesis is that video technology, especially video games, augments skill in reading visual images as representations of three-dimensional space. The presence of print (and later photographic) technology is historically associated with the development of conventions of perspective. Such conventions both allow and require the three-dimensional representations. Video games and television go beyond print and photography in their presentation of two-dimensional representations of three-dimensional space. The consumer must demonstrate not only an ability to interpret static two-dimensional images in the third dimension, but also dynamic images. Video games go farther still; the player must not only interpret, but also mentally transform, manipulate, and relate dynamic and changing images. It is the transfer of this skill to spatial contexts outside the game that is the focus of the present research. The question is: Can video game practice develop transferable skills in manipulating three-dimensional spatial representations?

Other studies have shown that spatial skills are developed both through informal activities and formal training (Baenninger & Newcombe, 1989). Indeed, Salomon (1974) showed an effect of dynamic televised representations of mental paper folding on performance with the static stimuli of the mental paper-folding test. Following a suggestion by Lowery and Knirk (1982–1983), many studies indicated that video games are among the training experiences that develop spatial skills (Dorval & Pepin, 1986; Gagnon, 1985; Greenfield, deWinstanley, Kilpatrick, & Kaye, 1994; McClurg & Chaillé, 1987; Okagaki & Frensch, 1994; Subrahmanyam & Greenfield, 1994), as well as spatial knowledge (Forsyth & Lancy, 1987). Of these, only McClurg and Chaillé used a task that involved mentally manipulating an object in three-dimensionally represented space. Their study used a mental rotations test (mentally turning a three-dimensional object represented in two-dimensional space) and involved fifth, seventh, and ninth graders; our test used a mental paper-folding test (mentally folding a two-dimensional object represented in two-dimensional space to form a three-dimensional object; based on Shepard & Feng, 1972) and involved college students.

Whereas all other previous studies of cognitive effects of video games (Greenfield, Camaioni, et al., 1994; Greenfield, Dewinstanley, et al., 1994; Subrahmanyam & Greenfield, 1994) were carried out in laboratory or classroom settings, the studies presented here were unique in utilizing the ecology of a video arcade. Study 1 was also unique in harnessing naturally occurring play for a systematic study. Unlike other studies, this one utilized subjects who actually play the "experimental" video game in real life. Study 1, therefore, had an unusual degree of ecological validity and complemented the experimental control of Study 2.

The importance of spatial skills as a form of representational competence goes beyond video games to the computer medium more generally. Greenfield (1984, 1993) summarized evidence that spatial skills were crucial to computer activities as diverse as word processing (Gomez, Egan, & Bowers, 1986) and programming (Roberts, 1984; Webb, 1984) in adults, adolescents, and children. Skills of spatial representation involved in word processing include understanding the sequential nature of text and how deleting and inserting text affects this sequence. Spatial representation is also required to understand the relation between the visible and invisible portions of the text. (In relation to programming, it should be noted that both Roberts, 1984, and Webb, 1984, did their respective research with LOGO, an iconically represented programming language; the role of spatial skills in learning more verbal or symbolic programming languages remains to be seen.)

The anthropological study of games has demonstrated that a culture's games socialize children in accord with the needs and adaptational requirements of a particular society (Roberts & Sutton-Smith, 1962; Werner, 1979). Video games provide many children with their first introduction to computers (Kiesler, Sproull, & Eccles, 1983). By promoting the spatial skills required for humans to interface effectively with computer technology (e.g., understanding how objects on the screen can be manipulated by input devices), video games can socialize children to adapt to a society in which computers have become central.

STUDY 1

Materials

The video game chosen for this experiment was The Empire Strikes Back. The game was selected for its graphic representation of three-dimensional space on a two-dimensional screen. The game gives the player the perspective of a starship pilot flying through space. The player's task is to shoot enemy ships while avoiding asteroids and enemy fire so as to accumulate points and advance in difficulty level.

For this experiment, spatial ability was defined by a subject's ability to correctly answer problems on an 8-item multiple-choice test of mental paper folding constructed by Brannon and Lohr for this study. The paper-and-pencil test required subjects to mentally refold drawings of unfolded cubes. This test is similar to that used by Shepard and Feng (1972) in their study of mental paper folding. The test is shown in Figure 1.

Below are drawings each representing a cube that has been "unfolded." Your task is to mentally refold each cube and determine which one of the sides will be touching the side marked by an arrow.

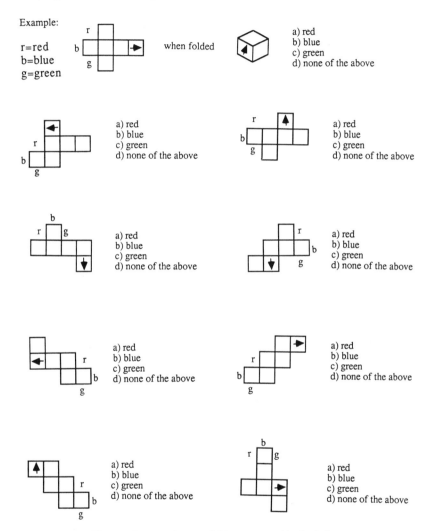

Figure 1. Mental paper-folding test used in Study 1.

Subjects and Procedure

The subjects for this study were 24 male UCLA undergraduates. To locate subjects, Brannon and Lohr watched The Empire Strikes Back machine in the UCLA video arcade and approached players as they finished playing a game, noting their scores. All of the players and therefore all of the subjects were made. In essence, the subjects were young men who played this particular game in their everyday life.

Potential subjects were asked to participate in a student research project and were informed that it would involve completing an 8-item test. Subjects took about 2 to 5 min to complete the test, with the average subject taking 3 min. Each subject was given as much time as needed to finish the test.

Analysis and Results

Game scores were used to divide the subjects into more and less skillful players; a score of 100,000 points was used as the criterion. In order to reach 100,000 points, a player had to complete a whole "round" and reach the next level, which seemed like a reasonable criterion to distinguish more and less skillful players. For the mental paper-folding test, a score of 6 out of 8 was considered to indicate good spatial skills; a score of below 6 was considered to show relatively weak spatial skills. The criterion score of 6 was used because it seemed reasonable that people with good spatial ability could fold all of the items, except for perhaps the two items that required the six folds (the maximum), to complete. Approximately half the subjects fell into each of the spatial skills groups.

There was a close relationship between scores on mental paper folding and video game scores. Seventeen out of 22 (or 77%) high video game scorers were also classified as high scorers on the spatial skills test. Conversely, 16 out of 18 (or 89%) low video game scorers also scored poorly on the spatial skills test. A chi-square test (corrected for continuity) showed this association between video game scores and spatial scores to be statistically significant on the .0001 level, $\chi^2 = 14.83$. Looking at the association the other way around, 89% of high spatial test scorers were also high video game scorers; only 24% of low spatial test scorers were high video game scorers.

Discussion

The Empire Strikes Back was notable for requiring players to navigate through three-dimensional space represented on a two-dimensional screen. The test of visual-spatial skills, mental paper folding, was also one that demanded visualizing three-dimensional movement from a two-dimensional display. At the same time there were differences between the requirements of the two situations. Probably the most important difference was that the video game was dynamic, whereas the spatial test was static. A second distinction was a difference in medium: the computer screen versus paper and pencil. Despite such differences in the stimuli and, consequently, the representational requirements of the two situations, the results strongly indicated that there was a unitary spatial skill that was evoked both in the video game and in the spatial test situation. One aspect of this common element was expressed by Loftus and Loftus (1983, p. 60) who wrote: "The visually represented objects on the screen are constantly changing, and the person who is able to mentally track these changes, and who can imagine what the configuration of objects will be in several seconds hence, is in a better position than the person who doesn't have these abilities." Similarly, mental paper folding requires the subject not merely to understand a pattern as it is now, but to imagine how it will look under a future transformation.

A major thesis concerning spatial skills and video games is that this medium is building on the everyday cognitive skills stimulated by television viewing. A study by Pezdek, Simon, Stoecert, and Kiely (1987) confirmed this relationship. Parallel to our findings concerning video game play, they found that skill in comprehending television (but not skill in comprehending radio or written material) was strongly correlated with performance on mental paper folding.

What we did not know from the results of Study 1 was anything about the causal relations between spatial skill and mental paper folding. Our hypothesis was that video game expertise could function as informal education for the development of skill in manipulating two-dimensional representations of three-dimensional space. Study 2 was designed to test this hypothesis.

STUDY 2

Design and Hypothesis

Before the experiment began, subjects were randomly assigned to an experimental or control group. Both groups were given a pretest and posttest of mental paper folding. The experimental group, but not the control group, played The Empire Strikes Back as a treatment condition; the number of games played and time spent playing were determined by the rate of progress to criterion. The control group did not have any experimental treatment; they merely took the pretest and posttest at the same time as the experimental group. At the end of the posttest, the control group played 10 games of The Empire Strikes Back as a way of assessing their level of video game expertise.

The experimental hypothesis was that the experimental group would make greater pretest–posttest improvement in mental paper folding than would the control group, as a function of their mastery of the "three-dimensional" video game The Empire Strikes Back.

Materials

The video game was the same as in Study 1. New paper-folding tests were constructed with similar items, but the number of items was doubled from 8 to 16 and the test was timed in order to create a greater range of scores. The additional items for the test were rotated and transformed versions of items from Study 1. Two forms, A and B, matched for the number of "mental folds" required by each item, were constructed. The same array of basic cube configurations was used on both forms; what varied from form to form were the questions asked and the orientation of the configurations. Subjects who received Form A in the pretest were to receive Form B in the posttest, and vice versa.

Subjects

Subjects for Study 2 were UCLA undergraduates, mostly 18- to 20-year-olds, recruited from the introductory psychology subject pool. Because of the absence of female video players in the first sample, we were interested in exploring gender differences in Study 2. We therefore did not mention video games in our recruitment material; we indicated only that the experiment involved "play." Our sample ended up with 18 men and 40 women—58 subjects in all. The greater number of women than men in Study 2 simply reflected the greater number of women in introductory psychology classes.

Procedure

Groups of subjects (approximately 7 to 10 per group) met to take the pretest and receive their random assignment to the experimental or control group. Alternating subjects received Form A or Form B and were asked to read instructions on the cover page of the test; these involved working a sample item. The experimenter directed the students: "You'll have 4 minutes to solve as many of the 16 problems as you can. If you get stuck on one, you may skip it and go to another. Don't guess because there is a penalty for wrong answers." Following the pretest, the control and experimental groups were separated; each met with an experimenter to hear the rest of the instructions.

Experimental Procedure. The experimental subjects were told to play the video game The Empire Strikes Back at the UCLA arcade at their own convenience, and were given $10 worth of marked quarters with which to do so. The quarters were painted purple and each set of 40 quarters were marked with an identification number associated with a particular subject. The experimenter explained the location of the game and the difficulty level at which they were to play. Subjects were given the task of practicing The Empire Strikes Back until they reached a score of 265,000 three times in a row; they were provided with sheets on which to record their scores. When they reached criterion, they were to call an experimenter who would verify their performance. They were also to call if they had not reached the criterion and needed more quarters.

The time frame for the experiment was the 10-week academic quarter. Subjects were pretested over the first 3 weeks of the quarter. At the end of Week 5, the experimenters began to call experimental subjects to encourage them to play more, in cases where a subject's quarters had shown up rarely or not at all in the machine. Most subjects were called two or three times during Weeks 6, 7, and 8. By the end of Week 8, fewer than one quarter of the experimental subjects had called for verification of the criterion. At that point, all of the experimental subjects were called and told to finish using their quarters, at which point the experimenters would watch them play one game regardless of their scores. As soon as subjects reached criterion (or during Weeks 9 and 10 if the criterion had not been reached), they were given the posttest. Following the posttest, each subject was given a questionnaire, which mostly inquired about previous video game experience.

Control Procedure. After the control subjects finished their pretests, they were told that they were finished with the first part of the experiment and that they would be called in about 2 weeks concerning the second part. We planned to give them the posttest with the experimental subjects; as seen in the previous description of the experimental procedure, 2 weeks turned out to be too short a period of time for the experimental subjects to reach the point of taking the posttest, so the control subjects had to wait longer.

Experimental and control subjects were posttested together, as they had been in the pretest. Subjects who had Form A on the pretest were given Form B, and vice versa. (In the case of two subjects, the wrong form was administered on the posttest because of experimenter error.) Following the posttest, control subjects were given the same questionnaire as the experimental subjects. Control subjects were then given marked quarters to play The Empire Strikes Back for 10 games. All agreed to do so by the next day and to put their score sheets in an envelope that was taped to the side of the machine. These 10 games were meant to assess the control group's initial level of video game expertise. The scores would be comparable to those for the experimental subjects' first 10 games during the experimental treatment. We assumed subjects were generally honest in reporting their scores, as they were told it did not matter how they performed on the game; therefore there was no situational source of a motivation to lie.

Analyses and Results

First, there was a large and statistically significant gender difference in the proportion of men and women reaching criterion. Whereas 75% of the men reached criterion on The Empire Strikes Back when tested by the experimenter, only 24% of the women did so. (A two-tailed chi-square test showed this difference to be significant at the .02 level.) It was not a question of the women practicing the game less than the men did. In fact, the reverse was true. On average, the women played 67 games and the men 49 games in the course of our experiment. A t test indicated that this difference was significant at the .05 level of probability, $t(29.2) = 2.30$.

In their normal lives, however, men already had more video game experience. Most men reported playing video games monthly, whereas most women reported playing only once per year. A chi-square test indicated that this association between gender and video game experience was significant at the .0001 level, $\chi^2(2, N = 54) = 26.01$. A correlational analysis showed that there was also a significant positive relationship between reported video game experience and initial performance on The Empire Strikes Back, $r(49) = .30, p < .025$.

Confirming the results of Study 1, we demonstrated an association between initial video game performance and spatial skill performance. There was a significant positive correlation between the highest of each subject's first 10 scores on The Empire Strikes Back and pretest performance on mental paper folding, $r(52) = .29$, $p < .025$. However, we were unable to demonstrate the predicted experimental effect: According to a 2 (Video Game Practice vs. No Practice) × 2 (Pretest vs. Posttest) repeated-measure analysis of variance (ANOVA), there was significant pretest–posttest improvement in mental paper folding, $F(1, 50) = 28.18$, $p < .001$. Practice in playing The Empire Strikes Back, however, did not improve mental paper-folding test scores more than the opportunity to practice this spatial skill during the pretest itself.

One possible reason for the lack of experimental effect was that the amount of practice in our treatment condition was not enough to produce far transfer to a static pencil-and-paper test. Perhaps far transfer might occur as a result of video game expertise built up over a longer period of time. The highest of the first 10 scores seemed a good measure of initial video game skill level and, therefore, also a measure of accumulated video game expertise. Knowing that there was a significant positive correlation between this measure and initial spatial test performance, we decided to use path analysis or, more precisely, structural equation modeling (Bentler, 1989) to ascertain the dominant direction of effects: from spatial skill to video game performance or from video game performance to spatial skill.

At the same time, we knew that males play video games more and, therefore, have more opportunities to build up expertise. In addition, males have been shown to have stronger spatial skills in a number of different tests (see Okagaki & Frensch, 1994; Subrahmanyam & Greenfield, 1994, for reviews of this literature). Our own repeated-measures ANOVA indicated that gender had a significant effect on mental paper-folding performance, $F(1, 50) = 5.82$, $p < .025$. We therefore constructed and tested different structural models that included gender, reported frequency of video game play, video game experience within the experimental (experimental vs. control group status), initial video game performance, and mental paper-folding performance (both pretest and posttest).

The most comprehensive causal model is shown in Figure 2. This model was derived by the application of Bentler's (1989) EQS program. The paths were tested as a single model derived from the major hypothesis of the study—that video game expertise would develop spatial skills. This model turned out to fit the data quite well, $\chi^2(10, N = 49) = 10.22$, $p = .42$ (Comparative Fit Index = .996; Bentler, 1990). In structural equation modeling, a large, nonsignificant probability level indicates a good fit with the model; a small, significant probability level indicates the absence of a fit (Bentler, 1989). According to this model, gender influences initial video game performance, a measure of accumulated expertise (i.e., boys perform better than girls), which, in turn, influences mental paper folding (pretest score).

The model also shows that the experience of receiving experimental video game practice does not affect posttest score (see nonsignificant path in Figure 2

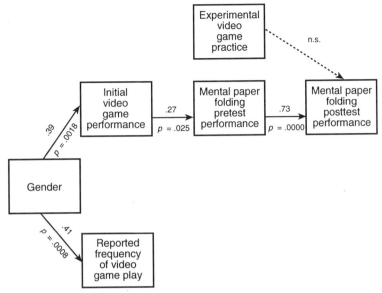

Figure 2. Structural equation model (Bentler, 1989) of causal relations among gender, video game expertise, video game experience, experimental video game practice, and mental paper folding. The depicted model is based on the subset of subjects (*N* = 49) that had no missing data in any of the six variables used in the model.

from experimental video game practice to mental paper-folding posttest performance). That is, the structural equation model confirms the absence of an experimental effect revealed in the repeated-measures ANOVA.

Because of findings in this and previous research concerning gender differences in spatial skills, we wondered whether gender was also having a direct effect on spatial skills. We therefore carried out a Lagrange Multiplier test for the path from gender to pretest paper-folding; the results, $\chi^2(1, N = 49) = .999$, $p = .32$, indicate that this causal path is not statistically significant. Therefore, gender does not influence this particular spatial skill directly, but through its influence on video game expertise.

Alternative models were also tested. An important alternative was the same model with an opposite direction of influence: from initial spatial skill to video game expertise, rather than vice versa. The causal link from mental paper-folding pretest performance to initial video game performance was statistically nonsignificant.

A Lagrange Multiplier test (Bentler, 1990) for additional parameters showed a statistically nonsignificant link between reported frequency of video game play and initial video game performance. Given the significant positive correlation between these two variables reported earlier, it seemed likely that reported experience was simply overwhelmed by the gender factor as a predictor of video game expertise. The fact that the significant relationship between reported experience and initial video game expertise was removed in a partial correlation in which gender was controlled substantiates this interpretation. Gender may mediate the relationship between practice and skill, as the differential success of men and women in reaching the experimental criterion in our study suggests.

Another Lagrange Multiplier test (Bentler, 1990) indicated that whereas initial video game expertise had a direct influence on initial spatial test performance (pretest), it did not directly influence posttest spatial performance. As shown in Figure 2, posttest performance, not surprisingly, was directly influenced by pretest skill level and the opportunity to practice mental paper folding during the pretest.

In order to obtain a more precise understanding regarding the appropriateness of the model in Figure 2 for both experimental and control groups, a two-group structural model was run. This model was identical to that shown in Figure 2, except that each of the parameters was estimated separately in each of the two groups, subject to the constraint that the estimates in one group would be identical to those in the other group, $\chi^2(21) = 32.07$, $p = .058$, Comparative Fit = .760. That is, the model fit statistically, but the fit index was somewhat on the low side. The Lagrange Multiplier test on the model showed that all but one of the parameters could be statistically considered to be equal across groups, but that the error or residual variance of reported frequency of video game play could not be considered statistically equal, LM $\chi^2(1) = 11.8$, $p = .001$. The variance of reported video game play was higher for the experimental groups. However, a nonsignificant Lagrange Multiplier test for the path from experimental video game practice to reported frequency of video game play in the Figure 2 model indicated that this difference in variance was a random phenomenon rather than one caused by the experimental treatment itself.

Because of the variance difference between experimental and control groups in reported frequency of video game play, a final model was run in which all parameters except this residual variance were forced to be estimated equally. This model fit exceedingly well, $\chi^2(20) = 12.73$, $p = .89$, Comparative Fit = 1.000.

DISCUSSION

Although we were not able to demonstrate the predicted experimental effect of *short-term* practice and mastery of The Empire Strikes Back on mental paper folding, we were able to use structural equation modeling to show a causal relationship between video game expertise, acquired over the *long-term*, and mental paper folding. There are a number of reasons why the experimental treatment may have failed, even though the theoretical analysis was correct.

First of all, the distance between the transfer test and the video game treatment was greater than in other studies (Greenfield, Camaioni, et al., 1994; Greenfield, deWinstanley, et al., 1994; Subrahmanyam & Greenfield, 1994). In all of those studies, the medium of the test stimuli matched the video medium of the game practice; in the research presented here, test stimuli were printed on paper, whereas game stimuli were presented on a video screen. Indeed, Okagaki and Frensch (1994) found that practice in mastering the game Tetris transferred to both computer screen and paper-and-pencil tests for male subjects, but to only screen-based tests for females. Hence, transfer distance for spatial skills may be narrower for females than it is for males—an interesting possibility. However, transfer distance (measured in terms of the similarity of the medium of test to the video game medium) may not be the whole story. Gagnon (1985), Dorval and Pepin (1986), and McClurg and Chaillé (1987) all found transfer from video game practice to spatial skills assessed through paper-and-pencil tests in female, as well as male, subjects.

A more important clue as to the absence of an experimental effect may lie in the fact that 76% of the female subjects failed to attain a criterion level of mastery of the video game itself, despite significantly greater practice in the course of the experiment. Because most of our subjects were women, it might be fair to state that the treatment itself failed, rather than the treatment effect.

Why the treatment itself failed is an interesting question. To the extent that there is a reciprocal influence of spatial skill on video game mastery, it might be because some women did not have the spatial skills to benefit from game practice and so failed to reach criterion, even with additional practice. Given the results of other studies of spatial skills in which female spatial skill benefited equally (Dorval & Pepin, 1986; McClurg & Chaillé, 1987; Subrahmanyam & Greenfield, 1994) or more (Gagnon, 1985) from video game practice, in comparison with male spatial skill, this does not seem to be a likely explanation.

One possible factor is the violence of The Empire Strikes Back. Malone (1981) found that the addition of thematic violence to a video game was a turn-on for boys but a turn-off for girls. The female preference for less aggressive themes was confirmed in a study of men and women by Morlock, Yando, and Nigolean (1985). Neither Okagaki and Frensch (1994) nor Subrahmanyam and Greenfield (1994) used a violent video game (for this very reason, in the case of Subrahmanyan & Greenfield). By contrast, the violence of The Empire Strikes Back may, on the average, have been a motivational turn-off for the women in our study.

On the other hand, this factor cannot be the total answer either: Gagnon (1985) used only violent games (one two-dimensional, one three-dimensional), and McClurg and Chaillé (1987) used one violent and one nonviolent game as experimental treatments in their studies. Yet female spatial skills and, in the case of Gagnon's (1985) study, female video game skills benefited as much or more than male skills did. Nonetheless, although the mental rotation performance of both boys and girls benefited from video game practice in McClurg and Chaillé's (1987) study, the benefit was considerably greater for boys than for girls following the violent game, but slightly better for girls than for boys following the nonviolent game. Dorval and Pepin (1986) used a three-dimensional violent game, Zaxxon, in their study; yet they found that males and females improved equally on their spatial task, the space relations test of the Differential Aptitude Tests.

One factor that might explain the different results with respect to gender in our study is that the subjects did not know that they were going to be in a video game experiment. Although the write-ups did not say so explicitly, it is likely that both Dorval and Pepin's (1986) and Gagnon's (1985) volunteer subjects were so informed. Hence, through self-selection, female motivation to play video games in those studies could have been greater than it was in the study presented here. In conclusion, it may be that violence made The Empire Strike Back unmotivating (cf. Malone, 1981) and, therefore, difficult for novice female players who lacked positive motivation to play video games.

Both studies confirmed a linkage between video game expertise, as demonstrated on a dynamic video game that requires navigation through three-dimensional space represented on a flat screen, and performance on a static spatial test that requires three-dimensional mental manipulation of a two-dimensional stimulus. Thus, this relationship between video game expertise and spatial skill performance had generality across two different kinds of populations: (1) arcade video players and (2) a student sample unselected for their video game interests. Although gender was a factor in the spatial test results, the structural modeling indicated that it operated by influencing video game expertise, which, in turn, developed spatial test performance; gender did not have a direct effect on the spatial test results.

By themselves, these studies suggested that practice over an extended period of time was necessary for the cultivation of spatial skills. However, motivational factors were confounded with short-term practice effects (or noneffects) in the research presented in this article. However, two other lines of investigation presented in this issue (Okagaki & Frensch, 1994; Subrahmanyam & Greenfield, 1994) found strong effects of short-term video game interventions on the cultivation of skills in manipulating spatial representations. Hence, the negative motivational effect of a violent video game on females who had not chosen to be in a video game experiment would seem to account for the failure of the treatment itself (i.e., lack of mastery of the video game by most of the women in the experimental condition). The failure of the treatment itself in turn could well account for the lack of an experimental effect in a sample that was predominately female.

As a cultural tool or artifact, these studies join others in this issue and elsewhere in demonstrating that video games are potent tools for cognitive socialization on a mass level for a variety of representational skills. In the case of spatial skills such as the dynamic representation of three-dimensional space on a two-dimensional screen, video games build on expertise utilized in an even more popular medium, the artifact of television (Pezdek et al., 1987). By showing that a video game can develop spatial skills similar to those utilized in other computer applications such as word processing (Gomez et al., 1986) and programming (Roberts, 1984; Webb, 1984), the results of these two studies confirm the anthropological emphasis on games as a socializer for adult roles in a particular society (Roberts & Sutton-Smith, 1962; Werner, 1979). They are a potent example of cognitive development resulting jointly from individual factors and processes of cultural appropriation (Saxe, 1991).

However, the cultural artifacts appropriated by subjects in Saxe's (1991) studies were not interactive. The metaphor for cultural learning through interactive processes is cognitive apprenticeship (Rogoff, 1991). In this model, the interaction is with another human model. Computer technology in general and video games in particular provide for the first time an opportunity for interactive apprenticeship by inanimate objects (although it is certainly significant that video games and other computer objects are created by human beings). The results of these studies and others are such that we have identified a form of cognitive apprenticeship that has the potential to be mediated entirely by an inanimate cultural artifact.

REFERENCES

Baenninger, M., & Newcombe, N. (1989). The role of experience in spatial test performance: A meta-analysis. *Sex Roles, 20,* 327–344.

Bentler, P.M. (1989). *EQS structural equations program manual.* Los Angeles: BMDP Statistical Software.

Bentler, P.M. (1990). Comparative fit indexes in structural models. *Psychological Bulletin, 107,* 238–246.

Bruner, J.S. (1965). The growth of mind. *American Psychologist, 20,* 1007–1017.

Bruner, J.S. (1966). On cognitive growth. In J.S. Bruner, R.R. Olver, & P.M. Greenfield (Eds.), *Studies in cognitive growth* (pp. 1–67). New York: Wiley.

Bruner, J.S., & Olson, D.R. (1973). Learning through experience and learning through media. In G. Gerbner, L.P. Gross, & W.H. Melody (Eds.), *Communications technology and social policy.* New York: Wiley.

Condry, J., & Keith, D. (1983). Educational and recreational uses of computer technology: Computer instruction and video games. *Youth and Society, 15,* 87–112.

Dorval, M., & Pepin, M. (1986). Effect of playing a video game on a measure of spatial visualization. *Perceptual Motor Skills, 62,* 159–162.

Forsyth, A.S., Jr., & Lancy, D.F. (1987). Simulated travel and place location learning in a computer adventure game. *Journal of Educational Computing Research, 3,* 377–394.

Gagnon, D. (1985). Videogames and spatial skills: An exploratory study. *Educational Communication and Technology Journal, 33,* 263–275.

Gomez, L.M., Egan, D.E., & Bowers, C. (1986). Learning to use a text editor: Some learner characteristics that predict success. *Human–Computer Interaction, 2,* 1–23.

Greenfield, P.M. (1983). Video games and cognitive skills. In *Video games and human development: Research agenda for the '80s* (pp. 19–24). Cambridge, MA: Monroe C. Gutman Library, Graduate School of Education.

Greenfield, P.M. (1984). *Mind and media: The effects of television, video games, and computers.* Cambridge, MA: Harvard University Press.

Greenfield, P.M. (1993). Representational competence in shared symbol systems: Electronic media from radio to video games. In R.R. Cocking & K.A. Renninger (Eds.), *The development and meaning of psychological distance.* Hillsdale, NJ: Erlbaum.

Greenfield, P.M., Camaioni, L., Ercolani, P., Weiss, L., Lauber, B.A., & Perrucchini, P. (1994). Cognitive socialization by computer games in two cultures: Inductive discovery or mastery of an iconic code? *Journal of Applied Developmental Psychology, 15,* 59–85.

Greenfield, P.M., deWinstanley, P., Kilpatrick, H., & Kaye, D. (1994). Action video games and informal education: Effects on strategies for dividing visual attention. *Journal of Applied Developmental Psychology, 15,* 105–123.

Guberman, S.R., & Greenfield, P.M. (1991). Learning and transfer in everyday cognition. *Cognitive Development, 6,* 233–260.

Kiesler, S., Sproull, L., & Eccles, J. (1983). Second class citizens. *Psychology Today, 17,* 41–48.

Loftus, G.R., & Loftus, E.F. (1983). *Mind at play: The psychology of video games.* New York: Basic Books.

Lowery, B.R., & Knirk, F.G. (1982–1983). Micro-computer video games and spatial visualization acquisition. *Journal of Educational Technology Systems, 11,* 155–166.

Malone, T.W. (1981). Toward a theory of intrinsically motivating instruction. *Cognitive Science, 5,* 333–370.

McClurg, P.A., & Chaillé, C. (1987). Computer games: Environments for developing spatial cognition? *Journal of Educational Computing Research, 3,* 95–111.

Morlock, H., Yando, T., & Nigolean, K. (1985). Motivation of video game players. *Psychological Reports, 57,* 247–250.

Okagaki, L., & Frensch, P.A. (1994). Effects of video game playing on measures of spatial performance: Gender effects in late adolescents. *Journal of Applied Developmental Psychology, 15,* 33–58.

Pezdek, K., Simon, S., Stoecert, J., & Kiely, J. (1987). *Individual differences in television comprehension. Memory and Cognition, 15,* 428–435.

Provenzo, E.F. (1991). *Video kids: Making sense of Nintendo.* Cambridge, MA: Harvard University Press.

Roberts, J.M., & Sutton-Smith, B. (1962). Child training and game involvement. *Ethnology, 1,* 166–185.

Roberts, R. (1984, April). *The role of prior knowledge in learning computer programming.* Paper presented at the Western Psychological Association, Los Angeles, CA.

Rogoff, B. (1991). *Apprenticeship in thinking: Cognitive development in social context.* New York: Oxford University Press.

Rogoff, B., & Lave, J. (Eds), (1984). *Everyday cognition: Its development in social context.* Cambridge, MA: Harvard University Press.

Rushbrook, S. (1986). *Messages of video games: Socialization implications.* Unpublished doctoral dissertation, University of California, Los Angeles.

Salomon, G. (1974). Internalization of filmic schematic operations in interaction with learners' aptitudes. *Journal of Educational Psychology, 66,* 499–511.

Solomon, G. (1979). *Interaction of media, cognition, and learning.* San Francisco: Jossey-Bass.

Saxe G.B. (1991). *Culture and cognitive development: Studies in mathematical understanding.* Hillsdale, NJ: Erlbaum.

Shepard, R., & Feng, C. (1972). A chronometric study of mental paper folding. *Cognitive Psychology, 3,* 228–243.

Sigel, I.E., & Cocking, R.R. (1977). Cognition and communication: A dialectic paradigm for development. In M. Lewis & L.A. Rosenblum (Eds.), *Interaction, conversation, and the development of language: The origins of behavior* (Vol. 5, pp. 207–226). New York: Wiley.

Subrahmanyam, K., & Greenfield, P.M. (1994). Effect of video game practice on spatial skills in girls and boys. *Journal of Applied Developmental Psychology, 15,* 13–32.

Vygotsky, L.S. (1962). *Thought and language*. New York: Wiley.

Vygotsky, L.S. (1978). *Mind in society.* Cambridge, MA: Harvard University Press.

Webb, N.M. (1984). Microcomputer learning in small groups: Cognitive requirements and group processes. *Journal of Educational Psychology, 76,* 1076–1088.

Werner, E.E. (1979). *Cross-cultural child development: A view from the planet Earth.* Monterey, CA: Brooks/Cole.

Chapter 11

Action Video Games and Informal Education: Effects on Strategies for Dividing Visual Attention

PATRICIA M. GREENFIELD
PATRICIA DEWINSTANLEY
HEIDI KILPATRICK
DANIEL KAYE
University of California, Los Angeles

Mass media constitute an important aspect of the informal educational environment provided by our culture. As such, they can be expected to affect processes of "everyday cognition" (Rogoff & Lave, 1984). Although basic cognitive processes are universal, cultural tools (Vygotsky, 1962) have the power to encourage selectively some cognitive processes, while letting others stay in a relatively undeveloped state. We use the term *cognitive socialization* (Greenfield, 1989) to refer to the influence of cultural tools on the development and exercise of skills for processing and communicating information. Media in general (Bruner & Olson, 1974; Greenfield, 1984; Salomon, 1979) and the computer in particular (Papert, 1980) are potent cultural tools for the selective sculpting of profiles of cognitive processes.

Among all the forms of computer technology, there is one that touches people on a mass scale and, even more important, touches them during the formative years of childhood when cognitive development is taking place. This form of

Experiment 2 was carried out with the aid of a grant from UCLA College Institute when Patricia M. Greenfield was the recipient of a Bunting Science Fellowship from Radcliffe College and the Office of Naval Research. Manuscript preparation was done with the aid of the Gold Shield Faculty Prize and a grant from the Spencer Foundation, awarded to Patricia M. Greenfield. We would like to thank Laura Weiss for creating the graphs, Lisa Kendig Black for help in preparing the manuscript, and Laurel Smith for statistical assistance.

Patricia deWinstanley is currently at Oberlin College. Heidi Kilpatrick is now with Mattel Corporation, Los Angeles. Daniel Kaye is currently with Applause, Inc., Los Angeles.

Correspondence and requests for reprints should be sent to Patricia M. Greenfield, Department of Psychology, University of California, Los Angeles, 405 Hilgard Avenue, Los Angeles, CA 90024–1563.

technology is the action video game. For example, a study in 1985–1986 by Rushbrook (1986) showed that 94% of 10-year-old children in Orange County, Southern California, played video games. Eighty-five percent of these children considered themselves good, very good, or expert players.

Action video games were designed to entertain, not to educate. Informal education is often characterized, however, by its unintentional effects. In any case, our interest does not lie in either the intended or unintended educational *content* of video games. It lies instead in the unintentional cognitive effects of the *forms* of the medium, forms that are derived from computer technology and that can be used to transmit a wide range of content, designed either to entertain or to inform (Greenfield, 1983, 1984). Content can be defined as the topical themes transmitted by a medium. For example, violent battle is one frequent content theme of action video games; geometric puzzles constitute a less frequent content area. Forms are defined as the design features of a medium that transcend particular content (Rice, Huston, & Wright, 1982). Interactivity and dynamic iconic imagery are examples of two formal features that are important in action video games.

We extended and subjected to scientific study Marshall McLuhan's (1964) dictum, "The medium is the message" as we focused on the cognitive "messages" of the video game medium. Because they are not a part of formal education, any cognitive effects of video game forms might be expected to appear primarily in the domain of "everyday," rather than that of school-related cognition.

Up to now, research has investigated the cognitive effects of video game experience on inductive discovery skills (Camaioni, Ercolani, Perrucchini, & Greenfield, 1990; Greenfield, Camaioni, et al., 1994), on the decoding of dynamic computer graphics (Camaioni et al., 1990; Greenfield, et al., 1994), on visual-spatial skills (Chatters, 1984; Dorval & Pepin, 1986; Forsyth & Lancy, 1987; Gagnon, 1985; Greenfield, Brannon, & Lohr, 1994; McClurg & Chaillé, 1987; Subrahmanyam & Greenfield, 1994), on eye–hand coordination (Drew & Waters, 1986; Favaro, 1983; Gagnon, 1985; Griffith, Voloschin, Gibb, & Bailey, 1983), and on reaction time (Clark, Lanphear, & Riddick, 1987; Orosy-Fildes & Allan, 1989). The results have generally been positive in all areas, although the positive impact on eye–hand coordination has been demonstrated for elderly people (Drew & Waters, 1986), but not young adults (Favaro, 1983; Gagnon, 1985). A number of cognitive skills related to video game expertise are useful in dealing with computers and high technology more generally (Compaine, 1983; Greenfield, 1989, 1993; Strover, 1984).

The U.S. military noted the similarity between the skills required to pilot an aircraft and those required to play video games (Nawrocki & Winner, 1983). For example, the army and, especially, the navy participated in and funded research on video games as performance tests (Carter, Kennedy, & Bittner, 1980; Jones, Dunlap, & Bilodeau, 1986; Jones, Kennedy, & Bittner, 1981; Kennedy, Bittner,

& Jones, 1981). Researchers established a high correlation between performance on a flight simulator configured for aircraft carrier landing and performance on the Atari home video game Air Combat Maneuvering (Lintern & Kennedy, 1984).

One reason for the correlation might be the skill of divided attention that we isolated for study in this article. Indeed, many flight tasks involve divided attention. For example, a pilot told us that trying to keep track of a lot of different things—for example, a row of six engine dials—is a lot like a video game. One would imagine that air traffic controlling, also similar to video games (Jones, 1984), would involve skilled use of divided attention. Thomas Longridge, a member of the Human Resources Laboratory at Williams Airforce Base, used an aircraft carrier landing game for research on pilot judgment (Trachtman, 1981).

The military have recognized other areas of relevance for video games, such as recruitment and training (Provenzo, 1991). The U.S. Army modified the Atari game Battlezone for use in military training (Nawrocki & Winner, 1983; Tracht-man, 1981). The U.S. Navy designed its own video game, a war game called NAVTAG, intended for tactical training of junior officers (Jones, 1984), and the British Navy has used a computer-based antisubmarine training game in a similar vein (Kiddoo, 1982); the U.S. Army has done something of a similar nature (Compaine, 1983). During the Gulf War, Commodore Tom Corcoran called the complex process of monitoring electronic screens to distinguish friends from foes in the air "an enormous video game with life-or-death consequences" (Healy & Fritz, 1990, p. A12).

In an effort closely related to our research, video games have been used to expand the effective field of visual attention for brain-damaged patients suffering from left neglect (Murphy, 1983). Such patients, as a result of paralysis on their left side, do not pay attention to the left side of the visual field. Video games that require scanning various locations were found to help repair this deficit of visual attention.

The research presented here focuses on the relation between video game expertise and divided visual attention. The hypothesis of the research came from the observation that in most video games, a player must be able to deal with events occurring simultaneously at several locations on the video screen (Gagnon, 1985; Greenfield, 1984). It was therefore hypothesized that: (a) video game experts would be better than nonexperts at tasks requiring divided visual attention, and (b) video game experience would play a causal role in improving performance on such tasks.

THE MEASUREMENT OF ATTENTION

Posner, Snyder, and Davidson (1980) conducted a series of studies designed to examine the effects of attention on the detection of signals in a visual field. In general, they found that response times to indicate the presence or absence of a target were reduced when subjects received information about the probable location of the target in the visual field. That is, if the stimulus occurred in an expected location (i.e., where the subject had been told there was an 80% probability of a stimulus occurring), responses were faster than if a stimulus occurred in a neutral location (i.e., where there was a 50% probability of a stimulus occurring). Likewise, if a stimulus occurred in an unexpected location (i.e., where there was a 20% probability of the stimulus occurring), responses were slower than if the stimulus occurred in a neutral location.

The increased response time for the unexpected location and the decreased response time for the expected location have been referred to as *cost* and *benefit,* respectively. The finding that, relative to a neutral location, the allocation of attention to a probable location leads to benefit, and the nonallocation of attention to an improbable location leads to cost, has been found by other researchers as well (e.g., Bashinski & Bacharach, 1980; Eriksen & Yeh, 1985; Posner, Nissen, & Ogden, 1978).

Like the study conducted by Posner et al. (1980), our experiments had a neutral condition in which the targets were equally likely to appear briefly in either one of the two locations, and a probable/improbable condition in which the target was much more likely to flash in one of the two locations. It was hypothesized that video game novices would show a pattern of cost and benefit

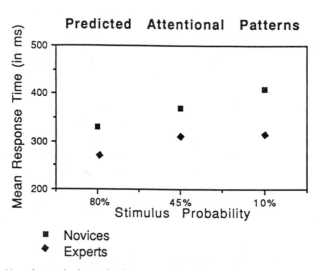

Figure 1. Hypothesized relationship between video game expertise and strategies for dividing attention. As in the experiments that follow, 80% represents a high-probability location, 10% a low-probability location, and 45% a neutral location.

similar to that reported in the attentional literature. That is, it was predicted that video game novices would be faster at responding to the probable target, when compared to the neutral targets, and slower at responding to the improbable target.

However, it was hypothesized that video game experts would show a pattern of cost and benefit quite different from that reported in the attentional literature. Again, it was hypothesized that video game experts would also be faster at responding to the probable target, when compared to the neutral targets; yet they would *not* be slower at responding to the improbable target. That is, it was predicted that the experts would show a benefit at the probable location without suffering a cost at the improbable location. This makes sense when one considers that in order to play a video game well, players must be able to focus most of their attention on the starship, the robot, or the Pac-Man (the probable target), as well as to maintain some of their attention on other objects (the improbable target). The hypothesized relationship between video game skill and strategies is shown in Figure 1. Lastly, because video game experts simply have more practice in manually responding to flashes on a screen, it was hypothesized that they would be faster than video game novices at responding to all the targets.

EXPERIMENT 1

Method

Subjects. There were 34 male undergraduates at UCLA who participated in the video game portion of this experiment in partial fulfillment of an introductory psychology course requirement. All subjects were right-handed and had normal or corrected vision. Of these subjects, 16 (8 were video game experts, 8 were video game novices) were asked to return to complete the attention portion of the experiment. The selection of the 16 subjects was based on the criteria described later.

Selection Criteria. Video game ability was assessed with the Apple IIe version of the game Robot Battle. This game was chosen because of its face validity. That is, in the game Robot Battle robots attack the player from all directions. It seemed that in order to play the game successfully, one would need to allocate one's attention across the playing screen. Furthermore, extensive pilot testing of this game showed that subjects' scores on Robot Battle were highly correlated with the number of video games that the subjects had played and the number of hours spent playing these games, both rs (17) = .67, ps < .001.

Subjects were asked to play two games of Robot Battle on an Apple II computer. Subjects scoring above 200,000 on either game or below 20,000 on both games were asked to return for the attention portion of the experiment. Pilot testing indicated that these cutoff points were sufficient in that a substantial number of subjects met these criteria, but not so many as to make the categories of expert and novice meaningless.

Attention Task. For the attention portion of the experiment, subjects were seated in front of the terminal screen; a chin and head rest were adjusted so that their eyes were exactly 12 in. from the screen. They were then shown where to place their fingers on the keyboard. The lights were turned off, and the subjects were allowed to adapt to the dark while they read the instructions. The instructions, presented via the computer, provided information about the percentage of trials that the target would appear at each location as well as instructions for initiating and responding to each trial. Subjects were encouraged to ask the experimenter about anything that was unclear. The experiment was conducted in a darkened room, with the experimenter present at all times.

A luminance detection task requiring a choice reaction time response was used to elicit a measure of attention. Stimuli were presented on a Northstar Horizon microcomputer in white against a black background. There were two possible target stimulus locations, each indicated by a pair of short horizontal lines (.36°) located 1° above and below the target location. The two target locations fell on a horizontal axis in line with the center of the screen and were separated by 14° of visual angle.

The target was an asterisk that increased in luminescence, thereby giving the appearance of a brief flash (33 ms). It was located between the set of bars on the right or the left, or on both sides simultaneously. There were two conditions that differed in the probabilities associated with the target's appearance at a given location. In one condition, the target appeared at one location on 80% of the trials, at the other location on 10% of the trials, and at both locations simultaneously on 10% of the trials. In the other condition, the target appeared equally often at the two locations (on the right 45% of the trials, on the left 45% of the trials). On 10% of the trials the target appeared at both locations simultaneously.

The subjects initiated each trial by pressing the space bar. Following a variable interval of 500 to 1,500 ms, one or both of the asterisks flashed between the set or sets of bars. Subjects responded to the asterisk or asterisks as quickly as possible with a choice reaction: They pressed the left key with the right forefinger if the left target stimulus was detected, the right key with the right middle finger if the right target was detected, and both keys with both fingers simultaneously if both targets were detected.

Response times were recorded by the computer. The screen cleared following each response. When the bar markers returned, subjects began another trial. Trials were repeated when the response times were too fast (i.e., an anticipation response). Subjects were encouraged to rest between blocks of trials and could stop at any point during the experiment by not pressing the space bar.

Eight blocks of 50 trials each (plus 20 practice trials that occurred only at the beginning of each condition) were given to each subject. Before the first block of trials, each subject was told that the asterisk would flash on the left side 45% of the time, on the right side 45% of the time, and on both sides 10% of the time (Condition 1). Before the fifth block of trials, half of the subjects were told that the asterisk would flash on the right side 80% of the time, on the left side 10% of the time, and on both sides 10% of the time. The other half of the subjects were told that the asterisk would flash on the right side 10% of the time, on the left side 80% of the time, and on both sides 10% of the time (Condition 2). In this way the side of the screen for the most probable location was counterbalanced across subjects for Condition 2.

Data Analysis. Duncan (1980) showed that when subjects are required to respond to two separate stimuli simultaneously, they suffer a decrement in performance relative to conditions in which subjects are required to respond to only one stimulus. Furthermore, he suggested that this decrement was not due to the inability to attend to two locations; rather, it was due to a response incompatibility. Therefore, the trials in which two targets appeared were not analyzed.

In keeping with Hertzog and Rovine's (1985) suggestions for data analysis, planned comparisons were run. The two 45% probability locations of Condition 1 were combined in order to compare them with the 80% and 10% locations of Condition 2.

Results

The means for the equal probability condition and the unequal probability condition for both the experts and novices are presented in Figure 2. As was expected, the video game novices' mean reaction time (RT) was longer for the 10% location compared to the 45% location (cost), and their mean RT was significantly shorter for the 80% location compared to the 45% location (benefit), $t(7) = -1.18, p < .07$, and $t(7) = 1.97, p < .05$, respectively. The power to detect an effect of the magnitude that was obtained was .30, which may explain why only trend level significance was reached in the 10% to 45% comparison. However, the direction of the effect was very consistent, as evidenced by 6 of the 8 subjects showing the same pattern, $p < .05$, by binomial probability.

It was also hypothesized that video game experts would show a benefit in the probable location but would not show a cost in the improbable location. Again, as was expected, video game experts' mean RT was significantly shorter in the 80% location when compared to the 45% location, $t(7) = 2.68, p < .05$. Video

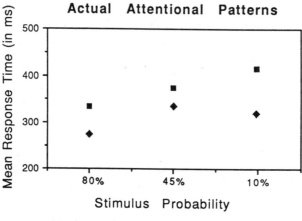

Figure 2. Actual relationship between video game expertise and strategies for dividing attention: Experiment 1.

game experts' mean RT for the 10% location was *not* significantly different from their mean RT for the 45% location.

Finally, video game experts' RTs were significantly faster than video game novices' RTs for the 80% location and the 10% location, $t(14) = -2.07$, $p < .025$, and $t(14) = -2.18$, $p < .025$, respectively. There was no difference between experts and novices in the even probability condition. The error rate did not exceed 4% in any of the analyzed conditions.

Discussion

The expectation that video game ability would be predictive of cost–benefit patterns was supported. Both novices and experts showed benefit to a probable location, a finding that is consistent with the attentional literature to date. This indicates that, regardless of any specific abilities, people in general can use information about target probability to focus their attention. The finding that novices showed a cost to an improbable location is also consistent with the attentional literature. However, the experts did not show the cost to the improbable location that has been found by other researchers (Bashinski & Bacharach, 1980; Eriksen & Yeh, 1985; Posner et al., 1978; Posner et al., 1980).

The focusing of attention has been likened to the focusing of a zoom lens on a camera (Eriksen & Yeh, 1985). As one focuses the zoom lens, the resolution at the periphery becomes less and less acute. Therefore, when attention is focused on an expected location, the resolution at an unexpected location is low. The zoom lens model is supported by the pattern of cost–benefit shown by the novices as well as the cost–benefit patterns found by other researchers (Bashinski & Bacharach, 1980; Eriksen & Yeh, 1985; Posner et al., 1978). However, when the experts focus their attention, one possibility is that they do not lose resolution in the periphery.

A study conducted by Shulman, Wilson, and Sheehy (1985) found that reaction times increased as the distance between the target and the focus of attention increased. Furthermore, Shulman et al. suggested that the distance effect was indicative of a gradient of attention, called an attentional field, that extends from the focus of attention outward. They qualified their findings with the suggestion that "attentional field sizes [could] be expected to vary with task demands and the spatial distribution of spatial attention" (p. 64). Moreover, in light of the present experiment, it also can be suggested that attentional field sizes can be expected to vary with the expertise of the subjects.

The question remains, did video game players have a greater attentional field that facilitated performance with video games, or did the playing of video games develop the greater attentional field demonstrated by the experts?

EXPERIMENT 2

The second experiment was designed to answer these two questions: To what extent was the strategic deployment of divided spatial attention a function of video game expertise? To what extent did attentional skills facilitate the development of video game expertise? With this in mind, we designed an experiment in which the attention task used in Experiment 1 served as the pre- and posttest for a new experiment. Between the pre- and posttest, an experimental group spent 5 hr playing a video game requiring the allocation of attention to many points on the screen. The major goal of the study was to see whether the experimental group subjects improved their attentional skills as a result of video game practice. This prediction was tested by comparing the experimental group with a control group that did not receive any experimental treatment between the pre- and posttest.

Following the pattern of Experiment 1, we divided subjects into groups of more and less experienced players (although the criteria were a little different, as will be seen). On the basis of Gagnon (1985), we predicted an effect of experimental practice on attentional skills in the less experienced group only. For the more experienced players, it was thought that the video game experience provided by the experiment would not significantly improve their attentional skills beyond the large amounts of practice they had already received in the real world. However, because our main goal was to detect an experimental effect rather than to discriminate between experts and novices, we did not restrict our groups to the two extremes of video game skill used in Experiment 1, but used all subjects. Consequently, we labeled the two groups in this experiment less experienced and more experienced rather than novice and expert, the labels used in Experiment 1.

Method

Subjects. Subjects were 40 male undergraduate students at UCLA. All subjects were right-handed and had normal or corrected vision. On the basis of a subsample of 20 for whom ages were available, the mean age of the sample was 19 years. Students participated as fulfillment of a partial requirement for an introductory psychology class and received nominal monetary compensation when the time required for the experiment exceeded class requirements.

Apparatus

The video game portion of the experiment was conducted on a Robotron arcade video game machine fixed at conventional arcade settings (i.e., level of difficulty). The apparatus used to measure attention was the same as in Experiment 1.

Design and Procedure

Group Assignment. Subjects were randomly assigned to either an experimental or a control group, with an equal number of subjects per group. The experimental group received 5 hr of practice at a video game; the control group did not play the video game beyond the initial five games used for assessment of skill. During the first experimental session, subjects' performance on an attention task, which served as a pretest, and on a video game (Robotron) was tested. The testing order of the attention task and video game was counterbalanced such that half of the subjects in each group received the attention task first and half were tested on the video game first.

Subjects within the experimental and control groups were also assigned to a more skilled or less skilled player category based on their best performance in five games of Robotron. Those above the median were classified as more skilled; those below the median were classified as less skilled.

Attention Task. The attention task was exactly as described in Experiment 1. The pretest and posttest consisted of eight blocks of 50 trials, four blocks per condition. Each condition was preceded by 20 practice trials. All subjects began with the 45%/45%/10% condition (Condition 1). For Condition 2, the side of the most probable target was counterbalanced such that the most probable location was at the left for half the subjects and at the right for the remaining subjects. The side of the most probable target was reversed for each subject during a second session, the posttest.

General Procedure. Using the procedures just described, we spent the initial experimental session assigning subjects to an experimental or control group, evaluating video game skill (more or less skilled), and assessing visual attention with the computerized task (pretest attention measure). All subjects returned 1 to $1\frac{1}{2}$ weeks later for a second attention task session (posttest attention measure). During the period between the first and last sessions, the experimental group received 5 hr of practice playing Robotron. Practice sessions were usually held on consecutive days, with subjects playing 1 to $1\frac{1}{2}$ hr per session. The video game practice sessions began 1 to 3 days following the initial session.

Results

A primary focus in analyzing the data was to test for the possible effects of video game training on performance on a visual attention task. Whereas a cost–benefit analysis was used to conceptualize the results of Experiment 1, the addition of the temporal element in Experiment 2 led us to focus our analysis on the change in attentional performance at each probability level of the target stimulus (10%, 45%, 80%). Change in attentional performance could occur as a result of repeated testing (when it occurred in both the control and experimental group) or it could occur as a result of the video game treatment (when it occurred in the experimental group alone).

As in Experiment 1, a cost–benefit analysis was used to conceptualize and analyze attentional performance at one point in time. In the cost–benefit analysis, response time in the 45%/45% condition, where both locations were equally likely to contain the target, served as a baseline, exactly as in Experiment 1. Table 1 shows that for each group at both pretest and posttest, an attentional

TABLE 1
Mean Response Time (in ms) as a Function of Treatment Group, Game Skill, Session, and Stimulus Probability

| | Stimulus Probability | | | | |
	80%	45%	10%	Benefit	Cost
Experimental Group					
More Skilled Players					
Pretest	254.14	280.33	312.28	26 ms	32 ms
Posttest	240.82	258.85	289.86	18 ms	31 ms
Less Skilled Players					
Pretest	259.41	300.02	326.23	41 ms	26 ms
Posttest	253.40	272.11	280.71	19 ms	9 ms
Control Group					
More Skilled Players					
Pretest	244.23	291.37	311.16	47 ms	20 ms
Posttest	222.42	255.68	293.43	33 ms	38 ms
Less Skilled Players					
Pretest	270.95	296.83	299.06	26 ms	2 ms
Posttest	251.21	265.22	290.62	14 ms	25ms

benefit, relative to the equiprobable baseline, occurred for responding to the target at the 80% probability location, whereas an attentional cost was incurred at the 10% probability location. The repeated-measures analysis of variance (ANOVA) and post-hoc tests reported later indicate that this pattern is statistically significant.

A 2 (Treatment: Experimental, Control) × 2 (Skill: More, Less) × 2 (Session: Pretest, Posttest) × 3 (Stimulus Probability: 80%, 45%, 10%) mixed model repeated-measures ANOVA was performed on the entire data set to examine the overall effects. Treatment and skill served as between-subjects variables; sessions and stimulus probability served as within-subjects measures. Because the purpose of the 45%/45% condition was to obtain a baseline measure of response latency when the target stimulus was equally likely to occur at either of the possible locations, the data from these two targets were averaged for this and all subsequent analyses, as in Experiment 1.

There was an overall decrease in response latency from the pretest to the posttest (287.17 ms and 264.53 ms, respectively), as reflected in the significant main effect of session, $F(1, 36) = 35.02$, $p < .001$. A main effect of stimulus probability was also observed, $F(2, 72) = 132.11$, $p < .0001$, showing at the very least that subjects were able to use the probability information. Mean RT for the 10%, 45%, and 80% targets was 300.42 ms, 277.55 ms, and 249.57 ms, respectively. This pattern indicated the expected cost at the 10% target and the expected benefit at the 80% target. According to Newman-Keuls tests, both cost and benefit were significant at the .05 level.

A significant interaction was found for Session × Stimulus Probability, $F(2, 72) = 3.44$, $p < .05$, reflecting the fact that performance improved least at the 80% location, the location at which performance was best on the pretest. Newman-Keuls tests indicated that the 10% and 45%, but not the 80%, probability targets showed a significant improvement from pretest to posttest.

More important, there was also a significant interaction between video game skill and stimulus probability, $F(2, 72) = 5.83$, $p < .005$, showing that, overall, superior performance of the more skilled players was observed only for the 80% and 45% probability targets (see Figure 3). According to Tukey tests, the difference between the more and less skilled players attained statistical significance at the .05 level only for the 80% probability targets. However, a significant three-way interaction between treatment group, game skill, and stimulus probability, $F(2, 72) = 3.39$, $p < .05$, indicated significantly lower response times for the more skilled players in the control group at the 45% probability location and significantly lower response times for more skilled players in the experimental group at the 80% probability location. Note that this three-way interaction is much weaker than the two-way interaction shown in Figure 3.

Experiment 2 replicates the general finding of Experiment 1 insofar as experienced players had faster response times in both studies. However, whereas the specific locus of the effect was the 10% probability location in Experiment 1, the loci were the 80% and 45% (equiprobable) targets in Experiment 2.

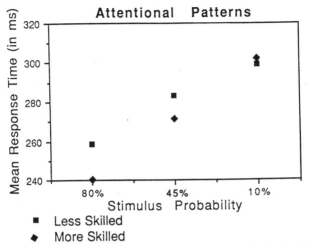

Figure 3. Relationship between video game expertise and strategies for dividing attention: Experiment 2.

A significant Treatment × Session × Stimulus Probability three-way interaction, $F(2, 72) = 5.58$, $p < .005$, showed that video game practice selectively improved performance on the 10% target as predicted (Newman-Keuls test, $p < .05$). Because of this significant reduction, video game practice decreased the response time cost for a low-probability target location (see Figure 4, Table 1). The control group significantly improved performance for the neutral (equiprobable 45%) targets (Newman-Keuls test, $p < .05$), thus increasing response time cost at the low-probability location (see Figure 4, Table 1).

In other words, the experimental video game treatment moved players from a cost–benefit pattern of attention that, at pretest, was relatively more like that of novices in Experiment 1 to a pattern that, at posttest, was relatively more like that of experts in Experiment 1 (cf. Figure 2, Figure 4). At the same time, the control group moved from a cost–benefit pattern that, at pretest, was similar to that of the experts in Experiment 1 towards one that, at posttest, was more like that of the Experiment 1 novices.

Discussion

Experiment 2 replicated findings from Experiment 1 and from previous research (Bashinski & Bacharach, 1980; Eriksen & Yeh, 1985; Posner et al., 1978; Posner et al., 1980) that there is attentional facilitation when a target stimulus appears in an expected position and attentional inhibition when it appears in an unexpected position. We were not able to demonstrate, as we had in Experiment 1, that more skilled players are able to monitor the least probable (10%) location better than less experienced players; in Experiment 2, both more and less experienced players showed attentional cost in responding to a target in the 10% location (Figure

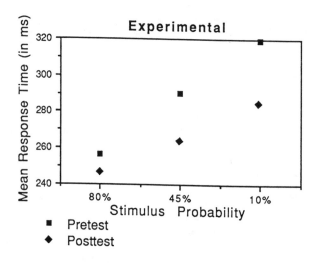

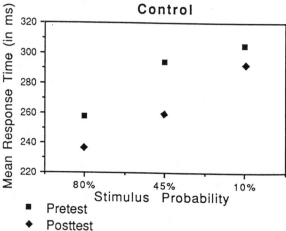

Figure 4. Effect of video game practice on cost–benefit patterns in the allocation of visual attention.

3). However, the experimental treatment did succeed in lowering the relative cost on the 10% target.

Experiment 2 also showed that repeated attentional testing improves overall visual monitoring performance. In line with the previous discussion, the across-the-board attentional improvement (i.e., at all probability levels) could have resulted either from expansion of the visual field, improvement in RT, or both.

Because expansion of the visual field generally leads to a lower visual resolution (Eriksen & Yeh, 1985), improvement in reaction time seems the most likely explanation.

GENERAL DISCUSSION

The results obtained with the expert video game players in the first study indicate that video game expertise is most highly associated with the reduction of cost in attending to a low-probability location in a task that demands divided attention. Recall that the 10% location occurred in the condition in which the target appeared 80% of the time in the alternative location. Compared with novices, video game experts were faster responders at both the low and high probability locations in the 80%/10% probability condition. They were not, however, significantly faster in the 45%/45% condition, when targets were equally likely to appear at either location.

Experiment 2, however, yielded a somewhat different pattern of findings. Again, the more skilled players had faster reaction times than did the less skilled players, but this time the superiority was observed only on the 80% and 45% probability targets. One hypothesis was that the different pattern of results in the two studies was due to the fact that Experiment 1 used extremes of video game skill, whereas Experiment 2 did not. However, follow-up analyses based only on extreme subjects in Experiment 2 did not succeed in replicating the cost–benefit pattern of Experiment 1. Therefore, it does not appear that the more selective sample of Experiment 1 was responsible for the different cost–benefit pattern of more skilled video game players in Experiment 2.

Given the results of the first study, the next question was whether video game play promoted or simply utilized strategies for deploying attention to more than one location. Experiment 2 showed that although experimental video game practice did not improve attentional performance overall, practice on a video game requiring visual monitoring of more than one location could develop strategies for reducing the relative attentional cost of monitoring the location of a low-probability target. Video game players themselves reported using strategies of visual attention, sometimes as a function of increased experience (Gagnon, 1985; Small, 1983; "Video Games," 1985).

Our results are partially in line with the results of a study of the effects of action video game play on the choice RT of older people (over age 60). As a result of playing a minimum of 14 hr of Pac-Man and Donkey Kong over a period of 7 weeks, subjects improved, relative to a control group, in a task that paralleled our equiprobability attention task; this result parallels the relative superiority of the more skilled video game players with the 45% target in Experiment 2. However, the largest effect of video game practice in Clark et al.'s (1987) study appeared in the more strategic RT task, in which the right hand had to respond to a stimulus on the left while the left hand had to respond to a stimulus on the right. This latter result agrees with our finding of a strategic change in the pattern of attention deployment as a result of experimental video game practice.

However, Clark et al. (1987) found a clear-cut experimental effect, whereas we did not. The discrepancy can perhaps be explained by the fact that subjects in Clark et al.'s study had a minimum of 14 hr of video game practice, whereas our subjects had only 5 hr of practice. Five hours of practice was perhaps not enough to affect such an overlearned, automatic skill as RT. Another possibility is that young people, such as the subjects in our studies, are at the peak of their RT because of youth and everyday life experiences, whereas older people, such as those in Clark et al.'s study, lack both the youth and the practice to keep their RT functioning at an optimal level.

From the point of view of research in attention, the results add another example to those gathered by Neisser (1976) that practice can lead to strategic improvement in what Neisser termed dual attention. Indeed, the research literature on divided attention implicitly recognizes the effects of practice on attentional strategies; experiments generally stabilize performance through thousands of trials and report the results of only the last session.

Even more relevant, Biocca (1989) showed that visual attentional strategies acquired from print literacy *transfer* to television viewing. In analogous fashion, our study showed that practice could also lead to a transfer of dual or divided attention strategies to a new task. This transfer seems to be an example of what Salomon and Perkins (1987) termed "low-road" transfer—that is, automatic transfer of an overlearned skill to a closely related situation. It contrasts with "high-road" transfer, conceptually based transfer that has potentially greater breadth of application.

From the point of view of attentional theory, the effect of video games appears to provide an example of attention as perception: "We choose what we will see by anticipating the structured information it will provide" (Neisser, 1976, p. 87). Gagnon (1985) reported that when game play became rapid, many frequent players "claimed to focus their gaze at the center of the play field in order to see the entire screen at once" (p. 272). Indeed, Shapiro (1990) succeeded in improving performance on an action video game by training subjects to focus their peripheral rather than central attention on peripherally appearing objects while eliminating unnecessary eye movements.

If this were a general strategy for increasing the effective (although not actual) visual field, one would expect improved performance by more skilled video game players under all conditions in our test, a result that did occur if we consider both Experiment 1 and Experiment 2. One might also expect that this strategy, combined with a reduction in visual resolution at the periphery of the field, as in Eriksen and Yeh's (1985) model, would lead to reduced cost at the low-probability location, along with reduced benefit at the high-probability location. This was exactly the pattern of results shown by our experimental group.

Taken together, the two studies showed that skilled or expert video game players had better skills for monitoring two locations on a visual screen and that experimental video game practice could alter the strategies of attentional deployment so that the response time for a low-probability target was reduced. Although the results of the two experiments were not entirely consistent, together they provided evidence that video games are a tool of informal education for the development of strategies of divided attention in both the short and long term. In the long term, both studies provided evidence that more skilled video game players had better developed attentional skills than less skilled players, although the results were stronger in Experiment 1. In the short term of our experimental treatment, 5 hr of video game practice significantly affected the strategic aspect of divided visual attention, as shown in improved skill in monitoring the low-probability target.

This new mass medium of the action video game thus seems to provide informal education for occupations that demand such skills in divided visual attention—for example, instrument flying, military activities, and air traffic control. For the same reason, the games may provide a positive influence on performance in sports such as basketball or ordinary activities like driving a car where skilled performance requires the monitoring of multiple visual locations. Our two studies showed that strategies for dividing visual attention are part of the cognitive "message" of action video games.

REFERENCES

Bashinski, H.S., & Bacharach, V.R. (1980). Enhancement of perceptual sensitivity as the result of selectively attending to spatial locations. *Perception and Psychophysics, 28,* 241–248.

Biocca, F.A. (1989, May). *The effect of literacy training on spatial attention to television and video monitors.* Paper presented at the annual meeting of the International Communication Association, San Francisco, CA.

Bruner, J.S., & Olson, D.R. (1974). Learning through experience and learning through media. In D.E. Olson (Ed.), *Media and symbols: The forms of expression, communication, and education* (pp. 125–150). Chicago: University of Chicago Press.

Camaioni, L., Ercolani, A.P., Perrucchini, P., & Greenfield, P.M. (1990). Video-giochi e abilita cognitive: L'ipotesi del transfer [Video games and cognitive ability: The hypothesis of transfer]. *Giornale Italiano di Psicologia, 17,* 331–348.

Carter, R.C., Kennedy, R.S., & Bittner, A.C. (1980). Selection of performance evaluation tests for environmental research. *Proceedings of the 24th Annual Meeting of the Human Factors Society.*

Chatters, L. (1984). *An assessment of the effects of video game practice on the visual motor perceptual skills of sixth grade children.* Unpublished doctoral dissertation, University of Toledo, OH.

Clark, J.E., Lanphear, A.K., & Riddick, C.C. (1987). The effects of videogame playing on the response selection processing of elderly adults. *Journal of Gerontology, 42,* 82–85.

Compaine, B.M. (1983). The new literacy. *Daedelus, 112,* 129–142.

Dorval, M., & Pepin, M. (1986). Effect of playing a video game on a measure of spatial visualization. *Perceptual and Motor Skills, 62,* 159–162.

Drew, D., & Waters, J. (1986). Video games: Utilization of a novel strategy to improve perceptual motor skills and cognitive functioning in the non-institutionalized elderly. *Cognitive Rehabilitation, 4,* 26–31.

Duncan, J. (1980). The locus of interference in the perception of simultaneous stimuli. *Psychological Review, 87,* 272–300.

Eriksen, C.W., & Yeh, Y. (1985). Allocation of attention in the visual field. *Journal of Experimental Psychology: Human Perception and Performance, 11,* 583–597.

Favaro, P.J. (1983). *The effects of video game play on mood, physiological arousal and psychomotor performance.* Unpublished doctoral dissertation, Hofstra University, Hempstead, NY.

Forsyth, A.S., Jr., & Lancy, D.F. (1987). Simulated travel and place location learning in a computer adventure game. *Journal of Educational Computing Research, 3,* 377–394.

Gagnon, D. (1985). Videogames and spatial skills: An exploratory study. *Educational Communication and Technology Journal, 33,* 263–275.

Greenfield, P.M. (1983). Video games and cognitive skills. In *Video games and human development: Research agenda for the '80s* (pp. 19–24). Cambridge, MA: Monroe C. Gutman Library, Graduate School of Education, Harvard University.

Greenfield, P.M. (1984). *Mind and media: Effects of television, video games, and computers.* Cambridge, MA: Harvard University Press.

Greenfield, P.M. (1989). I videogiochi come strumenti della socializzazione cognitiva [Video games as tools of cognitive socialization]. *Psicologia Italiana, 10,* 38–48.

Greenfield, P.M., Brannon, C., & Lohr, D. (1994). Two-dimensional representation of movement through three-dimensional space: The role of video game expertise. *Journal of Applied Developmental Psychology, 15,* 87–103.

Greenfield, P.M., Camaioni, L., Ercolani, P., Weiss, L., Lauber, B.A., & Perrucchini, P. (1994). Cognitive socialization by computer games in two cultures: Inductive discovery or mastery of an iconic code? *Journal of Applied Developmental Psychology, 15,* 59–85.

Griffith, P., Voloschin, P., Gibb, G.D., & Bailey, J.R. (1983). Differences in eye–hand motor coordination of video-game users and non-users. *Perceptual and Motor Skills, 57,* 155–158.

Healy, M., & Fritz, S. (1990, August 20). Navy's surveillance of 2 Iraq tankers tightens. *New York Times,* pp. A1, A12.

Hertzog, C., & Rovine, M. (1985). Repeated measures analysis of variance in developmental research: Selected issues. *Child Development, 56,* 787–809.

Jones, M.B. (1984). Video games as psychological tests. *Simulation and Games, 15,* 131–157.

Jones, M.B., Dunlap, W.P., & Bilodeau, I. (1986). Comparison of video game and conventional test performance. *Simulation and Games, 17,* 435–446.

Jones, M.B., Kennedy, R.S., & Bittner, A.C., Jr. (1981). A video game for performance testing. *American Journal of Psychology, 94,* 143–152.

Kennedy, R.S., Bittner, A.C., Jr., & Jones, M.B. (1981). Video-game and conventional tracking. *Perceptual and Motor Skills, 53,* 310.

Kiddoo, T. (1982). Pacman meets GI Joe? *Soldiers, 37*(9), 20–23.

Lintern, G., & Kennedy, R.S. (1984). Video game as a covariate for carrier landing research. *Perceptual and Motor Skills, 58,* 167–172.

McClurg, P.A., & Chaillé, C. (1987). Computer games: Environments for developing spatial cognition? *Journal of Educational Computing Research, 3,* 95–111.

McLuhan, M. (1964). *Understanding media: The extensions of man.* New York: McGraw-Hill.

Murphy, S. (1983, November 25). Techniques useful in helping brain-damaged: Video games give medicine an assist. *Los Angeles Times,* p. IX11.

Nawrocki, L.H., & Winner, J.L. (1983). Video games: Instructional potential and classification. *Journal of Computer-Based Instruction, 10,* 80–82.

Neisser, U. (1976). Attention and the problem of capacity. In *Cognition and reality: Principles and implications of cognitive psychology* (pp. 79–107). New York: W.H. Freeman.

Orosy-Fildes, C., & Allan, R.W. (1989). Psychology of computer use: XII. Videogame play: Human reaction time to visual stimuli. *Perceptual and Motor Skills, 69,* 243–247.

Papert, S. (1980). *Mindstorms.* New York: Basic Books.

Posner, M.I., Nissen, M.J., & Ogden, W.C. (1978). Attended and unattended processing modes: The role of set spatial location. In H.L. Pick & I. Saltzman (Eds.), *Modes of perceiving and processing information* (pp. 137–157). Hillsdale, NJ: Erlbaum.

Posner, M.I., Snyder, C.R., & Davidson, B.J. (1980). Attention and the detection of signals. *Journal of Experimental Psychology, 109,* 160–174.

Provenzo, E.F. (1991). *Video kids: Making sense of Nintendo.* Cambridge, MA: Harvard University Press.

Rice, M.L., Huston, A.C., & Wright, J.C. (1982). The forms of television: Effects on children's attention, comprehension, and social behavior. In J.D. Pearl, L. Bouthilet, & J. Lazar (Eds.), *Television and behavior: Ten years of scientific progress and implications for the eighties* (Vol. 2, pp. 24–38). *Technical reviews.* Rockville, MD: National Institute of Mental Health.

Rogoff, B., & Lave, J. (Eds.). (1984). *Everyday cognition: Its development in social context.* Cambridge, MA: Harvard University Press.

Rushbrook, S. (1986). *"Messages" of video games: Socialization implications.* Unpublished doctoral dissertation, University of California, Los Angeles.

Salomon, G. (1979). *Interaction of media, cognition, and learning.* San Francisco: Jossey-Bass.

Salomon, G., & Perkins, D.N. (1987). Transfer of cognitive skills from programming: When and how? *Journal of Educational Computing Research, 3,* 149–170.

Shapiro, K.L. (1990). Attention in visual space affects oculomotor performance. In D. Brogan (Ed.), *Visual search.* London: Taylor & Francis.

Shulman, G.L., Wilson, J., & Sheehy, J.B. (1985). Spatial determinants of the distribution of attention. *Perception and Psychophysics, 37,* 59–65.

Small, J. (1983). *Final term project on cognitive development.* Unpublished manuscript.

Strover, S. (1984, May). *Games in the information age.* Paper presented at the International Communication Association, San Francisco, CA.

Subrahmanyam, K., & Greenfield, P.M. (1994). Effect of video game practice on spatial skills in girls and boys. *Journal of Applied Developmental Psychology, 15,* 13–32.

Trachtman, P. (1981). A generation meets computers on the playing fields of Atari. *Smithsonian, 12,* 51–61.

Video games. (1985, June 10). *The New Yorker,* p. 36.

Vygotsky, L.S. (1962). *Thought and language.* Cambridge, MA: MIT Press.

Author Index

Subject Index